Second Language Learning and Teaching

Issues in Literature and Culture

Series editor

Mirosław Pawlak, Kalisz, Poland

More information about this series at http://www.springer.com/series/13879

Jacek Mydla · Małgorzata Poks
Leszek Drong
Editors

Multiculturalism, Multilingualism and the Self: Literature and Culture Studies

 Springer

Editors
Jacek Mydla
University of Silesia in Katowice
Sosnowiec
Poland

Leszek Drong
University of Silesia in Katowice
Sosnowiec
Poland

Małgorzata Poks
University of Silesia in Katowice
Sosnowiec
Poland

ISSN 2193-7648   ISSN 2193-7656 (electronic)
Second Language Learning and Teaching
ISSN 2365-967X   ISSN 2365-9688 (electronic)
Issues in Literature and Culture
ISBN 978-3-319-61048-1   ISBN 978-3-319-61049-8 (eBook)
DOI 10.1007/978-3-319-61049-8

Library of Congress Control Number: 2017944296

Printed on acid-free paper

This Springer imprint is published by Springer Nature
The registered company is Springer International Publishing AG
The registered company address is: Gewerbestrasse 11, 6330 Cham, Switzerland

Contents

Editors and Contributors

About the Editors

Jacek Mydla is Assistant Professor at the Institute of English Cultures and Literatures, University of Silesia, Poland. He holds an MA in philosophy (the Catholic University of Lublin) and in English (the University of Silesia), as well as a Ph.D and a postdoctoral degree in literary studies. He conducts research and lectures in the history of British literature, specifically Gothic fiction and drama, and theory of narrative. His book-length publications are as follows: *The Dramatic Potential of Time in Shakespeare* (2002), *Spectres of Shakespeare* (2009; a study of appropriations of Shakespeare's drama by early English Gothic authors and playwrights), and *The Shakespearean Tide* (2012; a study of representations of human time in Shakespeare's plays). Forthcoming is a book on the ghost stories of M. R. James. In his recent articles, in Polish and English, Mydla has been concerned with romantic drama, British empiricism in the eighteenth century, and the uncanny and supernatural in fiction.

Małgorzata Poks, PhD, is Assistant Professor in the Institute of English Cultures and Literatures, University of Silesia, Poland. Her main interests concern spirituality, civil disobedience, Christian anarchism, contemporary US literature, US–Mexican border writing, and animal and environmental studies. She is a recipient of several international fellowships and has published widely in Poland and abroad. Her monograph *Thomas Merton and Latin America: A Consonance of Voices* was awarded "the Louie" by the International Thomas Merton Society.

Leszek Drong is Associate Professor in the Institute of English Cultures and Literatures at the University of Silesia, Poland. He is head of the Department of Rhetoric in Culture and the Media and director of the Centre for the Study of Minor Cultures. His major publications include *Disciplining the New Pragmatism: Theory, Rhetoric and the Ends of Literary Study* (Peter Lang Verlag 2006) and *Masks and Icons: Subjectivity in Post-Nietzschean Autobiography* (Peter Lang Verlag 2001) as well as numerous chapters concerned with autobiography, rhetoric, New Pragmatism (particularly Richard Rorty and Stanley Fish), and Irish fiction (James Joyce, Flann O'Brien, Sebastian Barry, Robert McLiam Wilson).

Contributors

Anthony David Barker University of Aveiro, Aveiro, Portugal

Kornelia Boczkowska Wydział Anglistyki UAM, Adam Mickiewicz University, Poznań, Poland

Joanna Bukowska The Faculty of Pedagogy and Fine Arts, Adam Mickiewicz University, Poznań, Poland

Urszula Gołębiowska University of Zielona Góra, Zielona Góra, Poland

Agnieszka Kliś-Brodowska Institute of English Cultures and Literatures, University of Silesia, Sosnowiec, Poland

Ewa Kębłowska-Ławniczak English Literature and Comparative Studies Section, Institute of English Studies, University of Wrocław, Wrocław, Poland

Ewa Klęczaj-Siara Casimir Pulaski University of Technology and Humanities in Radom, Radom, Poland

Agnieszka Łowczanin Department of British Literature and Culture, University of Łódź, Łódź, Poland; Instytut Filologii Angielskiej, University of Łódź, Łódź, Poland

Dorota Malina Chair of Translation and Intercultural Communication, Philological Department, Jagiellonian University, Kraków, Poland

Małgorzata Poks Department of American and Canadian Studies, Institute of English Cultures and Literatures, University of Silesia, Sosnowiec, Poland

Barbara Poważa-Kurko Witold Pilecki State School of Higher Education, Oświęcim, Poland

Jadwiga Uchman University of Łódź, Łódź, Poland

Andrzej Wicher University of Łódź, Łódź, Poland

Edyta Wood Institute of Modern Languages and Applied Linguistics, Kazimierz Wielki University in Bydgoszcz, Bydgoszcz, Poland

Introduction

It is a tired cliché to insist that multiculturalism is an important social and political phenomenon. Multiculturalism has been with us for so long that in most developed societies, we have grown disenchanted with its original appeal and promise. It has, *ad nauseam*, been studied, discussed, condemned, vindicated, and finally proved unfeasible (or has it?). Still, illusory as it may seem, the multicultural project has produced tangible consequences. These include an abundance of cultural productions which attest to the vibrancy of the multicultural utopia. What our book seeks to reflect is the richness of those productions and the potential of this utopia to inspire writers and other creators. *Multiculturalism, Multilingualism and the Self: Literature and Culture Studies* is a tribute to how the very idea of multiculturalism affects not only the fictional characters analyzed by the authors of the chapters in this volume but also individual selves who contribute to cultures and their variety.

Multiculturalism, Multilingualism and the Self: Literature and Culture Studies is the second of two volumes of chapters concerned with the effect of multiculturalism and multilingualism on the self.[1] In our book, the primary focus is on the notion of multiculturalism itself and its cultural representations. We deliberately seek to remove this notion from its most sensitive social and ethnic contexts in order to see how it has been transformed by creative imaginations of various cultural agents. The first part of the book ("Selves, Identities and Cultural Differences—Literary Perspectives") considers strictly literary representations of multiculturalism in the context of the self, while the second ("Multiculturalism and the Self—Cultural Perspectives") is concerned with culture at large (including such themes as the film industry and game studies).

This book does not take sides in any debate on multiculturalism. We are not interested in addressing specific political issues. But, of course, they are there at the back of each contributor's mind: The notion of multiculturalism has been

---

[1]The first volume, published by Springer and edited by Danuta Gabrys-Barker, Adam Wojtaszek, Dagmara Galajda, and Pawel Zakrajewski, is: *Multiculturalism, Multilingualism and the Self: Studies in Linguistics and Language Learning.*

implicated in heated controversies and variously qualified to amplify its impasses and imperfections. For example, Stanley Fish, in one of the most spectacular chapters on multiculturalism to date, distinguishes between "strong" multiculturalism and "boutique" multiculturalism. What he finds crucial about strong multiculturalism is the notion of difference: "The politics of difference is what I mean by strong multiculturalism. It is strong because it values difference in and for itself rather than as a manifestation of something more basically constitutive."[2] For a strong multiculturalist tolerance is the name of the game, this principled position seems so entrenched that Fish is inclined to describe it as *uniculturalist* in the final analysis.[3] Boutique multiculturalism, in turn, is in Fish's view an untenable position because, even though "boutique multiculturalists admire or appreciate or enjoy or sympathize or (at the very least) 'recognize the legitimacy of' the traditions of cultures other than their own," they "will always stop short of approving other cultures at a point where some value at their center generates an act that offends against the canons of civilized decency as they have been either declared or assumed."[4] Fish's conclusion makes our task clear: We need to make a sharp distinction between multiculturalism as a philosophical problem and multiculturalism as a demographic fact.[5] Beyond that, our book aims to explore some of the cultural consequences of this demographic fact.

In Part I of *Multiculturalism, Multilingualism and the Self: Literature and Culture Studies*, most of the chapters revolve around the issues of identity, integrity, and diversity. Ewa Kębłowska-Ławniczak's chapter discusses these in the context of Ivan Vladislavić's novel *The Restless Supermarket*, which also problematizes the effect of a multilingual environment on the self. Next, a Western traveler's encounter with North Africa is explored in "The Self Between 'Two Incongruous and Incompatible Cultures' in Paul Bowles's *The Sheltering Sky*" by Urszula Gołębiowska. What Gołębiowska pays particular attention to is the consequences of the intercultural encounter: the incompatibility of the Western self with African space and culture; an expulsion of the white characters from the desert in the form of death and mental disintegration. In another chapter, "Kazuo Ishiguro's *Buried Giant* as a Contemporary Revision of Medieval Tropes" by Joanna Bukowska, multicultural issues are approached from a temporal angle, and the operative words in Bukowska's discussion of Ishiguro's novel are memory and forgetfulness.

American multiculturalism seems to be a case apart. The USA, a country that prides itself on its multicultural identity yet continues to oppress its minority groups through political, economic, and symbolic violence, is the backdrop to Ana Castillo's *So Far From God,* which Małgorzata Poks discusses from a feminist perspective. Poks concentrates on the critical representations of both

---

[2]Stanley Fish, "Boutique Multiculturalism" in: *The Trouble with Principle* (Cambridge, Massachusetts; London, England: Harvard University Press, 1999), p. 60.

[3]Fish, p. 62.

[4]Fish, p. 56.

[5]See Fish, p. 63.

multiculturalism and Christian patriarchy in Castillo's novel. In another Anglophone country, the UK, Polish immigrants face serious dilemmas which are directly concerned with multicultural issues. Those dilemmas are explored in "Literary Presentations of Polish Immigrants in England: *Where the Devil Can't Go* by Anya Lipska and *Madame Mephisto* by A.M. Bakalar," by Barbara Poważa-Kurko. Jadwiga Uchman, in turn, in her chapter "'Convergence of Different Threads': Tom Stoppard's *Dogg's Hamlet, Cahoot's Macbeth*," is concerned with Stoppard's intertextual strategies which invite multilingual and, by extension, multicultural readings of his plays. In the last chapter in Part I, what comes to the fore in Andrzej Wicher's discussion of *The Canterbury Tales* by Chaucer as a multicultural work is the theme of cosmopolitanism seen in the character of the Shipman.

Part II of the volume, which places multiculturalism and the self in cultural perspectives, opens with Anthony D. Barker's wide-angled take on Hollywood representations of the world at large and the challenges posed by the arrival of sound to representing diverse language communities as well as marketing multilingual/multicultural films to foreign audiences. IMAX films, in turn, are the primary focus of Kornelia Boczkowska's contribution, which foregrounds the transnational and multicultural aspects of spaceflight in *Hail Columbia* (1982), *The Dream Is Alive* (1985), and *Destiny in Space* (1994). A relatively new arrival on the research scene, the interactive video game, may also be studied from the perspective of multiculturalism, as argued by Agnieszka Kliś-Brodowska. In her article, she develops an inquiry into the current state of research and outlines perspectives for further study.

Dorota Malina looks into the challenges posed by intercultural translations in her chapter "An Haughty Sniff versus a Spoonful of Sugar, or Who Is Mary Poppins?" Comparing the original book series with its Polish literary and American cinematic renditions, the author discusses the strategies employed by the respective translators and adapters and examines the resultant shifts in the main character's identity. The two final chapters in this volume shine a revealing light on the problematic character of US multiculturalism. While Ewa Klęczaj-Siara reads ethnic American children's literature in the perspective of ethnic authenticity, Edyta Wood is concerned with indigenous lives caught in between cultures as presented in the self-narratives of Sherman Alexie and Joy Harjo. All in all, both literary and cultural perspectives on the nexus of multiculturalism and the self yield a dazzling multiplicity: a kaleidoscope of options, visions, and positions. In all these contexts, multiculturalism expresses limitless potential for new patterns and narratives of identity.

Part I
Selves, Identities and Cultural Differences—Literary Perspectives

Fear of Multilingualism and the Uses of Nostalgia in Ivan Vladislavić's *The Restless Supermarket*

Ewa Kębłowska-Ławniczak

Abstract The article concentrates on the growing multilingual and multicultural diversity which Ivan Vladislavić's protagonist reads as impinging chaos. The fear of intelligibility enhances his efforts to defend the ordering standards associated with the English language. Indicating the conventional and arbitrary nature of standards indispensable for the protagonist's understanding of the world, the article traces their cultural limits. Further, it points to the fact that the protagonist must transcend his predilection for closure in order to respond to the multilingual environ. Finally, the article argues that, paradoxically, the discernible nostalgic undercurrent pervading South African literature and culture may facilitate the acceptance of a necessary disruptive, self-reflexive epistemology. Dwelling on the ambivalences of longing and belonging, travelling between the individual and the collective, between the present and the prospective future—the article proposes—nostalgia may become a screening device, a mediator that performs a comforting function.

Keywords Vladislavić · Multilingualism · Romanticism · Nostalgia

1 Introduction

Aubrey Tearle, a former proofreader and the protagonist of Ivan Vladislavić's novel, entitled *The Restless Supermarket*, aligns himself with the arbitrary and conventional system of standards he struggles to protect considering their correctness and transparency indispensable not only for his but also for a general

E. Kębłowska-Ławniczak (✉)
English Literature and Comparative Studies Section, Institute of English Studies,
University of Wrocław, ul. Kuźnicza 22, 50-138 Wrocław, Poland
e-mail: ewa.keblowska-lawniczak@uwr.edu.pl

© Springer International Publishing AG 2017
J. Mydla et al. (eds.), *Multiculturalism, Multilingualism and the Self: Literature and Culture Studies*, Issues in Literature and Culture,
DOI 10.1007/978-3-319-61049-8_1

understanding of the world.[1] The proofreader's efforts to oppose what is called the devolution of the English language[2] are futile and alienating. Moreover, Vladislavić seems to be pointing to their cultural limits. The growing disparity between Aubrey Tearle's belief in linguistic purity and the tangible materiality of language sign, including the materiality of the very texts submitted to the protagonist as a proofreader, facilitate the discovery of the limits. Tearle, whose professional obsession extends due to his hermeneutic sensibility, proofreads not only texts but also the city of Johannesburg and its inhabitants. His task is supposed to keep "the grey matter supple" the same way physical exercise should keep the body fit (RS,[3] p. 64). Textualising the body of the increasingly alien conurbation, Tearle infects the precious language standards. The more and more formless urban materiality— an aurally, visually and haptically experienced detritus—endangers the proof-reader's sense of order. Some names become "tawty" (p. 20), a word Tearle is unable to find in any reference work, while others are reduced to monosyllabic chunks or "unfeeling stump[s] like Gav or Ern or Gord" (p. 20). In order to respond to the alienating otherness of the multilingual environ the protagonist must make an effort to transcend his predilection for closure. The article argues then that the pervasive sense of loss (including the loss of standards) and disappointment sustain a distinct and complex nostalgic undercurrent. Dwelling on the ambivalence of longing for what has been lost and the dilemma of belonging, travelling between the individual and the collective, between the present and the past, the present and the prospective future, nostalgia may become a screening device, a useful mediator that performs a paradoxically comforting function.

2   Multilingualism in South Africa

Ivan Vladislavić's *The Restless Supermarket* addresses a culturally and linguisti-cally complex situation in post-apartheid South Africa where multilingualism poses a many-faceted dilemma. In 1953 The Bantu Education Act instituted mother tongue education in African languages but with a separatist and discriminatory purpose. Introduced in agreement with what is called Herderian or Romantic ide-ology of European nation-states (Woolard, 1998, p. 16), instruction in indigenous languages prevented the speakers from mixing rather than recognized the

---

[1]Tearle's approach is mediated by codes and conventions and therefore his reading, Marais writes, is neither direct nor immediate (p. 102).

[2]Helgesson refers to a spectrum of figurative meanings the term conveys. The *minoritisation* of English in (post)Apartheid South Africa is essential (p. 778). However, devolution refers also to the process of handing over and delegating powers of decision concerning, for instance correctness and propriety, to the new "owners" of the language. Towards the end of the discussion, I refer to this passing of ownership in regard to memory.

[3]All in-text references to *The Restless Supermarket* by Ivan Vladislavić use the following abbreviation: RS.

uniqueness of their cultural heritage. This policy led to an exclusion of young speakers from the mainstream of social life by imprisoning them in their culturally distinct, essential ethnic identities and linguistically "pure" communities, "nation-states" or Bantustans. A more empowering solution would have been offered to the young South African pupils, the users of more than nine languages (now 12 are recognized as official) had the learners been given an opportunity to choose between the indigenous languages and English as medium of education. The multilingual policy implemented in South Africa, as Weber writes, "was fuelled by an ideology of white supremacy and fear of linguistic and cultural heterogeneity" (p. 128). Under these circumstances, somewhat ironically, the multicultural policy forced the speakers of indigenous languages into marginalisation. On the other hand, an exclusive use of the English language, instead of the indigenous, would reduce, though in a different way, the important heritage of the native languages and threaten to impose a uniformity and neutrality articulated by cosmopolitan liberalism, a policy which disregards cultural and linguistic variety. For the white inhabitants, this difference-blind policy could serve as a weapon against bewilderingly rapid change and an increasing sense of insecurity.

The changes Vladislavić documents in his writing affected many spheres of life resulting in urban and linguistic forms of hybridity reflected, for instance, in yet another group of languages, i.e. in the multicultural and multilingual phenomenon of street lingo or urban vernaculars.[4] In *The Restless Supermarket* Vladislavić often refers to the vernacular, a language which has emerged along with urban alterations and which addresses the related social and cultural transformations in post-apartheid South Africa. What is called urban vernaculars consists in a mixture of languages that have emerged from the multilingual background. Their defining feature, according to Beck, is that their speakers "may not necessarily be able to develop full competence in each of the languages that make up the amalgam" (p. 25). Mixing lexicon and risking the loss of cultural integrity, the users of urban vernaculars show a general disrespect for rules. Like in the game of eponyms and their progenitors, played by Spilkin and Merle in Vladislavić's novel, rules are replaced by amusing combinations which bring together "Wellington" and "Plimsoll" (RS, pp. 91–92). The speakers are criticised by Aubrey Tearle, the character of a language purist, for their bad speech manners.

The thriving multilingual and multicultural diversity, which the embittered protagonist reads as impinging chaos, enhances his efforts to defend the ordering norms and, in that way, to save both the world, rapidly receding from grasp, and himself

---

[4]The terms are not precise. Kruger explains that street lingo, e.g. Flaaitaaal which combines Afrikaans morphology with lexical elements from Bantu is spoken by Black males (p. xx) and therefore emphasis is put on the black versus white. Mesthrie, whose study focuses on geographically specific communities, points to the fact that the component of Africaans is characteristic of Coloured communities rather than Black (p. 97), which involves much greater diversity. Urban vernaculars are used by young people. The sense of confusion and difficulty in classifying the eruptions of linguistic activity is reflected in Vladislavić's writing. In *The Restless Supermarket* he classifies as a lingo-user someone who speaks "isi-Sotho or whatever" (RS, p. 29).

from the danger of "being swept away" (RS, p. 74). The chaos he compares to *Sacco di Roma* (RS, p. 121) affects not only the universe of discourse but also the cityscape which, in its palimpsest, reveals bodies left unburied among "rusted pipes," "a reef of disorder" and a civilization that had gone to ruin (RS, pp. 12, 189). Soliloquizing on his own death in the area of Abel Road, he sees it as the ultimate loss of standards (RS, p. 239), "as a precipitate efflux of vocabulary and idiom... the whole adulterated brew spilt on the dirty macadam of an unmemorable corner of a lawless conurbation" (RS, p. 30). The potential dissolution of cultural and linguistic norms and the inevitable minoritisation of Standard English terrify the protagonist. The catastrophic visions strengthen his belief in the necessity of challenging the decline of standards in general by becoming a writer, i.e. a public intellectual. A former proofreader of telephone directories, he focuses on writing a book whose title advertises a local language competition: The Proofreader's Derby. A notebook for the time being, the manuscript contains a "System of Records," a collection of errors compiled by the conservative proofreader who decides to devote his retirement to the task of classifying and collating the *corrigenda* collected during the thirty years of his professional career (RS, p. 64). Spilkin, a retired optician and Aubrey's colleague from the Café Europa, originally a "club" (RS, p. 40), believes the book to be the true story of Aubrey Tearle's life, a peculiar form of life-writing in the form of index cards and, potentially, his intellectual autobiography (RS, p. 63). A perfect proofreader leaves no visible trace. Hence Aubrey hopes the book to become a visible and tangible memorial or heritage "through which [he] hope[s] to make a little mark, something of lasting value to which [his] name might be attached" (RS, p. 30), a monument to standards which need to be defended.

3   Sources of Linguistic Diversity

In *The Restless Supermarket*, the proliferation of non-standard linguistic diversity poses a threat to what the English language and literature have traditionally meant in South Africa, i.e. the romantic expression of inner truth. This disruptive diversity is enhanced by several factors, including the appearance of indigenous languages in public space, the arrival of the newcomers with their non-standard English (some from Yugoslavia and Poland), and by Americanisms spreading through popular media and global commerce. Aubrey Tearle classifies indigenous speech as inarticulate, animal-like "roaring and cursing," or "multilingual sobbing" (RS, p. 12), and thus an intrusion of the materiality of noise into the purity of the public realm. To him a streetwalker, who speaks in isi-Sotho, "cracks" and "tee-hees" (RS, p. 29). The deteriorating social standards and language manners affect also the protagonist, whom better words begin to fail. Even the proofreader "stoops" to such Wesselisms as "skop, skiet and donner" and their corollaries "snot and trane" (RS, p. 11), words originating in Africaans. The inflow of new vocabulary stimulates his linguistic investigations. Still, the origin of many words is disputable, for example "china" meaning "friend" (RS, p. 163) sounds either like Cockney English or evokes a well-known pun from William Wycherley's comedy of manners but, as it turns out, can be derived from Bantu *umshana*. The newcomers, i.e. the immigrants, tellingly called Bogeymen, Bohemians or vagabonds (RS, pp. 129, 138), speak in varieties of sub-standard English littered with malapropisms and barbarisms (RS, p. 139). As Tearle discovers, the newcomers are unable to tell the difference between "boff," "buff" and "boffin" (RS, p. 139). On top of that linguistic mishmash, Americanisms multiply, for example the "spin-off" often used by the migrants. And so are other imports like the "chow-chow" used by Wessels on departure and borrowed from pidgin Chinese (RS, p. 139). The narrator notices the fashion for products with labels on the outside and their popularity among the newcomers who turn themselves into unsalaried sandwich-men. The fashion brings new commercial vocabulary into the public sphere, e.g. leatherama, cupboard-a-rama, veg-a-rama, and Glarebusters. In a restaurant serving more cosmopolitan food and conforming to global standards Tearle learns that "English not so good" (RS, p. 86), which may apply to both language and food. Insisting on the need to have standards of correctness, the conservative proofreader declares that when it comes to current usage he is "with Dr. Johnson" (RS, p. 236). However, he fails to notice the contemporary context within which "Magic Johnson" refers to the American basketball star rather than to the author of the famous dictionary. The purity of standards Tearle advocates is negatively revised by current usage. Moreover, it hinders rather than assists good communication.

4 Apartheid Discourse

Tearle's fear of miscegenation concerns more than language and in this respect echoes the demand for purity inherent in apartheid discourse while his efforts to preserve the correctness of a language severed from social and political reality reveal a nostalgic attachment to the romantic legacy. To a considerable extent, the fear of heterogeneity evokes comments on blood-mixing and bastardization J.M. Coetzee discusses in "Apartheid Thinking" (p. 173). Quoting from Geoffrey Cronjé, Coetzee points to the Apartheid conviction that mixed areas become dying-places for the whites, while "living-higgeldy-piggeldy," like the "mishmash-society," are conditions of social disorder denoting a lack of distinctions and mental confusion (p. 172). In *The Restless Supermarket*, the once elitist Café Europe admits an increasing mixture of guests speaking non-standard English: indigents in balaclava, the "new blood" (p. 149), Continentals, Slavs, and mustafinas (p. 273). The essential dichotomies collapse: inside versus outside (p. 254), private versus public (p. 152), and intuition versus reason. Emotions are no longer conceptualised so that the semantic boundaries between them obliterate—tears and laughter melt. Merouv Bonsma, a hybrid of a typist and a pianist, appears to be a repository "filled" with a "jumble of music that had been poured into her, like leftovers into an olla podrida," an "indiscriminate broth" (RS, p. 75). Instead of proper dining hours and "square meals" the restaurants serve "brunch," a "bastardized" form of dining (RS, p. 157).

Compared to a terrorist attack on a Heidelberg tavern, the final party brings Café Europe, the "philosophers" club, to an end (RS, p. 281). Even Tearle emerges from the experience of the bash curiously contaminated, looking like "a badly printed half-tone" (RS, p. 280), a tramp or a scavenger.

5 Romantic Legacy and the Dictionary

Though evoking romantic concepts, Vladislavić is not just a romantic writer. Neither is he a ruthless deconstructor of the romantic tradition.[5] The romantic legacy is signalled on the outskirts of the novel in its epigraphs, i.e. in the threshold zone of the paratextual surround, only to be interrogated by the implied reader. *The Restless Supermarket* is divided into three parts: "The Café Europa," "The Proofreader's Derby (Corrected)," and "The Goodbye Bash." The opening part converges around the disappearing institution of a social club (RS, p. 13) whose meetings used to cultivate the art of conversation and which deteriorates into "a family" meeting formula (p. 40). Part Two turns out to introduce a utopian city of the mind Tearle calls a "generous elsewhere," not a "home" but a place where he roams in his imagination (p. 24).The utopian project called Alibia promptly shows symptoms of infection. The closing part is devoted to a carnivalesque party which conflates the idea of the titular "bash" with that of a reunion. The novel as a whole and its subsequent parts are preceded by epigraphs. As Genette observes, "[t]he presence or absence of an epigraph in itself marks the period, the genre, or the tenor of the piece of writing" (p. 160). The romantic period, as opposed to realism, indulges in epigraphic excess in an effort to "integrate" the novel "into a cultural tradition" (p. 160). The epigraph, Genette observes, is a "password of intellectuality" (p. 160). Hence epigraphic excess in *The Restless Supermarket* seems to foreground a pedantic intellectuality and anchorage in tradition (including the romantic tradition), whose loss Tearle mourns writing up the monument of his intellectual autobiography he calls "The Proofreader's Derby." "I long therefore I am" is the romantic motto (Boym 2001, p. 13) the protagonist does not articulate directly but implements in his writing. Considering the desire for tradition that Tearle declares, it must be noticed that the opening epigraph is autographic as it is signed by Aubrey Tearle, the fictional author. Autographic epigraphs tend to function as preface. Genette suggests that apart from a lack of modesty they reveal disguised authorship attributed to a character. Indeed, the opening epigraph of *The Restless Supermarket* is not a quotation but a prefatory comment on the standards of purity and correctness whose guardian is the dictionary. Hence a dictionary utopia becomes the bedrock and the source of the "inner truth"—a dwarfed version of the

---

[5]Helgesson refers to Coetzee as a writer "operating in the twilight of the romantic era" (p. 781) and its deconstructor. Vladislavić bypasses such projects and instead of focusing on the expression "of the inner self" (p. 782), he focuses on the materiality of the sign.

romantic legacy. The effect is mildly ironic. "Where can we always find happiness?" asks the epigrapher and the epigraphed in one. "In the dictionary," is the answer Aubrey Tearle provides. In that way the tradition the proofreader invokes is anchored in language as it is codified in *The Pocket Oxford Dictionary*, "the incomparable fourth edition, revised and reprinted with corrections in 1957, henceforth referred to as 'the *Pocket*'" (RS, p. 20). Interestingly, the tendency to consider dictionary codifications as norms or ideal models is American rather than British. In "The Goodbye Bash" the *Pocket* saves the proofreader's life when the bootboy's knife blade goes straight into "the heart" of the dictionary (RS, p. 271), rather than Aubrey Tearle's chest, making the protagonist feel immortal (p. 272). Indeed, his immortality depends on the dictionary. Recollecting earlier language codifications, Tearle remembers nostalgically the *Concise* (2nd edition, 1929) revised by Henry W. Fowler, where the contributions of an amateur, Major Byron F. Caws, were diligently acknowledged (RS, p. 286). Boasting expertise in etymology, Tearle identifies with the amateur lexicographer. Although "the *Pocket*" claims control over current English, when exposed to the vernacular, the dictionary turns out to be a mausoleum, a heritage incapable of telling the difference between "huge" and "Eug," the latter derived from "Eugene" (RS p. 248). The gap between pure voice and "material" sign is foregrounded. It is Eug, a user of the urban vernacular and a travesty of authority who corrects the retired proofreader, questions his sanity and restores communication between Tearle and the semantically unstable environment. Proofreading fails as a form of communication, communication analysis and supervision of cultural interactions. Thus the amateur lexicographer and etymologist discovers the limits of his standards.

The two epigraphs that follow are allographic and derive from Hazlitt's essays, "On the Conversation of Authors" and "On Pedantry," while the third comes from the Gospel of St Matthew 23:24. The last holds a line directed against pedantry understood as excessive attachment to useless knowledge and inspires a change of perspective. Nostalgically embedded in Hazlitt's essays, "Café Europa" and "The Proofreader's Derby" share in the complexity of discussions in and around the essays as well as in the concept of communication the institution of conversation cultivates. There are ample intertextual relations between Hazlitt's essays and Vladislavić's writing. However, immediately relevant to the present discussion seems to be the figure of a scholar, an unyielding radical whose world is reduced to the materiality of books rather than text and who reminds us of Vladislavić's proofreader. Hazlitt's scholar "hangs like a film and cobweb upon letters... like the dust upon the outside of knowledge" and "browses on the husk and leaves of books, as the young fawn browses on the bark and leaves of trees" (Hazlitt, 1913, p. 315). Though expressing critical opinion, both authors (Hazlitt and Vladislavić) remain mildly sympathetic (showing understanding) towards their subject. Hazlitt for example, finds the bookish scholar honest, simple-hearted, faithful and affectionate (p. 315). Pedantry is not only ostentatious display of erudition but, as Simon P. Barry claims, "a distinct affect that makes the pleasures... of professional life possible" (2012, p. 47). The South African writer points out the proofreader's pedantry but is not seriously interested in stigmatizing Aubrey Tearle for his blindness. Considering these links, the Hazlitt epigraphs provide a subtle anchorage in the romantic tradition of the pure voice but, what is perhaps more important, reveal what the protagonist truly misses. What significantly pervades "On the Conversation of Authors" and enters *The Restless Supermarket* is the powerful sense of nostalgia:

> Those days are over! An event, the name of which I wish never to mention, broke up our party, like a bombshell thrown into the room: and now we seldom meet…There is no longer the same set of persons, nor of associations. (Hazlitt, 1913, p. 306)

> When I think of those times now (casting some shadow from my mind), they are dappled with daylight sifted through the north-facing window of Café Europa. Like gold dust blown in off the dumps. … Four people around a table. A round table…. We got to know one another a little, and to like one another to the same modest extent. There was not much depth to our association…. I can scarcely recall a conversation now that could not be plumbed with a teaspoon… But it was stable, reliable, secure – qualities some of us only came to appreciate fully after we had been overwhelmed by flimsy, crooked things. (RS, p. 104)

Surrounded by cultural and linguistic chaos, by analogy to the tradition of polite conversation of authors practised in Hazlitt's essay, the elitist Café Europe, now called an "error" (RS, p. 13) in the new post-1993 text, is closing down. As opposed to many other locations mentioned by Vladislavić, Café Europe never existed. Hence, a mind-product, the meeting-place of intellectuals imagined by Aubrey Tearly, it can be easily wiped out from the unstable landscape of Hillbrow.

6   The Nostalgic Turn

Post-apartheid South African culture, Hook observes, is "awash with nostalgia" bringing together a broad spectrum of voices (p. 170). Memoirs, scholarly reminiscences, and popular youth culture reveal a diversity of attitudes to the relevance of nostalgia as critical instrument. The latter prospect owes much to Svetlana Boym's *The Future of Nostalgia* (2001). Aware of the wealth of conceptualizations, I will limit the references of nostalgia to what is strictly pertinent to my highly selective discussion of Vladislavić's novel. Hence worth emphasizing is the fact that in spite of the complex typologies, the neat differentiations between the reactionary and the progressive, the restorative and the reflective nostalgias, they are not mutually exclusive. While restorative nostalgia tends to be defensive in protecting the absolute truth, reflective nostalgia, travelling between the collective and the individual, calls the absolute truth in doubt and, according to Boym, holds an ethical and creative potential (p. xviii). Nostalgia itself, Hook explains, is not "alternatively progressive or reactionary, but the uses to which it is put [are]" (p. 173). The object of romantic nostalgia, as in Hazlitt's essay, is, to use Boym's formulation, "beyond the present space of experience" (p. 13). It is either in the past or in the timelessness of such utopias as dictionaries, projects like Café Europe and the protagonist's intellectual autobiography which is also utopian.

The immediate impulse to nostalgic recollection in *The Restless Supermarket* derives from anxiety (or fear) caused by a sense of loss and chaos. As Tearle observes, "the existence of the place was threatened" (RS, p. 15). However, the nostalgic response is not uniform, both restorative and reflective. The temptation to indulge comfortably in purely restorative "looking back" is disturbed by ironic comments, parody and travesty, which shows that the speakers do address the uncertain present rather than indulge and immerse themselves in the past. Walking on the edge of Hillbrow, Tearle finds the public space uninviting. It turns out that the "seating arrangements," the benches for whites only, have disappeared[6] while new ones have not been installed to discourage loiterers (RS, p. 21). Neither explicit Apartheid nostalgia nor a case of Apartheid *Nachträglichkeit* [belatedness], the extent to which the walker either misses the lost order or reflects on change remains unclear.[7] Vladislavić's unique focus on detail generates a multiplicity of amazing episodes and plots rather than a consistently satirical approach. As a result, the walker's daily constitutional evolves into a drift. The unpredictability of encounters prevents an ideologically homogeneous narrative and allows for ethical reflection. Pursuing his daily walk Aubrey notices that Hillbrow's standards have deteriorated and the densely populated area is becoming a "jungly flatland" with "Europa Caffy" as the "last outpost of symbolization" (RS, p. 17).[8] Here, due to the symbolic reference to topography, a subscription to apartheid discourse becomes more prominent. Still, it is not Tearle but Wessels who sentimentally waffles about the "good old days" while the protagonist reflects on the relations between the present and the past in terms of travesty (p. 15) and parody of his favourite genre, the letter to the editor (p. 17). The romantic nostalgic, says Boym, "directs his gaze not only backwards but sideways, and expresses himself in... ironic fragments" (p. 13). Paradoxically, Vladislavić's appropriation of the romantic tradition is also multi-faceted and complex.

As opposed to these "ironic fragments," a non-romantic form of nostalgic expression (Boym mentions philosophical and scientific treatises) appears in Aubrey's treatise, test or intellectual autobiography, "The Proofreader's Derby," a utopian construction called Alibia (alibi) which disintegrates as a result of a series of accidents. Crucial is the death of the printer's devil whose duty has been to carry

---

[6]The "whites only" bench appears in several texts. Manase refers to them as the "iconography of segregation" (p. 55). The bench becomes the subject and title of one of the short stories, "The WHITES ONLY Bench" included in Vladislavić's *Propaganda by Monuments* where its replica furnishes a fake museum exhibit. The false exhibit triggers off painful memories of Apartheid (Vladislavić, 1996, p. 66). Vladislavić retains the ambiguity and diversity of memories due to a whole spectrum of perceptions converging around false heritage.

[7]As observed by Kruger, Vladislavić skillfully maintains the tension between "an ironic and a loving treatment" of the city and its "sober documentation" avoiding in that way the explicitly political "barbs" so prominent in the writing of, for example, Salman Rushdie, to whom Vladislavić is often compared (Kruger, p. 188).

[8]In urban vernacular, the "jungly flatland" becomes a term for "dense apartment districts in Johannesburg inner city" (Kruger, p. xx). The area is hilly. Once again a simple reference to the Apartheid past and colonial imagery is misleading.

the galley proofs of that day's edition of *Alibian Star* for approval (RS, p. 196). On his way from the printing works to the council chambers the young man rides into a stone wall and dies. The broken type gets scattered around the body and the boy's scooter. The related incidents of the broken type and the damage in the ancient city wall result in a massive catastrophe preventing either fixity or closure. While language errors proliferate, buildings drift off their foundations and float away in spite of the land surveyor's intervention. The city in "The Proofreader's Derby," Tearle's monumental work and the second part of Vladislavić's novel, has its visual counterpart in the painting of Alibia on the wall of Café Europe: "The impending loss that grieved me most was Alibia, the painted city that covered an entire wall of the Café… It should be moved to a new location… packed, transported, and reassembled. The Yanks were all for that sort of thing, carving up the world and recycling it as atmosphere" (RS, p. 16).

Assuming that the narrative utopia of "The Proofreader's Derby" realizes a re-union imagined by the nostalgic—a reassembling of an inauthentic future-past oriented reality—its collapse is likely to generate further restorative repetitions, a string of simulacra, incapable of forming the identity of Fluxman, its protagonist and Tearle's *porte-parole* or "word carrier." If so, Tearle's project of an intellectual's autobiography becomes a mechanism producing nostalgia in accordance with Susan Stewart's claim that "nostalgia is a desire for desire" (RS, p. 23). As opposed to the European ambience, which "has to accrue over time" (p. 23), nostalgic atmosphere is an American commodity "pumped in overnight" (p. 23). Paradoxically, then, Tearle's project of an intellectual autobiography generates a "restless" supermarket, a globally conceived commercial re-union, a trivializing form of romantic sentimentality and a parody of pure values as, ultimately, *pecunia non olet*. Its restorative potential reveals itself in a case of plastic surgery performed on a pink rubber elephant: the replacement of Dumbo's ear. Though explicitly comic, the commercially generated production of nostalgia guarantees access[9] to the market independently of race, class, gender, culture or linguistic competence.

In his efforts to preserve and accommodate the past in the context of a too looming present, Aubrey Tearl reminds us of a famous antiquarian, John Aubrey, the author of the *Brief Lives and Miscellanies* (1690), who insisted that the dying English past should be respectfully studied (Stewart, 1984, p. 139) and incorporated into the present. However, neither the *corrigenda* nor the pieces of etymological knowledge (no matter whether false or true) collected by the pedantic scholar can be appropriated by the multilingual present. Hence the project of launching "The Proofreader's Derby" as an intellectual's autobiography at the final bash is postponed by its author who, gradually, becomes aware of its illusory defensive

---

[9]In *The Restless Supermarket* debates on multiculturalism, nativism and cosmopolitan liberalism form an undercurrent deserving a separate discussion. The desire for a difference-blind system (Citrin & Sears 2014, p. xviii) and the market as index of democratic reform are often though humorously proposed. For the same reason the title uses the metaphor of a supermarket open round-the-clock.

potential.[10] On the other hand, the very idea of a re-union, even if it means access to the global market, reappears in Vladislavić's novel in the form of various souvenirs. Souvenirs, Stewart writes, are objects whose reawakening signals an earlier rupture (Stewart, 1984, p. 143). The potential of souvenirs consists in the fact that by lending "authenticity to the past," they move history into private time where the time of their production yields to the moment of their consumption (Stewart, 1984, p. 144), a shift which facilitates micro-narratives of reconciliation. The souvenirs in "Café Europe" are "souvenirs on loan," pieces of the Berlin Wall peddled by Eastern European emigrants:

> The dust had hardly settled in Germany before the rubble of the Berlin Wall was up for sale. One of Bogey's country cousins arrived with a piece of it in his luggage, a bit of brick and a layer of paint-smeared plaster. Muggins had paid fifteen marks for it, according to the cardboard container, which also had picture purporting to show that the paint was a scrap of the garish bubble with which the entire wall had been coated. The Western side, that is. (RS, p. 161)

For some South Africans, Popescu claims, these pieces of rabble were "liberation relics" (p. 19) and proof of a successful transition from a totalitarian to a democratic system. Moreover, they were witness to the reunification of a divided nation. In "The Goodbye Bash" the appropriation of Joburg's rubble follows the patterns of Ostalgia[11] for sale:

> 'Apartheid is yesterday,' Bogey was saying. 'But things of apartheid is today. many things, rememorabilia ... benches, papers, houses.'

> He pressed a business card into my hand. Dan Boguslavić. apartheid memorabilia. import/export. ... There were all sorts of things for sale. benches, white only. easy to assemble. blankets, prison, grey. books, reference. (RS, p. 249)

Nostalgia business becomes a necessary stage in the "owning" and domestication of difficult memories, a process of reconciliation forcing the excess of things and memories into a tentatively harmonic form. These souvenirs allow Bogey, an immigrant, to become a businessman in his new life, to consume and to tame the alien environment. The "benches, white only" no longer belong to the museumized heritage and no longer breed heritage nostalgia to shape and maintain the collective memory of Apartheid and its trauma. Instead, by entering the "restless" market, they become a cheap, aesthetically dubious but popular commodity anyone can acquire.

---

[10]Vladislavić makes it clear that Mandela's life-story has been treated as fetish. However, the proofreader remembers with a pinch of irony that Mandela on leaving the detention place was given a good suit but bad glasses, which gives rise to Tearle's etymological speculations as well as comments on Madiba's myopia (RS, pp. 185–86).

[11]Ostalgia is a form of nostalgia experienced by people who lived in the Democratic German Republic. It concerns aspects of social life but is often revealed in an effort to preserve local customs, brands and products which become precious souvenirs. Vladislavić makes references to the process of unification and its consequences drawing analogies between Germany and South Africa. The idea of selling Joburg's rubble as souvenirs comes from Berlin.

7 Conclusion

Finally, by analogy to the appropriation of objects and their re-location/re-installation in the present, "The Goodbye Bash" stages a Dionysian party which conflates a farewell with still another re-union. The reunion becomes a fleeting version of the nostalgic longing. Its aim is to get characters back together in an entirely altered context of Café Europe. As Lizardi explains, in contemporary mediatized culture reunions are meetings without any promise or indication of further content to come (p. 66). They neither restore the past nor offer continuity. Hence, the reunion in Vladislavić's novel screens the past selecting objects and memories for appropriation in the present but leaves the future open to speculation by re-directing the protagonist's attention to the "dark spaces" in telephone directories, to the unknowable on the map of Johannesburg, and to languages that he "would never put to the proof" (RS, p. 298). Reunion requires that the proofreader, another fossil and souvenir, is relocated from his imaginary topography of Alibia to recognize the otherness of the unscripted Joburg whose lights "squirm and wriggle," like bookworms, in an unknown language rather than "twinkle" in a familiar manner.

References

Barry, S. P. (2012). *Romantic pedantry: Personifying the intellectual from Mr. Spectator to Rev. Casaubon* (Unpublished doctoral dissertation). Rutgers, The State University of New Jersey.

Beck, R. M. (2010). Urban languages in Africa. *Africa Spectrum, 45*(3), 11–41.

Boym, S. (2001). *The future of nostalgia.* New York: Basic Books.

Citrin, J., & Sears, D. O. (2014). *American identity and the politics of multiculturalism.* New York: Cambridge University Press.

Coetzee, J. M. (1996). Apartheid thinking. In J. M. Coetzee (Ed.), *Giving offense: Essays on censorship* (pp. 163–184). Chicago, London: University of Chicago Press.

Genette, G. (1997). *Paratexts: Threshold of interpretation.* Cambridge: CUP.

Hazlitt, W. (1913). On the conversation of authors. In J. Zeitlin (Ed.), *Hazlitt on English literature. An introduction to the appreciation of literature.* (pp. 301–315). Oxford: OUP.

Helgesson, S. (2004). 'Minor Disorders': Ivan Vladislavić and the devolution of South African English. *Journal of South African Studies.* Writing in Transition in South Africa: Fiction, History, Biography. Spec. issue. *30*(4), 777–787.

Hook, D. (2013). *(Post)apartheid conditions: Psychoanalysis and social formation.* Houndmills: Palgrave.

Lizardi, R. (2015). *Mediated nostalgia: Individual memory and contemporary mass media.* Lanham, Boulder, NY, London: Lexington Books.

Manase, I. (2009). Johannesburg during the transition in Ivan Vladislavić's 'The WHITES ONLY Bench' and *The Restless Supermarket. English Academy Review, 26*(1), 53–61. doi:10.1080/10131750902768416

Marais, M. (2002). Visions of excess: Closure, irony, and the thought of community in Ivan Vladislavić's *The Restless Supermarket. English in Africa, 29*(2), 102–117.

Mesthrie, R. (2008). "I've been speaking Tsotsitaal all my life without knowing it": Towards a unified account of Tsotsitaals in South Africa. In M. Meyerhoff, & N. Nagy (Eds.), *Social lives in language—Sociolinguistics and multilingual speech communities* (pp. 95–110). Amsterdam, Philadelphia: John Benjamins Publishing.

Popescu, M. (2010). *South African literature beyond the Cold War*. Houndmills: Palgrave.

Stewart, S. (1984). *On longing. Narratives of the miniature, the gigantic, the souvenir, the collection*. Baltimore & London: The Johns Hopkins UP.

Vladislavić, I. (1996). The WHITES ONLY Bench. *Propaganda by monuments and other stories* (pp. 51–56). Johannesburg: Random House.

Vladislavić, I. (2012). *The restless supermarket*. And Other Stories: London & New York.

Weber, J., & Horner, K. (2012). *Introducing multilingualism: A social approach*. Abingdon: Routledge.

Woolard, K. A. (1998). Introduction: Language ideology as a field of inquiry. In B. B. Schieffelin, K. A. Woolard & P. V. Kroskrity (Eds.), *Language ideologies: Practice and theory* (pp. 3–49). Oxford: OUP.

Author Biography

Ewa Kębłowska-Ławniczak is Associate Professor of English Literature and Comparative Studies at Wrocław University, Poland. She is the author of *Shakespeare and the Controversy Over Baroque, The Visual Seen and Unseen: Insights into Tom Stoppard's Art* and the more recent book *From Concept-City to City Experience: A Study in Urban Drama* (2013). She has edited and co-edited several monographs including the recent *Spectrum of Emotions: From Love to Grief* (2016). Since 2012 she is general editor of the journal *Anglica Wratislaviensia* and co-editor of Silesian Studies in Anglophone Literatures and Cultures (Peter Lang). She has published articles and chapters in monographs covering the field of contemporary drama, theatre and urbanity in fiction and non-fiction in the English language.

The Self Between "Two Incongruous and Incompatible Cultures" in Paul Bowles's *The Sheltering Sky*

Urszula Gołębiowska

Abstract Paul Bowles's 1949 novel *The Sheltering Sky* explores the writer's recurring theme—the Western traveler's encounter with North Africa. Centered on the experiences of an American couple, Port and Kit Moresby, the novel maps their journey into the Sahara Desert as they flee the decadent, post-World War II America. Against existentialist interpretations of the novel which interiorize the desert and leave out the native culture, this reading foregrounds the role of the space and intercultural encounter in the protagonists' experience. It is argued that the desert does not serve as a backdrop or a blank screen on which the characters project their fears and desires, but is produced as a space—Soja's "Thirdspace"—that exceeds its physical and imagined components and involves mystery, agency and the power to transform the travelers' lives. Analogously to the desert, the local culture is misapprehended, not just projected on; it is framed in conventional Orientalist tropes of opacity, unknowability, and exoticism. Colonialist attitudes, thus reenacted, erect a screen between the observer and the observed, the West and the East, preventing a meaningful encounter between the cultures. The incompatibility of the Western self with the local space and culture is figured in its expulsion from the desert—Port's death and Kit's mental disintegration.

Keywords Intercultural encounter · Space · The self · The other

1 Introduction

The American expatriate writer Paul Bowles was uniquely predestined to write about intercultural encounters, having spent most of his life in Tangier, Morocco, where he lived permanently from 1947 until his death in 1999. Unsurprisingly, many of his novels and short stories are set in North Africa and explore the impact of the local space and culture on the Western traveler. This recurring theme is

U. Gołębiowska (✉)
University of Zielona Góra, Zielona Góra, Poland
e-mail: u.golebiowska@gmail.com

© Springer International Publishing AG 2017
J. Mydla et al. (eds.), *Multiculturalism, Multilingualism and the Self: Literature and Culture Studies*, Issues in Literature and Culture,
DOI 10.1007/978-3-319-61049-8_2

explored in Bowles's famous 1949 novel *The Sheltering Sky*, which centers on an African experience of three Americans in post-war Algeria. Port and Kit Moresby, accompanied by their friend Tunner, are travelers, not tourists—a distinction Port insists on, as the tourist "accepts his own civilization without question; not so the traveler, who compares it with the others, and rejects those elements he finds not to his liking" (Bowles, 1990, p. 6). Among the things Port wishes to leave behind is the Second World War—"one facet of the mechanized age he wants to forget," as well as the vacuous Western life with its consumerism and spiritual emptiness (Bowles, 1990, p. 6). By renouncing the unwanted aspects of the West, Port implicitly expects to remake his identity, however, rather than transform his Western self, the journey exposes and intensifies its most problematic features. Port's escape from the West is driven by the traits he rejects—a need for power and intellectual control continue to inform the enterprise preventing the hoped for self-enhancing encounter with the alien culture. This essay aims to show that despite their efforts to leave the "civilization" behind, the travelers unwittingly reenact colonialist attitudes to the local reality and project their unconscious fears and desires on the space and culture. When considered vis-à-vis current discourses on the politics of cultural representation, Port's and Kit's constructions of the people and culture reproduce Orientalist perceptions of essentialized difference and opposition between the self and the other, the West and the East. The conventional Orientalist tropes of unknowability and exoticism in which the foreign culture is framed intersect with personal feelings and fantasies, resulting in a misapprehension of the local reality and the failure of the intercultural encounter staged in the novel. The West and the East remain, to use the narrator's formulation, "two incongruous and incompatible cultures," impossible to bring together and unlikely to understand each other (Bowles, 1990, p. 177).

2   Reenacting Colonialist Attitudes

The characters' representations of the local culture and the Arab other as radically different and unknowable are consistent with colonial and Orientalist discourses, the outside perspective from which the other is viewed being emblematic of such representations. According to Said (1979), Orientalism is "premised upon exteriority" whose "principal product ... is of course representation ... not a 'natural' depiction of the Orient" (pp. 20–21). From the detached position, the Arabs are homogenized and essentialized—perceived as sharing certain characteristic traits constitutive of their belonging to a group and, therefore, referred to in the plural form. They are assumed to have "a completely different philosophy" and a different conception of time, the latter serving as a rationalization when Port obtains bus tickets by means of bribery, usurping the seats of local bus riders: "What's a week to them? Time doesn't exist for them" (Bowles, 1990, pp. 133, 183). Despite this radical difference, Port has always "found the Arabs very *sympathetic*" (Bowles, 1990, p. 66—emphasis mine). The bland term "sympathetic" applied to all "the

Arabs" betrays a superficial nature and a sweeping generality of the appraisal, exposing at the same time the constructed nature of the representations of the cultural other, who "is never simply given, never just found or encountered, but made" (Fabian, 2000, p. 208). The inevitable distortion involved in the theorizing of the Other is particularly evident in the representations constructed by the French colonists Port and Kit meet in the course of their journey, whose demeaning images of the natives, emphasizing their difference from Europeans, allow the French to form a positive self-image and to justify the entire colonial enterprise. Different from and opposed to the self, the Arabs are also viewed as unknowable, consistently with the stereotypical label of the "mysterious Orient" attached to the region by generations of Orientalists (Said, 1979, p. 26). Port's early observation that "their faces are masks" is echoed in Kit's complaint that "[i]t's impossible to get into their lives and know what they're really thinking" (Bowles, 1990, pp. 14, 122). The other's inscrutability and difference perceived as essential features, preexisting, not contingent on the self's construction and thus immune to change, determine the encounter. The mysterious, unknowable other will remain the same irrespective of the travelers' efforts which, understandably, are not forthcoming.

The radical difference and unknowability of the other culture are highlighted in the text by the opacity of the language and incomprehensibility of social spaces, which derive primarily from the travelers' unwillingness to gain basic knowledge about the culture, as it would interfere with the mystery of the place. The language barrier irritates Port: Arabic words, *mehara*, *fondouk*, *bled*, *bordj*, left untranslated in the novel reproduce the impact of the unfamiliar language on the travelers and function as "textual interruptions" for the reader (Edwards, 2005, p. 325). The language, people's behavior, and underlying logic of local towns converge to produce the feeling of confusion. As Walonen (2016) observes, "unintelligibility is rendered as a failure of perception"—Kit's painful disorientation in the urban landscape of El Ga'a results from her inability to read the spatial codes according to which the town has been constructed. What she is faced with is a "confusion of discrete impressions lacking a unifying totality" and a place "devoid of intelligible sense" (p. 40). The unknowability and impenetrability of the place and people that Kit finds unsettling are valued by Port, as they constitute the opposite of the despised West and thus exactly what he thinks conducive to the project of restoring his "weary" soul (Bowles, 1990, p. 127). Understandably, he does not seek to diminish the sense of the other's inscrutability, to bridge the gap between the self and the other. Rather, he avoids gaining new information and knowledge—before going to El Ga'a, he decides not to mention the town to a French lieutenant "for fear of losing his preconceived idea of it"—wishing to preserve the mystery of the encounter (Bowles, 1990, p. 175).

The exoticization of the native culture is another aspect of the image constructed in the novel which suggests an analogy with the Orientalist perception of the East. Otherness is essentialized and packaged as involving mysterious qualities representing the opposite of the West, offering a respite from its sameness and promising the enrichment of the self. In representations constructed by the protagonists, the differences between the self and the other do not promote, as in some Orientalist texts, the construction of the other as inferior or evil in order to facilitate a positive self-definition of the Western subject. By contrast, Port seeks contact with the "exotic" other to escape his thinking, self-conscious self, hence his fascination with what appears to be an intuitive, impersonal side of the natives. In Ain Krorfa brothel, where he tries to be "part of the timelessness of the place," two prostitutes who are "very much present" do not appeal to him at all, but he is instantly attracted to a blind dancer with a "strangely detached, somnambulistic expression" and a "supremely impersonal disdain in the unseeing eyes" (Bowles, 1990, pp. 143, 141). The dancer's impersonal aura stands in direct contrast to Western self-consciousness and self-importance which Port longs to shed, hoping to access the mysterious qualities through the woman. The wish to be changed as a possible motivation for a sexual encounter with the cultural and racial other is confirmed by Bel Hooks (2015), who comments on contemporary trends in inter-racial sexual desire and contact among young white males. Her observation that the decision "to transgress racial boundaries within the sexual realm" is not motivated by the desire to dominate the other, but by a wish "to be acted upon ...[to] be changed utterly" illuminates Port's motivations and longings (p. 24). His desire for the "exotic" woman can be also read as the Orientalist tendency to form an "almost uniform association between the Orient and sex," the Orient signifying not only "fecundity but sexual promise (and threat), untiring sexuality, unlimited desire," with the colonized space frequently constructed as feminine and therefore expected to be dominated (Said, 1979, p. 188). The fascination with the exotic elements of the native culture, the perception of the people as mysterious and irrational others, not subjects but objects to be used, are all features of colonialist and Orientalist dis-courses shared by the protagonists. Even if their vision cannot be fully aligned with typical patterns of such representations—after all it is not marked by a sense of superiority, but by a recognition of the West's negative aspects—it still partakes in the Orientalist binary logic. Essentializing differences between the Orient and the Occident as well as viewing the self and the other as opposites promotes the division into the observing and the observed, the subject and the objectified other.

What underscores the impossibility of the intercultural encounter is thus the travelers' affiliation with the Western culture they apparently reject but which informs both their constructions and objectification of the other and drives the entire expedition, made possible by their American nationality and privileged financial status. Taking advantage of the dollar's purchasing power, Port consumes the landscape and culture, exerting a neocolonial economic power over the local people. Offering to pay for an encounter with the blind dancer, he mimics the ways colonizers have always related to the local culture: enjoying it without under-standing—"even though he could not understand a word of what was being said he enjoyed studying the inflections of the language"—or appropriating and consuming (Bowles, 1990, p. 143). His tension while arranging a meeting with the woman is evident in the narrator's remark that he was "too concerned lest his prey escape him" (Bowles, 1990, p. 142). The comparison to a predator, impatient to feed on his prey, emphasizes the instrumental treatment of the other and the fact that the self-other relations are largely a matter of power in the novel. Even if the relations of domination shift, exposing a general tendency to treat the other instrumentally on both sides of the cultural encounter, Port's advantage—his nationality and wealth—constitutes an additional barrier between him and a local reality, which he is unable to penetrate from a detached, sheltered position. Significantly, it is the loss of his American passport that shatters Port's illusion of separation and immunity, exposing him to the impact of the place (Edwards, 2005, p. 316). As he explains to the French official while reporting the theft, "ever since I discovered that my passport was gone, I've felt only half alive" (Bowles, 1990, p. 164). Strangely, his perception of the place changes as well: "He did not look up because he knew how senseless the landscape would appear. […] He knew how things could stand bare, their essence having retreated on all sides to the horizon, as if impelled by a sinister centrifugal force" (Bowles, 1990, p. 165). The loss of his passport deprives Port of the protection he has relied on: it not only weakens his sense of identity, but also exposes him to the physical environment, from which he has been sheltered by his Americanness. The desert becomes less a construction of his previous, protected position than a real space which his diminished self is no longer able to invest with meaning.

Analogously to their constructions of the local culture, the Americans' understanding of time and space only apparently contradicts the attitudes associated with imperial expansion. Admittedly, the Moresbys' rejection of time opposes the colonizers' temporalization of space—the perception of empty areas on the maps as territories to be colonized and incorporated into the Western time of civilization. In their flight from the West and its compromised ideals of rationality and progress, Port and Kit dispose of the idea of time altogether, which the narrator refers to as "a fatal error of coming hazily to regard time as non-existent. One year was like another year. Eventually everything would happen" (Bowles, 1990, pp. 5, 137). The rejection of the teleological Western time means that it is their movement through space in pursuit of an authentic local space unaffected by time and untouched by colonization that becomes their goal. Contrary to the colonial focus on time and progress, this desire to locate a timeless, "uncolonized" space resembles a tendency to overemphasize space present in postcolonial discourses. Seeking to counteract "the privileging of time over space that dominated the colonial period," those discourses focus on the reclaiming of postcolonial space from its inscription into Western history (Zacharias, 2016, p. 217). Unlike *place*—a concrete location embedded in history—*space*, from the perspective of empire, was viewed as "empty, set outside of history," waiting to be colonized and incorporated into the Western history of progress (Zacharias, 2016, p. 217–218). However, since time and space are inextricably bound and interrelated, this focus on space and neglect of time has inevitably led to time's return to haunt the postcolonial discourses which, due to the effacement of time, are doomed to reenact unwittingly the imperial model of linear progress that they intend to oppose (Zacharias, 2016, p. 218). Analogously, the protagonists' relentless movement into the desert and their nostalgic search for spaces "empty" of Western influences are reminiscent of the colonizers' quest for *terra nullius* to be situated on the map of empire, as well as their valuation of "pure" and "authentic" local culture. To use Rosaldo's (1989) term, the travelers are engaged in "imperialist nostalgia," whereby "people mourn the passing of what they themselves have transformed," which may take the form, as in the novel, of recreating the colonizing journey, mystifying at the same time the travelers' connection and complicity with colonial domination (pp. 69–70). Even Port's name is suggestive of neo-colonial expansion, Port Moresby being originally a harbor in Papua New Guinea, a site of competing interests of colonial powers and a location of American military bases during World War II. The novel suggests yet another analogy between the journey into the desert and colonization—in North Africa, Port is reminded of his ancestors' venture into the American wilderness: "it made him feel that he was pioneering—he felt more closely identified with his great-grandparents, when he was rolling out here in the desert" (Bowles, 1990, p. 108). The word "wilderness" applied to the desert suggests a perception of the Sahara as empty (Bowles, 1990, p. 166). Ignoring the fact that it is populated and filled with local culture helps to produce it as a blank screen on which to project one's fantasies and desires.

3   The Other Space and Culture as the Site of Projections

Port's movement through the desert is driven by Western conceptualization of space as material landscape for the travelers to admire and consume visually, which, in the novel, intersects with space as a mental construct. Port's fantasies projected on the desert endow it with magical qualities and potential, thus rendering it innocuous, even protective. His belief that the Saharan sky has the power to shelter the travelers from the encroaching nothingness is an illusion he confesses to Kit: "[T]he sky here's very strange. I often have the sensation when I look at it that it's a solid thing up there, protecting us from what's behind" (Bowles, 1990, p. 100). When asked what *is* behind, he answers: "Nothing … Just darkness. Absolute night" (Bowles, 1990, pp. 100–101). By contrast, for Kit the desert is menacing and threatening to engulf her Western identity. Both the magical and the ominous qualities that the characters project on the desert are featured in the tale about a tea party in the Sahara invoked at the beginning of the novel. It tells a story of three Arab girls who set out to the desert to have tea there, which they perceive as a magical event, capable of endowing their unfulfilling lives with meaning. While they search for the highest dune on which to settle and enjoy the best view, they waste the early morning hours when the sun is still low. The top is reached when it is too hot and the girls, unable to return, end up scorched to death. The tale, whose relevance to his life Port fails to recognize, provides an apt metaphor for the characters' journey and prefigures its outcome—the movement deeper into the desert and away from Western civilization becomes an impossible quest for ful-fillment for Port and a torturous journey into the "wilderness" for Kit. The girls' hopes parallel Port's illusion that an external event—a journey—might become life-altering, while the story's tragic end foreshadows his death and Kit's psychological disintegration. Ultimately, the desert emerges as a natural force, not caring and protective, but powerful and indifferent.

As produced in the novel, the desert is a real, physical space, not just a setting—a scenic backdrop against which the characters' drama unfolds and through which the trajectory of Port and Kit's movement can be charted on one of the maps Port studies "passionately" (Bowles, 1990, p. 6). At the same time, the Sahara is also an imagined space, a site of Port's hopes and desires and a symbolic place of the self's transformation. Thus, the desert is both physical and mental space and still more, which corresponds to Edward Soja's term "Thirdspace." In his conception of "Thirdspace," Soja (2009) goes beyond the duality of physical and mental space, real and imagined, positing a third term, which is not a sum of its binary components, not a simple synthesis of elements, but simultaneously "subjectivity and objectivity, the abstract and the concrete, the real and the imagined, the unknowable and the unimaginable, ... structure and agency, mind and body, consciousness and the unconscious ... everyday life and unending history" (p. 54). Conceiving the desert as "Thirdspace" allows to explore its mystery and material agency, capable of radically transforming the traveler's life. In a 1971 interview Bowles explains that the "transportation of characters to such ["exotic"] settings often acts as a catalyst or a detonator," precipitating the final outcome (Caponi, 1993, 123). The desert's power and agency are also emphasized by Alexa Weik von Mossner's ecocritical interpretation of the novel. Against the ideas of "psychoanalytic and existential interiorization of the desert," von Mossner (2013) argues that Bowles "foregrounds the complex material interactions of natural and cultural environments and their combined effect on the body and mind of the dislocated individual" (pp. 219–220). The theme of the impact of the Sahara is further elaborated in one of the writer's travel essays: it is the exposure to the vast Saharan sky, compared to which "all other skies seem fainthearted efforts," that exerts a profound impact on the traveler (Bowles, 1963, p. 133):

> Presently, you will either shiver or hurry back inside the walls, or you will go on standing there and let something very peculiar happen to you, something that everyone who lives here has undergone and which the French call *le bâpteme de la solitude*. It is a unique sensation, and has nothing to do with loneliness, for loneliness presupposes memory. Here, in this whole mineral landscape lighted by stars like flares, even memory disappears; nothing is left but your own breathing and the sound of your heart beating. The strange, and by no means pleasant, process of reintegration begins inside you, and you have the choice of fighting against it, and insisting on remaining the person you have always been, or letting it take its course. For no one who has stayed in the Sahara for a while is quite the same as when he came. (Bowles, 1963, pp. 133–134)

Bowles's description of the "baptism of the desert" emphasizes the mystery of the space which goes beyond a combined understanding of the space as material and imaginary. What is foregrounded in the writer's account is a certain passivity on the part of the traveler, who allows to be acted upon, and the Sahara's power, invoked again in Bowles's statement about the novel. "[W]hat I wanted to tell was the story of what the desert can do to us. That was all. The desert is the protagonist" (Caponi, 1993, p. 54).

The violence of Port's hallucinations and death from typhoid suggests a confrontation between the active Western ego pushing farther and farther south in search of its own enhancement and the indifferent but powerful environment. In his escape from time and change, Port constructs a timeless and immutable space which will yield to his project of charting and following a straight route through the Sahara —"it had been one strict, undeviating course inland to the desert, and now he was very nearly at the center" (Bowles, 1990, p. 205). Port's hallucinations enact this constant movement, his self finally unhinged delves into itself to encounter unlimited space and horror in an unpeopled universe: "It was an existence of exile from the world. He never saw [in his visions] a human face or figure, nor even an animal; there were no familiar objects along the way" (Bowles, 1990, p. 232). Walonen (2016) observes that the illness to which Port succumbs is "represented as a dissolution of selfhood" and figured spatially as a restless movement he experiences in his visions (p. 42). It is as if the loss of the passport has completed Port's efforts to disengage himself from his national and cultural affiliation in order to refashion his self in a freer, unencumbered mode. Paradoxically, the absence of an anchor that would hold him in place during his visions is a source of such terror that Port longs for "something to hang on to when his eyes shut.... So as not to go. To stay behind. To overflow, take root in what would stay there" (Bowles, 1990, p. 237). The hallucinations seem to recreate the sought after unanchored existence in an alien, hostile environment that does not support the Western ego, the ego intent on pursuing the quest for fulfillment on its own terms. By venturing into the desert, Walonen (2016) explains, Port "has entered into the vastness and absoluteness of a space that is asocial and perhaps even anti-social, one that overwhelms all attempts to control and domesticate it and blasts away all trappings of civilization, including the self" (p. 42). Ultimately, the desert, whose appeal to Port has resided in its presumed timelessness, extends beyond the immutable physical landscape and the static imagined space experienced in the mind to encompass the lived space—the place of the characters' embodiment, which entails temporality, change, and even destruction.

Unlike Port, Kit does not invest the local space and culture with hopes and desires, but responds with fear to the alterity she encounters. Constantly afraid of the future, reading omens and signs, she projects her sense of life's indifference on the space and on the other. When accidentally stranded in a fourth-class car on a train journey, Kit perceives the local men as wholly indifferent, "looking at her, but with neither sympathy nor antipathy. Nor even with curiosity" (Bowles, 1990, p. 81). Arguably, the impenetrability of the other can be viewed as primarily present in her relationship with Port, the self's isolation and unknowability being transferred onto the Arab other and seen as a troubling aspect of the intercultural encounter. Not only the other but also the environment takes on the qualities she imparts to it: the sun and the star-filled sky appear "monstrous" (Bowles, 1990, pp. 198, 236), making her feel alone in a pitiless universe. Dreading all change, when faced with the ultimate change, Port's death, she rejects conscious, anxious life in favor of an existence as a mere body. Leaving Port behind at the French fort in SBA and entering the desert, she crosses a threshold and abandons a "civilized" world, shedding her Western identity, language, and security, which is rendered symbolically in the scene of bathing in the fountain at night. "Washing off" her old self, Kit experiences a sense of total transformation and freedom echoing the conception of the "baptism of solitude." She feels that she will never experience "[t] hat kind of tension, that degree of caring about herself" (Bowles, 1990, p. 258). Bathing in the fountain, she also loses her watch, which signifies the abandonment of her life history, memory, and the former time-bound life. Kit's subsequent unconscious existence as a sexual slave in the house of Belqassim, a Touareg leader of the caravan she joins, becomes a shelter from the pain of conscious life and memory. However, living like a native, dressed in Belqassim's men's clothes to deceive his wives, she is no closer to the local culture for she experiences it at the level of the body. Kit illustrates Bowles's understanding of the impossibility of a conscious immersion in an alien culture: her choice of letting go of awareness means that she loses an anchor in her previous life and reaches a point of no return. When she finally escapes from Belqassim, she is no longer able to reenter her former life: brought to Oran by the American Consulate, she disappears again. Kit's mental disintegration, obviously a consequence of her inability to bear the conscious life of memory and pain, can also be read as a mark of the cultures' incompatibility, suggesting the impossibility of retaining the Western identity and becoming totally immersed in the local culture. At the same time, letting go of her self-conscious, anxious self becomes a life-saving measure. In the environment hostile to the Western ego, which physically destroys Port, it is the abandonment of her own that allows her to survive.

4 Conclusion

Even if *The Sheltering Sky* is not, as sometimes argued, primarily concerned with the meeting of cultures (Caponi, 1993, p. 184), it still articulates Bowles's skepticism as to the possibility of a positive intercultural encounter in North Africa. As in his other fictions, the local space is not posited as an ideal contact zone "productive of the attributes of hybridity and interculturality" as these "normative attitudes" would entail mystifications of power relations and the legacy of colonialism (Pease, 2011, p. 15). Instead, the characters misapprehend the space and culture, framing the local reality in conventional Orientalist perceptions of opacity, unknowability, and exoticism as well as projecting their inner fears and desires on the desert and the cultural other. Ultimately, neither Kit's encounter with the desert and the culture experienced at the level of the body, nor Port's intellectual control over his experience allow for a transformative contact between the two cultures. The colonialist attitudes and the inner conflicts that the characters enact in the course of the journey function as a screen preventing the encounter with the other. The Western ego's incompatibility with the local world is figured in its ultimate destruction—abandoned by Kit and annihilated in Port's death, it is out of place in the desert. While impossible in the fictional world of *The Sheltering Sky*, a measure of contact and understanding between the cultures could still be envisioned outside the novel and its political context and achieved through an engagement with the culture, something the writer himself practiced. In his renderings in English of oral stories told in an unwritten Moroccan dialect and in the quest to save disappearing Berber music recorded by Bowles all over the Sahara, the writer embodied the attitude that he denied his characters—that of a Westerner embracing North African cultures. While Orientalism, for which Bowles has been often criticized, is indisputably present in his works, stereotypical representations of local people in *The Sheltering Sky* are problematized rather than endorsed by the writer. The Arabs do not appear as a homogeneous group (despite being perceived in this way by the characters). In Brian T. Edwards's interpretation of the novel, the presence of Belqassim, a nomadic Touareg and a member of a tribe opposed to the Arab nation-state, offers a corrective to the common manner of presenting the Arab North Africa as homogeneous, easy to translate for the American market and ready for a neocolonial expansion. Situating Bowles's novel "outside an American Century framework," Edwards (2005) refers to the protagonist's death as the writer's "interruption of the American national subject" and a confirmation of the impossibility of a new American identity or a new attitude to the foreign (pp. 315, 323). In this view, the failed encounter with the native culture staged in the novel emerges as "disruptive to US thinking about North Africa, an interruption to the reapplication of the frontier myth" (p. 318). For Edwards, Bowles offers a challenge to the American relation to the region marked by neocolonial, imperialist ambitions of a new global power, and therefore undermines the national context in which to consider the novel. The writer himself, although frequently referred to as an American writer, is perhaps better captured by Edwards's (2005) alternative labels: "Moroccan Bowles; Bowles the archivist of Moroccan national culture; the Anglophone African writer" (p. 313).

References

Bowles, P. (1963). *Their heads are green and their hands are blue: Scenes from the non-Christian world.* New York: Harper.
Bowles, P. (1990). *The sheltering sky.* New York: Vintage.
Caponi, G. D. (Ed.). (1993). *Conversations with Paul Bowles.* Jackson: University Press of Mississippi.
Edwards, B. T. (2005). Sheltering screens: Paul Bowles and foreign relations. *American Literary History, 17*(2), 307–334. doi:10.1093/alh/aji017
Fabian, J. (2000). *Time and the work of anthropology. Critical essays 1971–1991.* Amsterdam: Harewood Academic Publishers.
Hooks, B. (2015). *Black looks. Race and representation.* New York and London: Routledge.
Pease, D. E. (2011). Re-mapping the transnational turn. In W. Fluck, D. E. Pease, & J. C. Rowe (Eds.), *Re-framing the transnational turn in American studies* (pp. 1–46). Hanover, NH: Dartmouth College Press.
Rosaldo, R. (1989). *Culture and truth. The remaking of social analysis.* Boston: Beacon Press.
Said, E. (1979). *Orientalism.* New York: Random House.

Soja, E. W. (2009). "Thirdspace. Toward a new consciousness of space and spatiality." In K. Ikas, & G. Wagner (Eds.), *Communicating in the Thirdspace* (pp. 49–61). London, New York: Routledge.

von Mossner, A. W. (2013). Encountering the Sahara: Embodiment, emotion, and material agency in Paul Bowles's *The sheltering sky*. *Interdisciplinary Studies in Literature and Environment, 20*(2), 219–238. doi:10.1093/isle/ist023

Walonen, M. K. (2016). *Writing Tangier in the postcolonial transition. Space and power in expatriate and North African literature.* London, New York: Routledge.

Zacharias, R. (2016). Space and the postcolonial novel. In A. Quayson (Ed.), *The Cambridge companion to postcolonial novel* (pp. 208–229). Cambridge: Cambridge University Press.

Author Biography

Urszula Gołębiowska works as assistant professor at the University of Zielona Góra. Her research interests focus on American fiction and the intersections between literature, culture and philosophy. She has written articles on the work of Henry James, Alice Munro and J.M. Coetzee. She is currently working on a book which explores convergences between Henry James's ethical insights and Emmanuel Levinas's ethics of alterity.

Kazuo Ishiguro's *Buried Giant* as a Contemporary Revision of Medieval Tropes

Joanna Bukowska

Abstract Kazuo Ishiguro's latest novel, dealing with the role of memory in the construction of individual and collective identity and in the settling or perpetuation of conflicts between individuals and nations, takes as its setting the early medieval land of Britons and Saxons, where peace and happiness are extremely fragile and where the potentially destructive forces might be unleashed at any time. The paper examines the representation of the multicultural narrative world of *The Buried Giant* as a mixture of diverse medieval tropes, such as perilous journeys, quests, Arthurian characters, ogres and dragons. Kazuo Ishiguro rewrites these staple elements of medieval romances to create a vision, which though fantastic, mythical and historically distant, may be interpreted as reflecting the pressures and tensions faced by the contemporary world, which resembles a rich cultural tapestry, made up of divergent ethnic, religious, and historical backgrounds.

Keywords Kazuo ishiguro · Medieval romance · Quest · Memory · Intercultural relations

1 Introduction

Kazuo Ishiguro's latest novel, *The Buried Giant*, published in 2015, is set in early medieval Britain, in which peace is temporarily sustained by magic amnesia. The spell of forgetfulness, cast by Merlin, King Arthur's wizard, withholds the slumbering conflict between Britons and early Saxon settlers on the eve of the full-scale invasion, which in time was to wipe out the Celtic population in eastern, southern and central Britain. While the representation of the processes which paved the way for the full-scale Saxon invasion abounds in marvels echoing the enchanted world of medieval romances, it can also be interpreted as the manifestation of Ishiguro's concern with contemporary multiculturalist policies and their challenges. In *The*

J. Bukowska (✉)
The Faculty of Pedagogy and Fine Arts, Adam Mickiewicz University, Poznań, Poland
e-mail: bjoanna@amu.edu.pl

© Springer International Publishing AG 2017   29
J. Mydla et al. (eds.), *Multiculturalism, Multilingualism and the Self: Literature and Culture Studies*, Issues in Literature and Culture,
DOI 10.1007/978-3-319-61049-8_3

Buried Giant, the roots of the conflict between Britons and Saxons are located in King Arthur's failed attempt to forestall Saxon raids by his own violent subjugation of the early Saxon settlers and the fiasco of his policy to ensure their peaceful coexistence with Britons by the enforced erasure of their traumatic memories. Like Ishiguro's other novels, *The Buried Giant* is set at, what Cheng (2010, p. 18) calls, "an interesting juncture of two or more cultural forces." Cheng (2010, p. 21) also explains the implications of the multicultural perspective: "At the intersection of two or multiple cultures, he construes a discursive site that at once enables individuals to reflect upon their personal losses and corrals societies into ideological contention so as to expose their respective fallacies." The multicultural perspective the author assumes in his fiction enables him to present misguided beliefs and detrimental policies from different angles and to combine aesthetics and ethics, whose interrelation becomes "central to Ishiguro's vision" (Matthews and Groes, 2010, p. 2).

In *The Buried Giant*, like in Ishiguro's earlier novels, each of which is set in a distinct narrative world, large-scale conflicts intertwine with dramatic confrontations between individuals and the vagaries of human memory structure both personal and communal responses to ineffable past. These "long running preoccupations" (Alter, 2015, p. 19) with memory and loss, are as often mentioned in the reviews of *The Buried Giant* as its fantastical elements, which are described as "likely to surprise" (Hopley, 2015) the readers familiar with his earlier fiction, and which are perceived as the reason for which this novel is received as "a more pronounced shift, even for an iconoclast like Mr. Ishiguro" (Alter, 2015, p. 19) and as "his most startling and audacious adaptation of genre yet" (Holland, 2015). Speaking about the novels preceding *The Buried Giant*, Murakami (2010, pp. vii–viii) singled out Ishiguro's ability to combine continuity and innovation as the most distinctive traits of his fiction:

> Ishiguro's most outstanding feature is that all his novels are so different; from one to the next, they are put together in different ways, and point in different directions. In structure and style, each is clearly meant to stand apart from other. Yet each also bears Ishiguro's unmistakable imprint, and each forms a small yet wonderfully distinct universe in itself. But that is not all. When all those little universes are brought together … a far broader universe – the sum of all Ishiguro's novels – takes vivid shape… Ishiguro has a certain vision, a master plan, that shapes his work – each new novel that he writes constitutes another step in the construction of this larger macro-narrative.

The Buried Giant, with its fantastic element, might also be interpreted as a new addition to the tapestry, which Ishiguro has been weaving throughout his literary career. With its early medieval setting, reinvented elements of the medieval romance, and its concern with tensions and conflicts between different ethnic groups, struggling for the same territory, the latest novel expands Ishiguro's earlier exploration of the field of human memory by considering the consequences of remembering and forgetting not only at the level of an individual but also of the collective consciousness. Ishiguro ponders in this novel the questions of how helpful the loss or the suppression of memories can be in healing old wounds and overcoming resentment, whether between husband and wife or between distinct cultures, and whether the harmony, order and peace achieved at that cost can ever be permanent. The contemporary relevance of these questions corresponds well with Ishiguro's description of himself as "a writer who wishes to write international novels," which contain "a vision of life that is of importance to people of varied backgrounds around the world…" and which explore "those themes that are of genuine international concern" (Brandmark n.d. as cited in Wai-chew, 2010, p. 16).

2 Method

This analysis of *The Buried Giant* explores the way in which Ishiguro rewrites characteristic tropes of medieval romances and incorporates their reinvented version into his representation of a Breton couple's struggle with hidden concerns in their marriage and into his vision of a potentially volatile coexistence of disparate cultural groups, whose antagonisms have been temporarily subdued. The study involves the construction of the setting, the motivation of characters and the structure of the plot. The analysis aims at revealing the implications of the traditional medieval motifs, such as a perilous journey or a quest, which are rewritten and reconceptualised in the contemporary narrative, dealing with the forcefully supressed conflicts, which remain latent and which may explode at the time when the memory of the old grievances is recovered. The subsequent discussion traces the ways in which the original implications of the elements of medieval culture incorporated into Ishiguro's novel enrich its meaning and exposes the degree of their transformation.

3 Results

The analysis reveals a number of different aspects for which *The Buried Giant* remains indebted to the medieval romance. The primary influence is evident in the role of a quest as the organising principle of Ishiguro's contemporary narrative. The protagonists of the novel undertake a perilous journey through wilderness endowed with the characteristic features of the magical forest of medieval romances. The episodes that apparently distract them from the chosen course of action prove in time to constitute an integral part of their quest. The actual voyage is accompanied by a metaphorical quest through the obliterated regions of their memory. The full significance of both dimensions of their quest and the bitter implications of its ending become apparent to the characters only after its completion. Medieval tropes provide, thus, the foundation for the structure of Ishiguro's novel and a key to its interpretation. Nevertheless, the narrative implications of these traditional motifs appear to be different. Unlike in the medieval stories of chivalric adventure, the completion of the quest in *The Buried Giant* does not restore order and harmony either at the individual or social level. Instead, as a metaphor of the struggle for the recovery of memory, the quest reopens old wounds and revives bitter divisions. The rifts in the marital relationship created by infidelity and resentment, as well as the enmity between Britons and Saxons caused by the slaughter of innocents cannot be healed by a magic spell, symbolising the suppression of painful memories. The reality of lingering hostilities whether within a family or a multicultural society seems to be too complex to be immediately resolved. The fantastic background rooted in the characteristic features of medieval romances allows, thus, Ishiguro to provide a distance from which he can investigate the psychological and social implications of any attempt to bring such festering antagonisms to a closure and to examine the role, which memory plays in this process. In incorporating the medieval elements into his novel, the author once again undertakes the game with generic conventions and their narrative adaptation. It appears, however, that by doing so, the writer attains much more than the narrative distance and freedom from historical constrains. Transformed as they might be, these medieval devices carry with them into the contemporary narrative their original implications and expose the meaning, which otherwise could not so clearly surface up. Derived from such a distant and distinct cultural period, they also additionally enrich *The Buried Giant*, which explores not only interpersonal but also intercultural relations.

4 Discussion

The universal character of the questions concerning the process of forgetting painful memories is underscored in *The Buried Giant* by the vagueness of its early medieval setting. Sub-Roman Britain plays in the novel the role described by Umberto Eco in his list of ten different contemporary reconfigurations of the medieval period as "a pretext," that is "a sort of mythological stage" (Eco, 1998: 68) on which universal or even contemporary issues are depicted. The scarcity of the historical data characterising the interim period between the departure of the Romans and the removal of the Celts wiped out by the massive Anglo-Saxon immigration allows the writer to imbue the historical setting with features reminiscent of the fantastic world of the medieval courtly romance.

Like the questing knights, the protagonists of *The Buried Giant* depart from their own community in order to find their son without knowing their route. Axl tells his wife Beatrice: "This village may only be a few days away as you say. But how will we know where to find it?" (Ishiguro, 2015, p. 28). The elderly Briton couple do not know where this village is located or how to reach it. Even if Beatrice remembers the way to the nearest Saxon village, they feel lost and engulfed by the featureless moors, stretching as far as the eye can see and as intimidating and beguiling as the magic landscape of medieval romances. The dimensions, density and hostility of the enchanted forest, first depicted in the twelfth century romances of Chrétien de Troyes, also left the questing knight clueless about where his adventure led him, since there was no one who could give him directions (Putter, 1995, p. 19).

Likewise, the wild territory that Axl and Beatrice have to traverse is depicted by the narrator of *The Buried Giant* as desolate and perilous space:

> A traveller of that time would, often as not, find himself in featureless landscape, the view almost identical whichever way he turned. A row of standing stones on the far horizon, a turn of a stream, the particular rise and fall of a valley: such clues were the only means of charting a course. And the consequences of a wrong turn could often prove fatal. Never mind the possibilities of perishing in bad weather: straying off course meant exposing oneself more than ever to the risk of assailants – human, animal or supernatural – lurking away from established roads (Ishiguro, 2015, p. 30.)

Afraid to take a false step and lose their way, Axl and Beatrice traverse the unmapped countryside in search of their son. The sense of disorientation engendered by the featureless scenery is enhanced by the mist, which not only enfolds the countryside but also obliterates their memories, which they struggle to regain. The physical journey proceeds, therefore, in a parallel way to their mental passage through the uncharted territory of their memory, as perilous and as full of pitfalls as the unknown countryside.

Axl and Beatrice's physical progress is imperilled by ogres and other forces of darkness, which occupy particular evil spots. Hence, they are determined "to cross the corner of the Great Plain as close to the noon as possible, when the dark forces of that place were most likely to be dormant" (Ishiguro, 2015, p. 29). Although, unlike the questing knights of romances, they feel more at risk on the Great Plain than in the woods, the uncharted territory they travel through seems to function in the novel as a symbolic equivalent of the wild forest depicted in courtly romances. Putter points out that in the medieval romances the wilderness constituted a symbolic space which functioned as an inverted image of the court, an uncivilised landscape where violence prevailed (2001, pp. 21, 26). Cooper also associates this space with chaos and disorder:

> The philosophers of the twelfth century school of Chartres adopted the word *silva*, forest, as their term for chaos, matter that had not been yet given created form; and it may not be coincidence that the quest romance was developing its own characteristic landscape of forest at the same time. The romance forest is the place that conceals brigands and monsters, where the knight's claims to chivalry are tested, his values and his sense of self challenged (Cooper, 2004, p. 70.)

The uncivilised space, in which lawlessness and violence prevail, provides the background for the perilous journey, which constitutes one of the most essential motifs of both *The Buried Giant* and medieval romances. Ogres that prowl the darkness in Ishiguro's novel, also appeared among the dangerous opponents, which the eponymous character of fourteenth century *Sir Gawain and the Green Knight* had to confront during his quest (*Sir Gawain and the Green Knight*, 1972, II, 720–723). The ogres depicted in *The Buried Giant* also create a sense of imminent danger awaiting man venturing outside the boundaries of human civilisation. Their attack on a group of Saxons, preceding Axl and Beatrice's arrival at a Saxon village, enables the author to introduce two characters, who inadvertently change the peaceful coexistence of Britons and Saxons. The bloody feud between both nations, which has been brought to an end by communal amnesia, will be renewed by Wistan, an undaunted Saxon warrior, who rescues Edwin, a boy kidnapped by ogres. Edwin joins Axl and Beatrice's quest because he cannot stay in his village due to Saxons' superstitious fear concerning the wound with which he returns from his captivity. Consequently, the episode featuring ogres also helps Ishiguro to underscore the cultural differences between Britons and Saxons. All Saxons with the exception of Wistan, who has been brought up among Britons, and Ivor, the ealdorman of Briton descent, are so afraid that Edwin's wound will lure more ogres to their village that they are determined to kill the rescued boy. The Britons and the Saxons are presented as neighbouring communities, living next to each other, but they do not constitute a homogenous society. The tensions are evident in Axl and Beatrice's fear to walk through the agitated Saxon crowd and in their search for shelter in Ivor's cottage.

The primary influence of the genre of the medieval romance seems to be evident, nevertheless, in the instrumental role played in the novel by the motif of a quest, defined by Sadowski "as a sequence of events and adventures involving the pro-tagonist(s), leading towards some goal or solution (1996, p. 52)." Sadowski further expands this definition by stating:

> The quest, therefore, describes a sequence of related events usually framed within the framework of fictitious, imaginary lifespan of a protagonist, or at least within a crucial part of his life, with particular emphasis on moments of transition. Such idealised biographies of the heroic type provide personal examples of individuals, who have overcome, or are struggling to overcome, the limitations of their human condition, through the experience of existential, often ritualised rites of passage … followed by a subsequent rebirth of a new man, readapted to the society with different parameters of personality (1996, p. 53.)

The perilous journey that Axl and Beatrice embark upon transforms not only their relationship but also the fragile peace between Britons and Saxons and the future of these nations. Their quest develops in the least expected way, and the protagonists change in the way they have not predicted or desired. From the beginning this quest has a double purpose: Axl and Beatrice want to be reunited with their son, whom they can hardly remember, and to recover their lost memories of the life they have shared. Setting off to find their son, they leave behind their own community they felt oppressed by. They not only want to regain their lost child but they also seek his protection. Their desire for integration into his society, realises, thus, one of the essential aims of a romance hero's quest, as discussed by Schmolke-Hasselmann (1998, p. 13).

These medieval influences are, however, not literarily incorporated into Ishiguro's novel but assume in it an alternative form. If the quest represented in *The Buried Giant* takes place simultaneously on the physical and psychological planes, then its medieval counterpart relates more to the physical and spiritual aspects of the narrative world. As the analysis of Chrétien's Arthurian romances makes evident: "The road that leads to knightly adventure is the way also to spiritual perfection" (Artin, 1999, p. 99), and "the meaning of love and adventure does not remain in the sphere of secular courtly ideals alone, but transcends those fictional ideas to partake of the meaning of their spiritual counterparts, grace and sacramental participations in the life of Christ" (Artin, 1999, pp. 98–99). Additionally, the dualism of the goals, pursued and achieved by errant knights is not overtly expressed in the romance narrative, but it emerges only as a result of the interpretation, as Artin (1999, p. 97) suggests, of "a total context of meaning" or "a web of connected meanings" since "the figure in romance is not simply a sign for something else; rather, the figure shares the meaning of some other thing or event" (Artin, 1999, p. 97). It was not necessary, therefore, for a knightly character to undertake a special spiritual pursuit, for his adventures to be understood in such sense, neither was it necessary for the poet to state his purpose explicitly, since, as Artin (1999, p. 94) asserts, the commonly shared knowledge of Christian theology guaranteed such interpretation of his narrative. Consequently, even if multiplicity of goals could be ascribed to both the pursuits undertaken by the protagonists of *The Buried Giant* and by the chivalric characters, the complexity of their quests concerned different spheres and were also represented in a different way.

Even if the characteristic elements of medieval fiction appear in Ishiguro's novel in a rewritten form, they shed new light on his representation of Axl and Beatrice's search for their fading memories and for their missing son. The narrative mode of the medieval romances, providing the background, against which the plot of *The Buried Giant* is presented, originated, as most of the medieval literature, in the oral tradition. As pointed out by Vance (1987, p. xiv), "The performance or the telling of stories in the oral societies is essentially commemorative." Since new stories originated as version of older stories, the reception of literature as well as the awareness of individual and national identity depended on the cultivation of collective memory, which, as Vance asserts (1987, p. xiv), the oral society valued much more than literate societies:

> For it is in this vast *memoria* that are contained all sacred texts, all the foundational myths, all the explanatory regresses that provide the members of particular collectivity with a hold on their lived experience and distinguish them from their neighbours (Vance 1987, p. xiv.)

The value assigned to memories in this mindset, is manifested through the narrative techniques, that are designed "to animate as many of the constitutive elements of *memoria* as possible" (Vance, 1987, p. xv). In these old oral societies and their narratives, memory was "no longer conceived as pure repository, but as an animating force itself" (Vance, 1987, p. xv). The concept of the shaping role of individual and collective memories underlines also the plot of Ishiguro's latest novel, in which memory is represented as both a powerful formative and destructive force, and which considers the equally influential implications of its suppression. Although it has been recognised as a recurrent aspect of all Ishiguro's novels, that "the narrators struggle against processes of misremembering, forgetting, and repression, to construct for themselves a story that draws together either the fragmented elements of their own identity, or the coherent account of the traumatic historical events (Baillie and Matthews 2010, p. 37), it is *The Buried Giant* that gives full expression to the agency of memory, which is not perceived only as an archive of the past, but as an untamed force, which, when mismanaged, can destroy both a family and a nation.

Both protagonists are troubled by the strange amnesia that also affects the community they live in. Beatrice confides to Axl that she can hardly recollect their son: "'Some days I remember him clear enough,' she said. 'Then the next day it's as if a veil's fallen over his memory. But our son's fine and a good man, I know that for sure'" (Ishiguro, 2015, p. 26). Axl is likewise worried about his inability to remember the boy:

> 'I don't recall his face now at all,' Axl said. 'It must all be the work of this mist. Many things I'll happily let go to it, but it's cruel when we can't remember a precious thing like that' (Ishiguro, 2015, p. 32.)

Axl in fact suspects that their predicament might be connected with the strange affliction of the whole community, evident in their failure to react joyfully to the unexpected return of a little girl who had got lost on the moors and whom they had been franticly searching for. It is Beatrice, however, who provides reasons for their journey:

> Now I think of it, Axl, there may be something in what you're always saying. It's queer the way the world's forgetting people and things from only yesterday and the day before that. Like a sickness come over us all... There is a journey we must go on, and no more delay... A journey to our son's village (Ishiguro, 2015, pp. 18–19.)

Beatrice becomes particularly determined to persuade Axl to go after the visit of a strange woman in black, who tells her that the couples who cannot recall the same memories are separated by a boatman during their ultimate voyage to the other-world. From the beginning of their journey, the aim to find their son becomes closely connected to the recovery of all their memories:

> Our memories aren't gone for ever, just mislaid somewhere on account of this wretched mist. We'll find them again, one by one if we have to. Isn't that why we're on this journey? Once our son is standing before us, many things are sure to start coming back (Ishiguro, 2015, p. 49.)

Beatrice is convinced that the recovery of these memories is essential to sustain their love and to prevent their ultimate separation. Initially Axl cannot see her point:

> How can our love wither? Isn't it stronger now than when we were foolish young lovers?

> But Axl, we can't even remember those days. Or any of the years between. We don't remember our fierce quarrels or the small moments we enjoyed and treasured. We don't remember our son or why he is away from us.

> We can make all these memories come back, princess. Besides, the feeling in my heart for you will be there just the same, no matter what I remember or forget. Don't you feel the same, princess?

> I do, Axl. But then again I wonder if what we feel in our hearts today isn't like these raindrops falling on us from the soaked leaves above, even though the sky itself long stopped raining. I'm wondering if without our memories, there is nothing for it but for our love to fade and die.

> God wouldn't allow such a thing, princess (Ishiguro, 2015, p. 49.)

Beatrice provides impetus for their action. She refuses to wait passively for what the future might bring. Motivated by her longing for her son and her love for her husband, she prefers to face the unknown, rather than be separated from the loved ones. What is at stake is not only the recovery of the past but also the prevention of future calamity. Axl's agreement to go is, however, instrumental in their final decision concerning their departure. The object of the quest seems at first to be specifically related to Axl and Beatrice and to concern their son, their memories and their love. It turns out in time, nonetheless, that its consequences will be extremely far-reaching, since it will change not only the nature of their relationship but also the peaceful coexistence of Briton and Saxon neighbours, who, remaining under the influence of Merlin's magic spell, have forgotten about their former enmity.

Already at the first stop in a Saxon village, Axl and Beatrice's quest becomes intertwined with the mission of Wistan, a Saxon warrior from the fens, who rescues Edwin, kidnapped by the ogres. When Edwin is entrusted into the custody of the Briton couple, Wistan offers to escort them during their dangerous passage to their next stop at the monastery. Axl and Beatrice, who are to take Edwin to their son's village, decide to make a detour to consult father Jonus about Beatrice's pain, as advised by a medicine woman in the Saxon village. Such diversions from the established object of the quest were also popular in the medieval romances, whose plot, as Cooper observes, often consists:

> of a series of adventures encountered along the way: adventures that are usually in some way related to the final object of the quest itself. A journey, however, allows for an easy addition of further adventure, for extra stopovers or digressions or diversions... (2004, p. 46.)

These apparent inconsistencies are resolved in the light of the overall development of the quest because in romances, as Artin points out, "real coherence of meaning lies elsewhere than in the surface of ...narrative" (1999, p. 91). The meaning emerges instead from the accumulation of significant details (Artin, 1999, p. 97).

Just like in the case of romance quests, Axl and Beatrice's fortuitous encounter with Wistan and their unintended visit in the monastery prove in time to constitute an integral part of their quest. Although Father Jonus does not cure Beatrice's affliction, he reveals to the couple that the cause of the amnesia affecting Britons and Saxons alike can be connected with the female dragon, Querig, inhabiting the local hills. As it also turns out, Wistan's errand is in fact a cover-up for his actual mission to slay the dragon. Willing to regain their lost memories, Axl and Beatrice are pleased with such prospects, and they enable Wistan to pass the Briton guards of Lord Brennus, sent to capture him before he can destroy the dragon. Consequently, they contribute to his ultimate success. When they renew their journey to their son's village, their passage down the river is brought to a sudden halt by the attack of pixies. The couple's flight from these magical creatures brings them to children, who raise a poisonous goat in order to destroy the dragon. Axl and Beatrice's agreement to help these children and bring their goat to the dragon's lair apparently causes another diversion, but in fact integrates their struggle against amnesia with Wistan's vindictive mission to slay the dragon. Ironically, their quest to restore order becomes united with Wistan's destructive plan to reopen old wounds and renew the feud between Saxons and Britons. The grim implications of Querig's destruction imbue the restoration of memory at both personal and communal level with equivocal value and prefigure the personal cost that the couple will have to pay for their regained memories.

As the journey starts bringing back to them some long forgotten images, their awareness of their own history expands and they are made to reconsider their feelings, which puts their love to the test. "The sense of values under test" is actually one of the romance characteristics singled out by Barron in his delineation of the genre (1987, p. 59). The couple's experience is also reminiscent of the ordeal that the errant knight was subject to in the wild forests of medieval romances. As Putter observes: "In the forest heroes are thrown back on themselves and meditate on their follies" (1995, p. 24). The space of the quest verifies the romance heroes' compliance with the shared ideal. Self-discovery is also perceived by Schmolke-Hasselmann as one of the most important aims of the knight's quest in medieval romances (1998, p. 13). The quest, as Cooper suggests, therefore, opens particularly easily into a metaphor, into what is commonly thought of as "a quest for identity…" understood as "social identity" but also "self-knowledge," which "is most likely in romance to mean discovering new capacities which enable you to reach that 'ideal version' of the self" (2004, pp. 49–50).

Axl and Beatrice's quest to reclaim their memory, hidden from their view by the breath of the dragon, gradually changes their attitudes to each other. At first they are determined to regain all their memories and to cherish every remembered moment. A little disagreement about their memories concerning some festivities, during which a stranger praised Beatrice's beauty, leads to Beatrice's commentary: "If that's how you've remembered it, Axl, let it be the way it was. With this mist upon us, any memory's a precious thing and we'd best hold tight to it" (Ishiguro, 2015, p. 85). When father Jonus, having revealed to them the cause of their personal and communal amnesia, asks philosophically "whether it is not better some things remain hidden from our minds," Beatrice responds:

> 'It may be for some, father, but not for us. Axl and I wish to have again the happy moments we shared together. To be robbed of them is as if a thief came in the night and took what's most precious from us' … 'What's to fear father? What Axl and I feel today in our hearts for each other tells us the path taken here can hold no danger for us, no matter that the mist hides it now. It's like a tale with a happy end, when even a child knows not to fear the twists and turns before. Axl and I would remember our life together, whatever its shape, for it's been a thing dear to us (Ishiguro, 2015, p. 172.)

Their confidence, however, dwindles in time as they assemble new bits and pieces of the life they have shared. On remembering being left alone at night, Beatrice insists on walking separately, and, at Querig's lair, she realises she has more to fear from the mist clearing than Axl. It is not, however, until the final moments of their quest that their love faces the ultimate confrontation with their newly regained memories of her infidelity, his bitterness, the ensuing departure of their son and his death in another village struck by the plague.

The final test comes when the boatman, who in the manner of the Green Knight, questioning Gawain about his winnings, cross-examines them about their bitter and sweet memories of their shared life before deciding whether they can sail away together or separately to the otherworld. Their failure to pass the test is determined by Axl's realisation how petty his revenge was when he prevented Beatrice from making a journey to their son's grave:

> 'I forbade her to go to his grave, boatman. A cruel thing. She wished us to go together to where he rested, but I wouldn't have it. Now many years have passed and it's only a few days ago we set off to find it, and by then the she-dragon's mist had robbed us of any clear knowledge of what we sought.'

> 'Ah, so that's it,' I say, 'that part your wife was shy to reveal. So it was you stopped her visiting his grave.'

> "A cruel thing I did, sir. And a darker betrayal than the small infidelity cuckolded me a month or two."

> 'Gain? There was nothing to gain, boatman. It was just foolishness and pride. And whatever else lurks in the depths of a man's heart. Perhaps it was a craving to punish, sir. I spoke and acted forgiveness, yet kept locked through long years some small chamber in my heart that yearned for vengeance. A petty and black thing I did her, and my son also' (Ishiguro, 2015, p. 172.)

Unlike in medieval romances, there is no happy ending and no return journey. The initial object of their quest, the reunion with their son, may only be attained after crossing the threshold of death. With a faint hope for this reintegration Beatrice allows the boatman to ferry her to the other shore. The self-knowledge Axl gains as a result of this quest prevents him from joining her. The price for the growth in self-awareness is separation.

The multiple aims of their quest turn out to be mutually exclusive. What Axl and Beatrice believed to be a means to an end proves to be an insurmountable obstacle. The restoration of their memory makes them painfully aware that their plan to find their son is infeasible. The wounds, which had been long forgotten, are reopened again and they have to confront the uneasy truth concerning their relationship. The resolution of their quest sheds a new light on their journey, which progresses towards their confrontation with death. Seemingly random or superfluous details, such as Beatrice's persecution in their home village and her incurable ailments, the couple's old age and their anxiety concerning the possibility of their future separation, the motif of widows and the ferryman, all acquire a new meaning after their quest is completed and when their ultimate destination is revealed. The motif of the protagonist's lack of awareness concerning the overall meaning of the quest, whose significance may be discovered only with hindsight also appeared frequently in medieval romances, in which the quest played a defining role. Cooper's observation concerning the structural function of the quest in medieval romances could apply equally well to its role in *The Buried Giant*:

> The aim of the quest, its poetic as well as its geographical end, is integral: that is, it defines what the entire story is about and ensures that the entire journey is something more than random, even though it may start haphazardly, by adventure, and proceed with adventures

that may prove equally adventitious. The achievement of the quest, or even failure to achieve it, will be not just another episode, but the informing principle of the whole romance. The start and finish of most such works are therefore locked together… The lucidity that the idea of the quest appears to possess is disturbed on many occasions by the protagonist's not quite knowing until the end of the story what the object of his quest actually is (Cooper, 2004, p. 47.)

In *The Buried Giant*, Axl and Beatrice's quest also constitutes the core of their story. Its progress is not linear but full of diversions, which the characters interpret as delays but which, in fact, are instrumental in bringing them to the lair of the dragon, Querig, which they plan to poison in order to regain their memories. When they meet Wistan at the end of their journey, they support him ardently because they perceive his determination to kill the dragon as conducive to their own aims. Even when the memories restored to them turn out to be very painful, they still believe that their love may survive, that both of them will be happily reunited with their dead son, and that the whole family will be together again on the island of the shadows. It is not, however, until the very final moments of their journey, when the ferryman insists on taking Beatrice alone to the otherworldly island and when Axl turns away without waiting for his return, that they are able to grasp fully the consequences of Querig's destruction, and, thus, the full significance of their quest.

The connection between the beginning and the end of the quest depicted in *The Buried Giant* is bitterly ironic. In the medieval romances the start and finish are usually complementary and tightly interlocked. *Sir Gawain and the Green Knight* begins with Gawain's response to the Green Knight's challenge and ends with Gawain's return to the court after he has passed the test but also received from his opponent a bitter lesson concerning his imperfections. In Middle English *Ywain and Gawain*, Ywain's initial chivalric victory and his wedding are followed by complications, which necessitate further verification of his loyalty as both a knight and a husband before order and balance are eventually restored. In *The Buried Giant*, the ending does not resolve the initial tension and does not restore the harmony. Yet, the final scenes of the novel are also related to its beginning by providing a very bitter conclusion to the opening events. Axl and Beatrice's quest to find their son ends with the discovery of the truth concerning his death. The quest for truth which was to fortify their relationship ends with their separation.

The assistance which they give to Edwin and Wistan and their support of Wistan's quest to destroy the dragon also bring unforeseen consequences concerning intercultural relationships. Wistan's completion of his quest proves to be destructive on a massive scale and fatal in particular to all Britons. When Wistan slays Querig, the dragon, the mist disappears and both Britons and Saxons become aware again of their old feud. The Saxons recollect the fact that their own aggression was subdued by King Arthur through violence and bloodshed and their desire for retaliation, which has been pent up for years by magically imposed amnesia, is eventually unleashed. The magic spell made them forget the reasons why they initially wanted to destroy the Britons but it could not guarantee long-lasting peace because the tensions caused by mutually inflicted wounds have remained unresolved and anger has kept festering even when it remained unacknowledged. Wistan's plan to incite the fury of the Saxon settlers succeeds and the Britons face annihilation at the hands of the vindictive Saxons, both living among them and invading Britain from their distant homeland.

This aspect of the plot also enables Ishiguro to introduce to his narrative world two principal characters of Arthurian romance, that is, King Arthur and his nephew Gawain, both of whom are presented as relics of the past who subscribed to the wrong set of ideals. Their representation in *The Buried Giant* drastically alters the medieval models of these characters, however diverse they might have been in the medieval tradition. Gawain, idealised in the earliest Arthurian texts as a perfect knight and a perfect lover, whose reputation is slightly undermined in the late medieval tradition (Schmolke-Hasselmann, 1998, pp. 104–140), is cast by Ishiguro into the role of the protector of the dragon, whose breath sustained amnesia among Britons and Saxons. His unilateral admiration for Arthur as a commander both merciful and gallant sets him at a direct contrast with Axl, who curses Arthur for attaining his victory over the Saxons by the breach of the promise to spare their villages. In his frayed and rusty armour, Ishiguro's Gawain becomes an embodiment of the obsolete view that violence can pave the way for peace and that this peace can be sustained by the erasure of the past from the collective memory.

5 Conclusion

Although *The Buried Giant* does not seem to recreate either the world of pre-Saxon Britain or the spirit of Arthurian literature, it remains greatly indebted to medieval culture by its incorporation of certain characteristic tropes of medieval courtly romance. It seems that the distance between the contemporary and the medieval world is greatest when Ishiguro rewrites the characters from Arthurian romance who are tailored to suit his representation of the universal theme. The influence of medieval tropes is most evident in the representation of the physical and mental quests, whose twists and turns take the characters through the unmapped countryside and the uncharted territory of their memory. However unexpected and bitterly ironic the result of these quests might be, they control the whole narrative of *The Buried Giant* and constitute its integral part. Just like in many of the medieval romances, the reader can only see in hindsight that what the characters eventually obtain is what they have been heading for throughout the quest even if they remained heedless of its actual objectives. Ishiguro's novel resonates, therefore, with the echoes of the medieval tradition, the author does not, however, literarily recreate the narrative world of the courtly romances, but borrows from them the structural elements, which are transformed and re-contextualised in his narrative. Despite being altered and designed to expose the thematic concerns expressed in *The Buried Giant*, the medievalist elements still carry with them the residue of their original implications, enriching the meaning of the novel and specifically exposing the formative and destructive agency of individual and collective memory. Set within the frame of the world of fantasy, the characters' ethical concerns gain a universal character.

The novel does not provide, however, an easy answer to the overarching theme of how individuals and multicultural societies can cope with past trauma. When the giant of painful memories is buried and forgotten, it may always stir and become awake at any time, wreaking havoc with peace, built on the insecure foundation of unresolved tensions. As Ishiguro shows, post-conflict trauma has to be handled with care both at the level of individual bonds and at the level of relationships between societies, cultures and ethnic groups. Memory constitutes an integral part of human identity and the suppression of painful memories cannot replace the arduous process of reconciliation. Sometimes the wounds need time to heel and then forgetfulness may help them to do so, but the original cause has, nevertheless, to be properly addressed as the giant needs to be tamed rather than buried alive.

References

Alter, A. (2015, February 20). *A new enchanted realm. The New York Times*. The New York edition, p. 19.

Artin, T. (1999). The allegory of adventure: An approach to Chrétien's romances. In P. Meister (Ed.), *Arthurian literature and Christianity* (pp. 86–106). New York, NY: Garland.

Baillie, J. & Matthews, S. (2010). History, memory and the construction of gender in a pale view of hills. In S. Matthews & S. Groes (Eds.), *Kazuo Ishiguro. Contemporary critical perspectives* (pp. 37–46). London, New Delhi, New York, Sydney: Continuum.

Barron, W. R. J. (1987). *English medieval romance*. London, England, New York, NY: Longman.

Cheng, C. (2010). *The margin without centre: Kazuo Ishiguro*. New York: Peter Lang AG.

Cooper, H. (2004). *The English romance in time: Transforming motifs from Geoffrey of Monmouth to the death of Shakespeare*. Oxford, England: Oxford University Press.

Eco, U. (1998). *Faith in fakes. Travels in hyperreality*. London, England: Vintage.

Holland, T. (2015). *The Buried Giant* review: Kazuo Ishiguro ventures into Tolkien territory, *The Guardian*, March 4, 2015, available at: https://www.theguardian.com/books/2015/mar/04/the-buried-giant-review-kazuo-ishiguro-tolkien-britain-mythical-past

Hopley, C. (2015). Fantasy forged in an evanescent landscape. *The Buried Giant* by Kazuo Ishiguro. *The Washington Times*, April 2, 2015, available at: http://www.washingtontimes.com/news/2015/apr/2/book-review-the-buried-giant

Ishiguro, K. (2015). *The Buried Giant*. Kindle edition.

Matthews, S., & Groes, S. (2010). 'Your words open windows for me': The art of Kazuo Ishiguro. In S. Matthews & S. Groes (Eds.), *Kazuo Ishiguro. Contemporary critical perspectives* (pp. 1–8). London, New Delhi, New York, Sydney: Continuum.

Murakami, H. (2010). On having a contemporary like Kazuo Ishiguro. Translated by T. Godson. In S. Matthews & S. Groes (Eds.), *Kazuo Ishiguro. Contemporary critical perspectives* (pp. vii–viii). London, New Delhi, New York, Sydney: Continuum.

Putter, A. (1995). *Sir Gawain and the Green Knight and French Arthurian romance*. Oxford, England: Clarendon Press.

Sadowski, P. (1996). *Knight on his quest: Symbolic patterns of transition in Sir Gawain and the Green Knight*. Newark: University of Delaware Press—London, England: Associated University Press.

Schmolke-Hasselmann, B. (1998). *The evolution of Arthurian romance. The verse tradition from Chrétien to Froissart*. Cambridge, England: Cambridge University Press.

Sir Gawain and the Green Knight. (1972). J.A. Burrow (Ed.). London: Penguin Books.

Vance, E. (1987). *From topic to tale. Logic and narrative in the middle ages.* Minneapolis: University of Minnesota Press.

Wai-chew, S. (2010). *Kazuo Ishiguro.* New York, NY: Routledge.

Author Biography

Joanna Bukowska obtained her PhD in British literature in 2003 from Adam Mickiewicz University in Poznań. Her doctoral dissertation was entitled "Between the concept of man and the concept of a romance hero. Semiotic and cultural analysis of characters in Thomas Malory's *Morte Darthur.*" Since 2006 she has been employed at the Faculty of Pedagogy and Fine Arts in Kalisz, an integral part of Adam Mickiewicz University in Poznań. Her research interests include: Middle English literature, medievalist literature, contemporary British fiction and literary theory.

Multiculturalism, the Foreign and Early Gothic Novels

Agnieszka Łowczanin

Abstract Many literary historians nowadays stress the importance of cultural exchanges between England and the Continent in the process of the creation of Gothic fiction in the last decades of the eighteenth century (Hale in *European Gothic: A Spirited Exchange, 1760–1960.* Manchester University Press, Manchester, pp. 17–38, 2002; Cornwell in *A new companion to the gothic.* Willey, pp. 64–76, 2012; Wright in *Britain, France and the Gothic, 1764–1820. The Import of Terror.* Cambridge University Press, Cambridge, 2003). Despite political tenccsions between England and France at that time, "the import of terror," as Wright has put it, was a two-way, fast-flowing literary traffic, which impacted on the shape of what is nowadays known as literary Gothic. French romances helped shape Gothic fiction, which was then translated into French and, with French being the *lingua franca* of the erudite elites, its radiation stretched from the Atlantic to the eastern reaches of the Continent. Polish intellectual elites read the early English Gothic novels in their French translations. In Poland, during the reign of the last king, Stanisław August, literary activity, translation included, was encouraged and supported by the monarch as part of the reformative educational scheme to improve the nation. This paper will attempt to look more closely at these multicultural and multilingual exchanges, with the aim of reading early Gothic fiction's predilection for the foreign as a consequence of the cosmopolitan atmosphere of the Enlightenment, which fostered interest in foreign literatures, made possible by mushrooming translations.

Keywords Gothic novels · Enlightenment · Cosmopolitanism · Translations · Anna Mostowska

A. Łowczanin (✉)
Department of British Literature and Culture, University of Łódź, Łódź, Poland
e-mail: alowczanin@yahoo.com

A. Łowczanin
Instytut Filologii Angielskiej, University of Łódź, ul. Pomorska 171/173, Łódź, Poland

© Springer International Publishing AG 2017   45
J. Mydla et al. (eds.), *Multiculturalism, Multilingualism and the Self: Literature and Culture Studies*, Issues in Literature and Culture,
DOI 10.1007/978-3-319-61049-8_4

1   Introduction

From its onset, literary Gothic had a predilection for the foreign. The proto-Gothic text, Horace Walpole's *The Castle of Otranto* (1764), set the tone. The story, which was originally published as a translation by a William Marshall of the sixteenth-century Italian manuscript of a Counter-Reformation monk, took place in the Italian principality of Otranto, and its plot featured crusades to the Holy Land and a Sicilian romance. Foreign ingredients are also present in the early Gothic novels that followed Walpole's. Their settings are foreign: in Ann Radcliffe and M. G. Lewis, considered the best exponents of the early stage of the genre, it is obligatorily France, Spain, Italy, or Sicily. And, consequently, their characters are foreign too: aristocratic villains, Marquises and Marchesas, or else, degenerate dupes of popish, that is foreign, institutions: nuns, prioresses and abbots.

This multicultural ingredient, Italian, French and Spanish, was read by its early perusers as the epitome of the dreaded Catholic Other, the culprit of hypocrisy, sin and moral degradation, and an idiom to express anxieties at home. The purpose here is to investigate the possible routes by which the foreign, in such an abundance, seeped into Gothic fiction. Therefore, early Gothic novels will be seen against the much broader canvas of European literary exchanges going on throughout the eighteenth century, and especially the trade between England and the Continent in the last decades of the eighteenth century. The contention here is that one of the ways of examining the foreign is to see it as an aftermath and legacy of the eighteenth-century atmosphere of intellectual openness, of the enlightened ideas of cosmopolitanism and internationalism, but also rationalism, which, importantly for the Gothic, "displaced religion as the authoritative mode of explaining the universe and altered conceptions of the relations between individuals and natural, supernatural and social worlds" (Botting, 1996, p. 23). Moreover, if, as Horner and Zlosnik remind us, "most critics would probably agree that Gothic writing always concerns itself with boundaries and their instabilities," "with the permeability of boundaries" (2005, p. 1), these boundaries can also be seen as those defining the limits of literary epochs, limits which are established not at the moment literary phenomena take place, but are imposed by later literary critics, and are, therefore, to be seen as often arbitrary divisions that overlap rather than follow one another in a clear-cut manner. It is in this sense that the Gothic, though undoubtedly a harbinger of Romantic imagination and an attempt "to explain what the Enlightenment left unexplained" (Botting, 1996, p. 23), should also be seen as the fruit of Enlightenment openness, and a product of the unprecedented translational activity that it bred.

Unearthing these multicultural connections at the roots of the Gothic genre and imagination, uncovering the flows that fostered its germination, is one of the ways to understand the presence of foreign ingredients in the early English Gothic novels. It is also one of the ways to understand the rapidity of the dissemination of the Gothic on the Continent. Interest in other cultures and multicultural activities promoted by enlightened ideology are seen here as important threads in the examination of the spread of the Gothic to Continental, especially Central-Eastern, Europe.

2   The Foreign in Early Gothic Fiction

A classic recipe for Gothic fiction is contained in a well-equipped toolbox filled with devices easily recognisable since the genre's inception. The tropes, which we now define as Gothic, seem to rest on a handful of conventions, tricks so well-defined and clichéd that along with the now canonical staple texts produced by the first Gothicists came their parodies composed by their early critically-and-artistically-inclined readers.

> Take—An old castle, half of it ruinous.
>
> A long gallery, with a great many doors, some secret ones.
>
> Three hundred bodies, quite fresh.
>
> As many skeletons, in chests and presses …
>
> Mix them together, in the form of three volumes, to be taken at any of the watering-places before going to bed,

writes an anonymous reader of *Spirit of the Public Journals* in 1797 (as cited in Botting, 1996, p. 44). In the same year, another anonymous contributor to *The Monthly Magazine*, signed as "A Jacobin Novelist," submits a piece entitled "The Terrorist System of Novel Writing," in which he bemoans the quality of contemporary novels:

> … alas! So prone are we to imitation, that we have exactly and faithfully copied the SYSTEM OF TERROR, if not in our streets, and in our fields, at least in our circulating libraries, and in our closets…
>
> …just at the time when we were threatened with a stagnation of fancy, arose Maximilian Robespierre, with his system of terror, and taught our novelists that fear is the only passion they ought to cultivate, that to frighten and instruct were one and the same thing…from that time we have never ceased to "believe and tremble"; our genius has become hysterical, and our taste epileptic (1797, pp. 102–104.)

Though yet again ridiculing the Gothicists' fondness for terror, this author's problem with Gothic fiction seems to be as much its prescriptiveness as its indebtedness to foreign influence. In this second piece of criticism the use of the first person plural pronoun stresses the collective experience of falling under the destabilizing foreign influence while admitting the author's participation in the process: "So prone are *we* to imitation" and "*we* have exactly and faithfully copied" (emphasis mine). The repetitive use of the personal pronoun "we," and the possessive pronoun "our"—as in: "*our* streets, *our* fields, *our* circulating libraries, and *our* closets"—underscores the ubiquity of experience: foreign influence in the terror-Gothic cloak has indiscriminately affected everyone and enveloped and polluted the country—its cities, countryside and its bedrooms.

The disgruntled reader bemoans the changing aesthetics of the novels, the doubtful tastes and expectations of the reading public, and attributes them to the political tensions of the decade. He is not the only one to point to the connection between the political and the literary: Marquis de Sade, the first commentator on

M. G. Lewis's *The Monk* of 1796, famously said that the novel was "the necessary fruit of the revolutionary tremors felt by the whole of Europe" (as cited in Sage, 1990, p. 49). In his opinion, contemporary novelists had no choice but to appeal to the supernatural and horror for imagery because only this would be absorbing enough for readers who were by then "familiar with the extent of the miseries which evil men were able to heap upon mankind." Undoubtedly, by the mid-1790s Gothic tropes "could no longer be presented naively; they had all been familiarized and sophisticated by the events in France" (Paulson, 1983, p. 221).

The aftermath of the laudable fall of the Bastille was the unpardonable reign of Terror, massacres of the aristocracy and the royal family in France, and in 1792 the declaration of war on England. So, while the foreign, especially the French—associated with excessive sophistication and Catholicism, their foppishness and popishness—might have been frowned upon in earlier decades when censure was mainly aesthetic and ideological, in 1790s England it became a political statement. Seen in this light, the comment on the detrimental foreign influence made by the anonymous reader of *The Monthly Magazine* is more than derision, it expresses aversion to, and danger caused by, the foreign.

If, in the very nature of the genre lies fascination with the mysterious and the obscure, which provides a more fertile breeding ground for the terrifying, the signature of the Gothic, then the foreign and the remote becomes a territory aesthetically privileged to the local and the familiar. Evoking visual and emotional effects of terror is, of course, in line with the theories of Edmund Burke, who, prior to the effusion of Gothic productions, speculated on the sublime, "the strongest emotion which the mind is capable of feeling" (as cited in Sage, 1990, p. 33). The preconditions for experiencing the sublime are: fear, as terror is its "ruling principle" (p. 34), and obscurity, because "[w]hen we know the full extent of any danger, when we can accustom our eyes to it, a great deal of the apprehension vanishes" (pp. 34–5). In this sense, the foreign, the remote and the unmapped might be seen as a desirable supply of exotic obscurity and unfamiliarity. For the readers of the 1790s the ruinous castle with a great many secret doors that the anonymous reader of 1797 speaks of was a much more plausible source of pleasing terror if set in remote Sicily rather than the Home Counties.

3   The Enlightened Cosmopolitanism and the Foreign in Gothic

Yet, literary Gothic abounded in foreign elements from its beginning, before Burkean ideas were recognized by such writers as Ann Radcliffe to provide the aesthetic foundations for their imagery and plots. I suggest the reason for this predilection for the foreign can be found when Gothic fiction is not treated separately, or marginally as it has been, as a "detour" on the way to Romanticism, but when it is seen against a broader canvas of readers' expectations and the literary atmosphere of the time.

As has been suggested in the introduction, at the time Gothic fiction was born intellectual inquisitiveness was in the air and it affected not only intellectuals. This resulted in an understanding of the necessity for a classical, that is foreign, education, carried out by the leisured and moneyed parts of societies in the form of the Grand Tour, practised by the upper classes in England and other European countries alike. The exposure to foreign culture and landscapes fed the literary imagination of such artists as Thomas Gray, Horace Walpole and William Beckford, all important for the early Gothic. Orientalism was becoming the vogue of the day, travel writing expanded and "decentred perception away from parochial, local and national topoi" (Scrivener, 2007, p. 8). The cosmopolitan atmosphere of the enlightened eighteenth century encouraged various forms of cross-cultural exchanges. The Enlightenment was "self-consciously international, and to be 'enlightened' (éclairé, aufgeklärt, illuminato, oświecony) almost by definition meant to be open to ideas from abroad" (Butterwick, 1998, p. 36).

The preface to the second edition of Walpole's seminal Gothic text, which appeared a year after the first publication of the story, in 1765, is the one in which the reading public learnt they had been hoaxed into believing *The Castle of Otranto* was a translation of an Italian manuscript retrieved "in the library of an ancient catholic family in the north of England" (1998, p. 5). Walpole admitted authorship, and, acknowledging local Shakespearean influence, elaborated on the creation of a modern romance. His mention of the national bard was a response to Voltaire's comments on Shakespeare made in his collective edition of Corneille of 1763, in which he complained that there is "scarcely a tragedy by Shakespeare where one doesn't find the jokes of coarse men side by side with the sublimity of heroes" (as cited in Clery, 1995, p. 118). Walpole's polemic with Voltaire became a "defense of Shakespeare in what was perceived by his patriotic admirers to be a climate of Voltaire-headed French hostility" (Townshend, 2012, p. 40).

4   Voltaire and Anglomania

However, Voltaire's much earlier text, *Letters Concerning the English Nation*, published in 1733 after his return from a three-year exile in England, contains comments on Shakespeare made in a markedly different tone. Here, Voltaire praises the bard, as, for example, in the closing remarks of Letter XVIII, "On Tragedy," where he admits that the "shining monsters of Shakespeare give infinite more delight than the judicious images of the moderns" (1778, p. 152). Apart from Shakespeare, Voltaire's *Letters* are observations on various aspects of life in England, its politics, church and philosophers; above all, however, they praise the English system of liberties. And although they also contain echoes of European criticisms of the English—as in the opening of Letter XI, "On Inoculation," which reads: "It is inadvertently affirmed in the Christian countries of Europe that the

English are fools and madmen" (1778, p. 63)—the versatility of this publication, the reputation of its author and his first-hand commentaries were significant because they were the first analysis of a foreign civilization and his "synthesis did much to make England fashionable" in Europe (Wade as cited in Butterwick, 1998, p. 47).

While it would be difficult to measure the extent to which Voltaire's work contributed to making England the vogue of the decades to come, the fact is that Anglomania and the more philosophic Anglophilia seeped into France and from there spread across the Continent. Gradually, European aristocrats began to favour English landscape gardening over French-Italian formal parks; later Rousseau did much to contribute to spreading the preference of heart to reason, nature to culture, innocence to experience, and consequently, Shakespeare and Richardson to Molière and Corneille (Schama, 1989, p. 149). In Germany, "[t]ranslations of English periodicals and literature, increasingly done from the original rather than French, mushroomed from the 1740s. They included 320 novels between 1740 and 1799" and Shakespeare was translated twice: in the 1760s and 1770s (Butterwick, 1998, p. 56).

5   The Age of Translations and the Gothic

With Latin having lost its importance in academic as well as in imaginative writing, in the eighteenth century vernacular languages were already well-established means of transmitting ideas. The enlightened age can safely be labeled as an era of translation throughout Europe and, as a consequence, "the first attempt of Europe's republic of letters to conduct a cosmopolitan conversation without a 'universal language'" (Oz-Salzberger, 2006, p. 386). The impact of the opening of this translational throughway on the germination and development of Gothic fiction was profound.

It is a critically attested fact that the development of the Gothic genre in England and its later proliferation on the Continent can, to a large extent, be attributed to this intellectual traffic, and an intense interest on both sides of the Channel in seeking inspiration and themes in each other's literatures (Hale, 2002; Wright, 2003). Terry Hale makes a claim that the Gothic novel was "substantially a *product*" of "considerable translational activity" and that "many of the conventions which we associate with the British Gothic novel today arose as a by-product of the translation process" (2002, p. 17). All the pivotal names of the first phase of the Gothic after Walpole made their way into the canon with translations and appropriations, often unacknowledged. One of the first examples is Charlotte Smith's 1785 translation of the Abbé Prévost's 1731 novel *Histoire du Chevalier des Grieux et de Manon Lescaut* under the title of *Manon L'Escaut: Or, The Fatal Attachment. A French Story* (Hale, 2002, p. 18). Similarly, Sophia Lee's *The Recess, or a tale of other times* published between 1783–5 is largely indebted to the Abbé Prévost's *Le Philosophe anglais: Histoire de Clèveland* of 1731, especially for its romance element (Hale, 2009, p. 220). Clara Reeve, the author of *The Old English Baron* of 1778, subtitled a "Gothic Story" and aimed at improving on Walpole's, in 1789 published *The Exiles; or, Memoirs of the Count de Crondstadt*, an unacknowledged adaptation of Baculard d'Arnaud's novel *D'Almanzi* (Wright, 2003, p. 39). Even the great enchantress, Ann Radcliffe, is indebted to inspiration from abroad. It has been critically acknowledged that her early work "demonstrates a discerning, skeptical and sustained engagement" with such continental authors as Bernardin de Saint-Pierre, Jean Jacques Rousseau and Madame de Genlis (Wright, 2003, p. 90). Among the French sources which Radcliffe herself points to as immediate stimulation for *The Romance of the Forest* (1791) in the opening sections of the novel, is a collection of criminal cases, *Les Causes Célèbres et Intéressantes*, published from 1734 by a French lawyer François Gayot de Pitaval, translated into English by Charlotte Smith in 1787, and used as the basis of her own collection of tales, *The Romance of Real Life* (Chard, 2009, p. 367).

That it was possible for these authors to publish works which by contemporary standards would be considered plagiarism can be taken as evidence relating to the attitude towards authorship and translation exhibited by publishers, critics and readers alike. For example, the review in *The Monthly Magazine* of Clara Reeve's *The Exiles* begins with the appraisal of the novel: it is considered "[a]n interesting and well conducted story" and it is only in the last sentence that its author points out that "[t]he principal incidents appear to be borrowed from a novel of the justly admired *M. D'Arnaud*" (*Monthly Magazine*, January 1789, p. 88). Although Reeve is clearly caught out for not acknowledging her source, as Angela Wright points out, this "observation was made without rancour or censure" (2003, p. 39).

With the exception of Ann Radcliffe, along with their own original productions, these female writers practised translation and creative appropriation, recycling other writers' work, whether they acknowledged it or not. In this way, they contributed not only to the flourishing of literary exchange between England and France, but also to increasing the readers' appetites and creating a demand for stories which were only beginning to be called Gothic at that time. Literary traffic between England and France went on unabashed in the decades which were formative for the Gothic genre, and its impact on solidifying Gothic conventions has only recently been fully recognized and acknowledged. Terry Hale has attested that the Gothic was "forged in the crucible of translation" (2002, p. 23); and in the recently published *Britain, France and the Gothic, 1764–1820*, Angela Wright has followed the same trajectory, giving ample evidence that "France and its eighteenth-century authors were formative in the creation of the Gothic in England (2003, p. 149).

6   The Gothic Strikes Back—Dissemination to the Continent

Despite serious political rifts and animosities between England and France, and despite the bad publicity Gothic romances generated as a consequence, the exchange of literature and thought continued and was fruitful. During the French Revolution and the Napoleonic Empire "the English Gothic novel was almost as popular in France as in Britain" (Hale, 2009, p. 223). English Gothic novels found their way into French with astonishing rapidity. *The Castle of Otranto* (1764) came out in French in 1767, Clara Reeve's *The Old English Baron* of 1778 after a decade had two different versions in French, and in the next three decades "practically every English Gothic novel of any distinction" made its way into French (Hale, 2009, p. 223). The most popular author of Gothic romances, both at home and abroad, was, of course, Ann Radcliffe. Her third novel, *The Romance of the Forest* (1791) was the first one to be translated in 1794. Then in 1797 the translations of three more of her books came out: *Castles of Athlin and Dunbayne* (1789), *A Sicilian Romance* (1790) and *The Mysteries of Udolpho* (1794). The last novel published in her lifetime, *The Italian* of 1797, had as many as two translations in the year of its publication in England, by the Abbé Morellet and Mary Gay (Hale, 2002, p. 224).

Altogether there were over a hundred English Gothic novels translated into French; however, "as the Gothic novel radiated out across Europe, the range of translated works became considerably restricted" (Hale, 2002, p. 31). Despite the growing Anglomania, English was not the lingua franca of the intellectual elites of the time. Therefore, the march of the Gothic across the Continent happened in most cases via their French translations. This is how, for example, the Italians read English Gothic romances, and, since French was undoubtedly the most popular of the foreign languages spoken by Polish aristocratic elites of the time, in the same form, via French translations and appropriations, they reached the territory of the largely Francophile Commonwealth of Poland and Lithuania.

7   The Enlightenment, the Last Polish King and the Gothic

Fascination with French, and later English, culture gradually affected affluent aristocrats, and through their patronage the developing class of literati, and, as Richard Butterwick attests, in central and eastern Europe Anglomania and Gallomania were often complimentary (1998, p. 56). Poland remained in very close contact with France and the range of French influences on Polish culture is beyond the scope of this essay. It suffices to say here that when the reign of the Saxon Wetting dynasty ended with the death of Augustus III, under the auspices of the newly-elected king, Stanisław August Poniatowski, the fog of ignorance began to slowly disappear and the period of the so-called "Saxon night," a term used to characterize the cultural backwardness, apathy and political anarchy of the reign of the two Wetting kings, officially came to an end (Butterwick, 1998, p. 23).

The future king's education encompassed a Grand Tour, which included a stay in France and in Britain in 1754, not yet a popular destination among Polish aristocrats of the time. It was during this visit, and thanks to the lifelong friendship which he had struck in Berlin with Sir Charles Hanbury Williams, that Stanisław Poniatowski became enamored with English culture, literature and theatre. In his memoirs, written in French and only recently translated into Polish, the future king makes interesting comments about the mid-eighteenth-century impact of French culture on the English as seen by a foreigner. He says:

> Twenty years ago, barely one in forty Englishwomen condescended to speak French, and all—not even excluding the red-haired—managed without rouge or powder, they did not look after their teeth, their manners and their dress stood in striking contrast to the French customs. Today, they have not only come closer to their neighbours in all these matters, but they have also introduced important changes in the manners of the Englishmen... I dare to think, that these two nations, who now visit each other much more often than in the old days, bestow mutual favours on each other. The French have become a little bit more cautious and less careless, whereas the English—if one believes that they adapt the French deportment only out of courtesy towards their ladies—will perhaps en passant mend the faults of their national upbringing, which at the start leaves them with so much liberty that later, for various reasons, they become too addicted to their own passions (Stanislaw August, 2013, p. 150, my translation.)

In the late 1750s, for over a year the future king worked as a secretary to Sir Charles, then the British Ambassador in Russia, and his correspondence of this time leaves no doubt that Williams helped to make Stanisław an Anglophile (Butterwick, 1998, p. 100). From 1764, when Stanisław Poniatowski ascended the throne, the Enlightenment, and with it intellectual openness, were encouraged at his court as the king attempted to "transform traditionalistic Poles into enlightened Europeans" (Taylor-Terlecka, 2002, p. 56). One of the ways of achieving this aim was to "reform the Polish world à l'anglaise," as he said in his memoirs. "Ever his own minister of culture and propaganda, the king took charge of the nation's spiritual life, his court playing the role of central office of arts and education. Culture was not an end in itself but a means" (Taylor-Terlecka, 2002, p. 56). Under his auspices the first ministry for education, the Commission for National Education, was created. Often, however, the cultural throughway led via France, as when the king founded a twice-weekly essay-periodical, *Monitor*, modelled broadly on the French edition of the English *Spectator*, *Le Spectateur ou le Socrate Moderne* (Sinko, 1956, p. 34), and the first professional national theatre, modelled on the Comédie Française.

The intellectual atmosphere was favourable and encouraged numerous translations. During the thirty years of the last king's reign over two hundred romances were translated, most of them from the French (Sinko, 1961, p. 7). All the big names of the English novel of the eighteenth century were rendered into Polish: Defoe, Fielding, Smollett, Swift, MacKenzie, Sarah Fielding, and Frances Sheridan. Richardson remains the only novelist who has never been translated into Polish; however, numerous copies of French translations of his novels in the libraries, and numerous allusions and references give evidence that he was widely read and very well known (Sinko, 1961, p. 81).

Yet, of the over a hundred Gothic novels translated from English into French, not a single one was translated into Polish in the eighteenth century. Lack of translations does not mean lack of demand for this type of fiction, because throughout the country, women, country gentlemen's wives and daughters who were their main readers, traditionally indulged in medieval and baroque romances of the seventeenth century (Taylor-Terlecka, 2002, p. 57), later in the mushrooming translations of contemporary ones, and they would have undoubtedly constituted an eager reading public for the novels of English provenance. It is difficult to determine why there is a complete lack of translations of English Gothic romances into Polish, even be it via French. Definitely part of the demand was satisfied by French translations. Another plausible reason might have been a systematic anti-romance campaign launched in the 1760s by the ever more influential *Monitor*, and continued well into the 1790s. Romances—and Gothic novels according to contemporary nomenclature were classified as such—were hailed not only as useless and incongruent with didactic models propagated by the state, but also as detrimental to the tastes and morality of the reading public. While all the other contemporary romances were subject to the same type of baiting, perhaps it was Gothic fiction's reputation for indulgence in the supernatural that discouraged the prospective translators, though the 1768 translator of Antoine Galland's *One Thousand and One Nights* (1704–1717) seemed undeterred by its predilection for horror, such as ghouls or haunted houses. The first Polish translation of a Gothic novel was of Ann Radcliffe's *The Romance of the Forest* (1791), which appeared only in 1829 and was translated from the French as *Puszcza, czyli Opactwo St. Clair.*

8   Polish Gothic: Anna Mostowska

In Polish literature of that time there is one writer whose fiction was definitely directly shaped by the English Gothic romances: Anna Mostowska, the Princess Radziwiłł, a contemporary of Ann Radcliffe. Mostowska came to maturity in the golden Stanisław era of literary flourishing and openness, in the aura of French- and Anglomania. She resided in the capital at the time of the Great Sejm (1788–1792), and intellectually benefitted from the times when Warsaw was the local smithy of talents, and a hub of political and literary life. She became enamoured with French and German literature, and translated stories by Madame de Genlis and Wieland, but the shape of her writing and her major literary influence is to be found in the English Gothic, especially in the romances of Ann Radcliffe. Explaining her literary fascinations in the preface to one of her stories, "Strach w zameczku" ("Fright in the castle"), Mostowska explained her literary provenance and mission:

> … Mesdames de Lafayette, de Riccoboni and a great number of authoresses and authors, the delight and diversion of their times…are worthy of everlasting remembrance; they now are…am I to reveal the truth? Utterly boring. If our mothers were easily moved by the lots of Clarissa, Pamela, etc., the exhausted feelings of our generation need more violent emotions. Dreadful spectres, visitors from the otherworld, tempests, earthquakes, ruins of ancient castles inhabited only by ghosts, packs of bandits armed with daggers and a traitor's poison, murder, prisons, and eventually, devils and witches—when all this is found together, only then do we have a romance fit for the taste of our era (Mostowska, 2014, p. 181.)

Examining the nature of English Gothic, Robert Miles concludes that it "cues us into some of the eighteenth-century sources of internal, Protestant, British unease" (2002, p. 86). Similarly, Mostowska's Gothic takes us into the depths of national anxieties. A foreign Gothic cloak supplied her with the aesthetic tools to uncover the hidden recesses of the complex composite state identity of the Commonwealth of Poland and Lithuania, in order to construct local cultural and historical meaning.

Mostowska uses the terror and the ghosts to communicate to the young gener-ations of her readers the most glorious moments of the past and that is why in four volumes she published, her stories are significantly subtitled: they contain a Polish, a Belarusian, a Ruthenian, a Lithuanian, and a Samogitian story. The purpose the author may have had in mind was to revive the multinational and multicultural spirit of the once territorially vast Polish-Lithuanian Commonwealth. And perhaps just as was the case with the magnetism of the myth of the Goths that the English were eager to revive in the eighteenth century to help define their national identity, in their own way, Mostowska's stories too aim at rekindling the political umbrella-identity of the now-lost, ethnically, linguistically and culturally composite state. In a similar manner, historical accuracy is done away with in favour of mythologised ancestry which informs the vivid collective imagination. And as in the counterpart English Gothic stories, historical truth resides here not in facts but in artifacts, in the way history and political decisions seep into and imprint themselves upon ordinary people's lives and collective consciousness.

9   Conclusion

I believe it is worth investigating this unexplored Central-Eastern European terri-tory of the Gothic, to demonstrate that "histories of the Gothic in cultures where it has long been thought the Gothic had no history worth telling" (Hale, 2002, p. 35) can challenge our conceptions of its mainly western European exchanges, and contribute to a better understanding of the nature and allure of this polymorphic genre. Early Gothic fiction, undoubtedly deeply rooted in national concerns, often investigates them via foreign topographies. Analysing the possible origins of the interest in the foreign, and seeing it as a consequence of the increased mobility of people and their receptivity facilitated by enlightened ideas of intellectual inquis-itiveness can help not only to chart a more precise map of European Gothic in its earliest stage, but also reveal certain shared preoccupations and techniques, which in turn can shed new light on the understanding of contemporary processes informing the rapidity of the spread of global gothic.

References

Botting, F. (1996). *Gothic*. London: Routledge.
Butterwick, R. (1998). *Poland's last king and English culture. Stanisław August Poniatowski 1732–1798*. Oxford: Clarendon Press.
Chard, Ch. (2009). Notes. In A. Radcliffe (Ed.), *The romance of the forest* (pp. 364–397). Oxford: Oxford University Press.

Clery, E. J. (1995). *The rise of supernatural fiction. 1762–1800*. Cambridge: Cambridge University Press.

Cornwell, N. (2012). European gothic. In D. Punter (Ed.), *A new companion to the gothic* (pp. 64–76). Willey.

Hale, T. (2002). Translation in distress: Cultural misappropriation and the construction of the Gothic. In A. Horner (Ed), *European gothic: A spirited exchange, 1760–1960* (pp. 17–38). Manchester: Manchester University Press.

Hale, T. (2009). Roman Noir. In M. Mulvey-Roberts (Ed.), *The handbook of the gothic* (2nd ed.) (pp. 220–226). London: Palgrave Macmillan.

Horner, A., & Zlosnik, S. (2005). *Gothic and the comic turn*. Basingstoke: Palgrave Macmillan.

Miles, R. (2002). Europhobia: The catholic other in Horace Walpole and Charles Maturin. In A. Horner (Ed.), *European gothic: A spirited exchange 1760–1960* (pp. 84–103). Manchester: Manchester University Press.

Mostowska, A. (2014). *Powieści, listy*. Łódź: Wydawnictwo Uniwersytetu Łódzkiego.

Oz-Salzberger, F. (2006). The enlightenment in translation: Regional and European aspects. *European Review of History, 13*(3), 385–409. Retrieved: 1 April 2016. doi:10.1080/13507480600893122

Paulson, R. (1983). *Representations of revolution, 1789–1820*. New Haven: Yale University Press.

Sage, V. (1990). *The gothic novel. A casebook*. London: Macmillan.

Schama, S. (1989). *Citizens. A chronicle of the French Revolution*. Harmondsworth: Penguin Books.

Scrivener, M. H. (2007). *The cosmopolitan ideal in the age of revolution and reaction, 1776–1832*. New York: Routledge.

Sinko, Z. (1956). *"Monitor" wobec angielskiego "Spectatora."* Wrocław: PAN.

Sinko, Z. (1961). *Powieść angielska osiemnastego wieku a powieść polska lat 1764–1830*. Warszawa: Państwowy Instytut Wydawniczy.

Taylor-Terlecka, N. (2002). Jan Potocki and his Polish milieu: The cultural context. *Comparative Criticism, 24,* 55–77. doi:10.1017/So144756402005450

The Terrorist System of Novel Writing. (1797). Anon. *Monthly Magazine,4,* 102–114. Web. Accessed 1 April 2016. Hathi Trust Digital Library. https://www.babelhathitrust.org.

Townshend, D. (2012). Gothic Shakespeare. In D. Punter (Ed.), *A new companion to the gothic* (pp. 38–63). Oxford: Wiley-Blackwell.

Voltaire. (1778). *Letters concerning the English nation*. London: J. and R. Tonson, D. Midwinter, M. Cooper, & J. Hodges. Retrieved from: https://books.google.pl

Walpole, H. (1998). Preface to the First Edition. *The castle of Otranto* (5–8). Oxford: Oxford UP.

Wright, A. (2003). *Britain, France and the gothic, 1764–1820. The import of terror*. Cambridge: Cambridge University Press.

Author Biography

Agnieszka Łowczanin teaches in the Department of British Literature and Culture at the University of Łódź. She specializes in eighteenth- and nineteenth-century fiction and has published articles on authors of this period, focusing on the politics, poetics and paradoxes of the Gothic genre. She co-edited a volume of essays *All that Gothic* (2014). She has organised two international conferences devoted to cultural and literary manifestations of Gothicism. She is currently working on a book that charts the movement of Gothic themes and motifs across national and linguistic boundaries, and traces European exchanges in the Gothic, especially English influences on Polish Gothic fiction in the early stages of the development of the genre.

The House Sofi Built: Critique of Multiculturalism and Christian Patriarchy in Ana Castillo's *So Far from God*

Małgorzata Poks

Abstract In *So Far from God*, Chicana author Ana Castillo focuses on the consequences of the colonial wound theorized by Gloria Anzaldúa in *Bordernalds/La Frontera*. Following the lives of four young Chicana women and their resourceful mother Sofi, Castillo's novel invites an interventionist reading of US multiculturalism. A country that prides itself on its multicultural identity and continues to oppress its minority groups through political, economic and symbolic violence has failed to live up to the promise of the dream of "liberty and justice for all." Adopting various strategies of survival in the modern world, from failed assimilation to open rebellion against the phallogocentric norm, the novel's female characters both fall victim to the continuing legacy of coloniality/modernity and struggle to build a viable alternative to their invisibility within the dominant culture. The paper demonstrates how Castillo appropriates the feminine in her decolonial use of Christian spirituality to endow her Chicana characters with agency. Drawing strength from the reintegrated feminine principle, Sofi and her Chicana *comadres* are capable of constructing a viable vision of a new world across class, race, and gender differences. The feminist utopia imagined in the pages of *So Far from God* is curiously reminiscent of the Zapatistas' dream of "a world in which many worlds fit."

Keywords Interculturalism · Hagia Sophia · Feminist · Spirituality · Mysticism

1 Introduction

In pre-contact times, the American hemisphere was home to a rich variety of cultures. From hunting-gathering to sophisticated farming societies and the advanced civilizations of Mesoamerica, indigenous peoples had adapted to every possible

M. Poks (✉)
Department of American and Canadian Studies, Institute of English Cultures and Literatures, University of Silesia, ul. Grota-Roweckiego 5, 41-200 Sosnowiec, Poland
e-mail: gosiapoks@gmail.com

© Springer International Publishing AG 2017
J. Mydla et al. (eds.), *Multiculturalism, Multilingualism and the Self: Literature and Culture Studies*, Issues in Literature and Culture,
DOI 10.1007/978-3-319-61049-8_5

geographical niche and spoke about 2000 distinct languages (Mintz & McNeil, 2016). This cultural diversity was lost at the time of colonization and the imposition of one hegemonic culture throughout the double continent. In the North, the unstoppable march of (Anglo-Saxon) Manifest Destiny created a powerful empire which soon appropriated the name of the hemisphere and, as empires would, defined its identity in monolithic cultural terms. The resulting melting pot was to melt all cultural differences into quintessential "Americanness," ironically defined in white, Anglo-Saxon, Protestant male terms. Although the USA has since embraced the policy of promoting cultural difference, in the second decade of the twenty-first century the struggle of "unmeltable" ethnics and other invisible minorities for the hegemonic culture's recognition of difference (the *e pluribus unum* of the country's motto) is still far from finished. This is best illustrated by the jingoist political campaign of Donald Trump, the US mounting hostility towards immigrants, especially Muslim "terrorists" and undocumented immigrants from south of the border, as well as the construction of the giant wall between the USA and Mexico (already called the Great Wall of America). To transform this Fortress America, in which the privileged few live in safe isolation from the internal and external "trespassers," into an inclusive American House with freedom and justice for all, multiculturalism alone will not do.

Identified with a top-down government policy that, at best, amounts to cultural relativism, multiculturalism tends to foster indifference to cultural diversity instead of the hoped-for curiosity about and interaction with the "other." A number of academics, especially from regions with significant indigenous populations like Canada and Hispanic America, have recently spoken in favor of interculturality as "an ideological principle clearly indicative of an 'other' thinking" (Walsh, 2012, p. 16). As a grassroots movement spurred by an upsurge of interest in indigenous epistemologies, interculturality challenges the presumed universality of western knowledge, demonstrating the latter's insufficiency in and of itself. As argued by Catherine Walsh from Universidad Andina Simón Bolívar, "interculturality points to the radical transformation of social structures and institutions, and the building of a Plurinational State" (2012, p. 17). An outline of such a state, which for the purpose of this article I will call an American House, in contrast to the previously introduced concept of Fortress America, can be found in Ana Castillo's 1993 novel *So Far from God*. This novel seeks to reclaim indigenous and other non-hegemonic knowledges, subalternized by colonization and patriarchal dominance, in an attempt to present a model of *buen vivir*, or living well, beyond the profit principle dominant in developed capitalist societies. Its central character, the Chicana matriarch Sofi, initially defined exclusively by relations of patriarchal dominance and called La Abandonada, as an allusion to her being abandoned by her husband, eventually becomes Sofi-La Mayor, a people's leader and an architect of an inclusive utopia, a house of wisdom open to all. At the end of the novel Sofi (*Sophia* in Greek) becomes a veritable saint (*hagia*) and martyr in the eyes of the community. Thus, it can be argued that biblical Wisdom, Hagia Sophia, literally manifests herself in the saintly character of Sofi.

In what follows I will demonstrate how Castillo appropriates the feminine in her decolonial use of Christian spirituality to endow her Chicana characters with agency. Drawing strength from the rediscovered feminine principle, Castillo's female characters are capable of constructing a viable vision of a new reality across class, race, and gender differences. The feminist utopia imagined in the pages of *So Far from God* is curiously reminiscent of the Zapatistas' dream of "a world in which many worlds fit."

2 Sophia and Decolonization of Christianity

Castillo has frequently relied on religious myths which are especially empowering for women—therefore usually unorthodox and creatively re-appropriated. It comes as no surprise then that Sofi's name evokes associations with Sophia-the wisdom figure of Hebrew Scripture. As Hagia Sophia, or Holy Wisdom, she is the central character in the Book of Proverbs, Psalms, Song of Songs, Ecclesiastes, Book of Wisdom, and the Wisdom of Sirach. One of the most often mentioned figures in Jewish Scripture (after Yahweh, Moses, David, and Job), Hagia Sophia is identified with the "dark but lovely" woman of the Song of Solomon (1:5) as well as with *natura naturans* (uncreated nature) personified in the feminine child who was present at the act of creation. In the *Book of Proverbs* Wisdom says:

> I was formed long ages ago,
>
> at the very beginning, when the world came to be.
>
> When there were no oceans, I was given birth,
>
> when there were no springs abounding with water;
>
> before the mountains were settled in place,
>
> before the hills, I was given birth,
>
> before he made the world or its fields
>
> or any of the dust of the earth.
>
> I was there when he set the heavens in place,
>
> when he marked out the horizon on the face of the deep,
>
> when he established the clouds above
>
> and fixed securely the fountains of the deep,
>
> when he gave the sea its boundary
>
> so the waters would not overstep his command,
>
> and when he marked out the foundations of the earth.
>
> Then I was constantly at his side.
>
> I was filled with delight day after day,

rejoicing always in his presence,

rejoicing in his whole world

and delighting in humankind (Prov. 8:23–31.)

By some identified with the feminine aspect of God, or—heretically—with the fourth person of the Trinity,[1] the biblical Sophia is a tender and caring, motherly counterpart of God the Father. Protective and rejoicing at the whole of creation, Sophia was known and prayed to by early Christians, but she gradually disappeared from the theological horizon at the time of the Gnostic heresy in the 13th century, her cult domesticated by and absorbed into the cult of the Virgin Mother of God. Additionally, as male theologians feared Sophia's potential fusion with pagan goddesses and tended to emphasize the masculine in religion, Holy Wisdom was absent from theological disputes until the late 19th century, when she resurfaced in the Russian Orthodox Church and, later, was rediscovered by Christian feminist theologians. Interestingly and somewhat paradoxically, even before she was rediscovered by feminists, she appeared in a series of dreams and mystic visions to Trappist monk Thomas Merton (1915–1968).[2] In his poem entitled "Hagia Sophia" Merton writes:

> There is in all visible things an invisible fecundity, a dimmed light, a meek namelessness, a hidden wholeness. This mysterious Unity and Integrity is Wisdom, the Mother of all, Natura naturans. There is in all things an inexhaustible sweetness and purity, a silence that is a fount of action and joy. It rises up in wordless gentleness and flows out to me from the unseen roots of all created being, welcoming me tenderly, saluting me with indescribable humility. This is at once my own being, my own nature, and the Gift of my Creator's Thought and Art within me, speaking as Hagia Sophia, speaking as my sister, Wisdom (1977, p. 363.)

As a member of a colonized minority, Castillo re-appropriates the sophianic tradition in her narrative of resistance to the dominant (white and masculine) culture's definition of "America." Through this act of epistemic disobedience toward religious orthodoxy and seeking to reclaim the wisdom tradition of the bible, Castillo herself becomes a lover of wisdom and a decolonial philosopher.[3] In his appropriation of Enrique Dussel's theory of transmodernity, US philosopher of Puerto Rican extraction Nelson Maldonado-Torres comments: "… the philosopher is called to be more than a 'functionary' (Husserl) or an 'interpreter' (Habermas), she is called to be an agent of de-colonization that furthers critical consciousness,

---

[1] The sophiology of Sergey Bulgakov, Nicolai Berdyaev, and Vladimir Solovyov are cases in point.

[2] In 1958 in his private journals Merton recorded several dreams about a lovely Jewish girl whose name was Proverb. He recognized in her the Wisdom figure of the bible and several years later, while in hospital, he was taken care of by a young nurse who looked exactly like the Proverb of his dreams. Merton developed a deep attachment to the nurse and this relationship helped him heal the emotional traumas of his childhood (Cunningham, 1996, pp. 176-17, 182; Daggy, 1998, pp. 243–329).

[3] In Greek *philosophos* means a lover of wisdom.

altericity, and the teleological suspension of identity through different episte-mologies" (2008, p. 234). This is exactly what Castillo does in *So Far from God*.

In an essay collection *Massacre of the dreamers*, published two years later (1995), Castillo explicitly embraces religious syncretism as empowering for women. In her discussion of Chicana spirituality, she shifts the theological point of gravity from religious transcendence, which is mostly advocated by the male guardians of orthodoxy, to the down-to-earth, most immanent aspects of religion as it is lived and experienced by the poor and oppressed, especially by third-world women who lack theological education. The latter's deep faith in divine inter-vention in the here and now helps them overcome the seemingly impossible obstacles of daily existence. Thus, religious immanence and earthly joy are much more relevant to disadvantaged communities than the "pie in the sky" promised by (privileged male) Church preachers. Castillo writes:

> We [conscientized Chicanas] must take heed that not all symbols that we have inherited are truly symbolic of the life-sustaining energy we carry within ourselves as women; so even when selectively incorporating what seems indispensable to our religiosity, we must ana-lyze its historical meaning, so that it validates our instincts to survive on our own terms. Moreover, survival should not be our main objective. Our presence shows our will to survive, to overcome every form of repression known to humankind. Our goal should be to achieve joy (1995, pp. 145–146.)

Although Christianity, especially Roman Catholicism, remains central to Chicana identity, Castillo draws a line between institutional religion and lived spirituality. While the former, as an extension of the dominant patriarchal mindset, perpetrates the subjugation of women to powerful male authorities, it is the latter, informed as it is by selectively appropriated rituals and religious symbols, that help the Chicana cope in a society "that does not give her humanity substantial value" (Castillo, 1995, p. 146). In other words, Chicanas' lived spirituality is inter-cultural and as such it is syncretic and subversive of the (white, man-made) religious system. Seeking "spiritual guidance no longer from a paternal white god figure but a brown or black mother …" (Castillo, 1995, p. 145), Chicanas—oppressed by the system—have little regard for doctrinal purity; instead, they creatively adapt ele-ments from ancestral religions and synthesize them into one empowering (inter-cultural) whole. Thus, in her "sheroic" (Castillo's coinage) struggle for self-confidence and fulfillment, the pious Chicana seeks guidance from the Mother principle as manifested in the most cherished Mexican religious icon, the brown Virgin of Guadalupe.

3 The Earth Mother and Indigenista Hermeneutics

The Virgin of Guadalupe is reported to have appeared near today's Mexico City to Juan Diego, a Nahua peasant, in 1531. On his way to church, the newly converted Indian met a beautiful mestiza woman speaking Nahuatl. Significantly, this meeting took place on the site of a former Aztec shrine dedicated to Tonanzin—"Our Sacred

Mother" in the Nahuatl language. The dark-skinned woman identified herself as the Mother of both the Christian god and the supreme Nahuatl god (Livingstone, 2008).

A popular indigenista interpretation maintains that the Virgin's name is a mispronunciation of Coatlaxopeuh, meaning "the one [feminine] who crushed the serpent's head" (Davíla, as cited in Leatham, 1989, p. 30). Gloria Anzaldúa (1999, p. 49) insists that Coatlaxopeuh, as well as the homonymous Coatlalopeuh, refer to the Aztec goddess Coatlicue, known as the Lady of the Serpent Skirt. In the late post-classical period, Coatlicue's power over life and death was too intimidating to the male-dominated Aztec culture, which split her into her more sinister aspect, embodied in Tlazolteotl, and Cihuacoatl, the benevolent Tonanzin (Anzaldúa, 1999, p. 49). Clearly, the masculine mind, whether pre- or post-contact, cannot bear ambiguity. But, more relevantly to the argument pursued, since in Christian theology the Virgin Mother of God is believed to be destined to crush the serpent's head (Gen. 3:15), indigenista activists see in Guadalupe Tonanzin (as she is often called) an iconic synthesis of the old and the new worlds. Thus, in indigenist hermeneutics, the Lady in Blue of the venerated Mexican icon is believed to represent the nurturing Mother Earth and is identified with the female aspect of the Nahuatl supreme deity Ometeol (The Lord and Lady of Duality). This is an important link with Sophia, the feminine aspect of Christian God.

In Hispanic America as well as among US Mexicans, Guadalupe Tonanzin has become an important emblem of indigenous struggles for justice and empowerment. She is also a symbol of the Zapatista movement, a native Maya, land- and justice-centered rebellion against corporate greed and neocolonial exploitation of indigenous peasants. Zapatismo demands the return of land stolen from the Maya owners, embraces nonviolence as a weapon of choice, and attempts to build a more just world in which "many worlds fit." What is of primary importance in this movement presided over by Mother Earth is that Zapatistas promote gender equality, encourage indigenous feminism and participatory, bottom-up democracy, and "rule by obeying" (their motto is *servir obedeciendo*).[4] I find the model of equality and autonomy advanced by this movement consonant with the all-inclusive utopia, a House built by Wisdom that Castillo envisions in the pages of *So Far from God*.

The Zapatista experiment seems to demonstrate the working hypothesis of Castillo's novel, namely, that the reintegration of the repressed female principle into the individual and collective psyche is capable of reinstating a harmony on which lasting peace can be built. The military (aggressive, masculine, patriarchal) metaphor of Fortress America can then be replaced by the welcoming (feminine and peaceful) metaphor of an American House with many rooms to suit everyone. Guadalupe Tonanzin as a manifestation of Sophia, the feminine aspect of God/Mother God who delights in humankind (Prov. 8:31), would want all her children to dwell together in a world where many worlds fit and where everyone can rejoice in the whole of creation.

---

[4]See, e.g., Mignolo, (2011, pp. 213–251).

4 Absent Lords and Caring Mothers—Return of the Goddess in *So Far from God*

The novel is set in a fictional border town of Tome and focuses on the life of an average Chicano family struggling for survival.[5] Rather typically for such a family, Sofi's husband, the charming and irresponsible Domingo, is mostly absent or merely passively present in the house. Etymologically, Domingo (from the Latin *domine*) is supposed to be the lord and master of the house. In reality, however, he is a compulsive gambler who disappears without a trace when the youngest daughter is born, leaving his wife alone in charge of the house, the family enterprise Carne Buena Carnecería, and their four daughters: Esperanza (Hope), Fe (Faith), Caridad (Charity), and the youngest, simply called La Loca Santa (the Holy Madwoman). When Domingo reappears many years later, broke, forlorn, and eager to live off his wife's money, Sofi takes him back without as much as a reproach. But when Domingo gambles off her family inheritance, Sofi does what she should have done twenty years before but did not for fear of being excommunicated by the Church and cursed by her parents: she sues for divorce. Conditioned since birth to serve the established patriarchal order, Sofi, who has meanwhile lost two of her daughters and launched her career as mayor of Tome, finally finds the courage to take control over her personal life and get rid of her useless husband. In symbolic terms, the growing visibility and independence of Sofi in the novel's narrative marks the eclipse of the patriarchal order and the return of the goddess. The inefficient Lord and Master (Dominus-Domingo) has been dislocated from his ontological place of privilege by his feminine counterpart (Hagia Sophia) embodied in the wise, longsuffering woman and grassroots activist struggling for community improvement, who nonetheless cares enough for her good-for-nothing husband to eventually let him stay in the unfinished cabin he started building for one of their daughters. In the new House constructed by feminine wisdom and centered on a community of females, compassion overrides justice, cooperation takes the place of aggressive competitiveness, and ultimately it is the good life (*buen vivir*) for all rather than the elite few that counts.

5 Failures of Capitalism and the Painful Construction of the House of Wisdom

Sofi owes her transformation—from a victim of the modern/colonial matrix of power to an empowered, conscienticized woman actively engaged in rebuilding her world—to motherhood. Her three eldest daughters: Fe, Esperanza and Caridad, are

---

[5]For interesting recent discussions of this novel see: Romero (2012, pp. 25–52), Spurgeon (2005, pp. 120–144).

named after the three theological virtues enumerated in Paul's First Letter to the Corynthians (13:13). Historically, Faith, Hope and Charity are also the names of early Christian martyrs and daughters of Sophia, herself a saint and a martyr. The real name of Sofi's youngest child remains unknown. On account of her cataleptic seizure and the following miraculous resurrection at the time of her burial when she was merely three, she is called La Santa (saint). Upon awakening in the coffin, the child is reported to have flown to the top of the church roof and proclaimed that she had been taken to heaven, purgatory and hell, and returned to earth to pray for others, the officiating priest included. But her odd manners, intolerance of human smell and her subsequent refusal to be seen, let alone touched, by anyone save her mother; the girl's preference for the company of horses and other animals; her disheveled appearance and numerous other oddities finally bring her the name La Loca, the "Santa" being dropped altogether. The most spiritual of the sisters, she, paradoxically, dies of the least likely disease to afflict her: AIDS.

While, on account of her cataleptic seizures, visions, and other supernatural abilities, La Loca is believed to be in intimate contact with spiritual reality, her sisters, at least initially, have little understanding for mysticism, but ultimately all three of them undergo martyrdom, falling victim to racism and gender and military violence. Their lives and deaths throw light on the failures of capitalism and the dominant culture's narrative of progress, revealing what Walter Mignolo calls the dark side of modernity.[6]

Esperanza, the most politically conscious of Sofi's children, becomes a TV reporter and is sent to Saudi Arabia to report on the First Gulf War. Kidnapped and tortured, she dies a martyr's death and is awarded a posthumous medal by the American army, which is an ironic twist of fate, given the youthful Esperanza's support for the Chicano Movement, her reporting on US-sponsored crimes against third-world countries, like the military coup against Salvador Allende and the ensuing political terror in Chile (Castillo, 1994, pp. 239–240), and her overall work "to change the system" (p. 142).

Caridad, as her name suggests, is absolutely selfless, unable to hate anyone, and perfectly beautiful. Abandoned by her true love (Memo), she gives her love indiscriminately to anybody who wants it. For this unbecoming generosity, Caridad is mutilated by anonymous attackers so badly she barely survives. Needless to add, the conniving (male) authorities do not find any culprit. When miraculously restored to full health, Caridad becomes a spiritual healer, falls in love with an unknown woman, and disappears for a year into solitude to meditate on her infatuation. Upon her return, the townspeople believe her to be a holy hermit and seek her blessings. While visiting an Acoma village with Esmeralda, her mixed-blood Indian beloved, Caridad is pursued by a jealous male admirer (Francesco el Penitente) and jumps down a cliff holding Esmeralda's hand. Instead of dying, however, they are both believed to have joined the Acoma female deity

---

[6]This idea is most fully developed in Mignolo (2011).

Tsichtinako, "deep within the soft, moist dark earth" where they can be "safe and live forever" (Castillo, 1994, p. 211).

The third daughter, Fe, is the most practical, predictable, and conformist of all Sofi's daughters. Working hard to attain the American Dream, Fe the perfectionist is ashamed of her family and seeks to distance herself from her humble beginnings. When her high school sweetheart unexpectedly abandons her on the eve of their wedding day, her meticulously planned life collapses. Fe loses her voice screaming loudly for weeks on end, but eventually she does marry an equally predictable cousin of hers, moves into her own dream house filled with all the dream gadgets, only to die of cancer a year later. Nobody told her or her Chicana co-workers at Acme International that they were polishing hi-tech weapon parts for the Pentagon with highly toxic chemicals. The loyal Chicana worker receives neither medical assistance nor financial compensation from her employer.

The lives of Fe, Caridad, and Esperanza are Castillo's creative appropriations of medieval hagiographic writings. With La Loca's life and death paralleling quite closely the mysterious life and death of another saint of medieval Christendom— Christina Mirabilis or Christina the Astounding (1150–1224)—it seems vital to understand why Castillo should reclaim those stories for her end-of-twentieth-century narrative which foregrounds the role of female mystic spirituality. Michelle Sauer of the University of Washington (2000) argues that in medieval Church mysticism gave a modicum of agency to women, an otherwise invisible and silenced group of believers. Medieval women-visionaries would be venerated by their contemporaries who believed the saintly females mediated ultimate reality and delivered divine warnings and other messages to the sinful world. Some, it should be added, assisted sinners in conversion, which was explicitly the priests' role, influenced world politics, or counseled popes.[7] Thus, subtly subverting the dominant relations of power, female visionaries and saints enjoyed a modicum of agency in the deeply patriarchal institution of the Christian Church. Moreover, they were often declared saints by communities of faith immediately upon performing what was considered to be a miracle, although recognition from Church authorities was either slow or not granted at all. The veneration of Christina Mirabilis, for example, has never been officially approved by the Church. By retrieving those narratives of female power and adapting them to the contemporary context, Castillo re-appropriates early Christian women's narratives of resistance to the patriarchal matrix of power. As the official Church more often than not allies itself with the colonizing forces which keep fragmenting Chicana/o society and sacrificing life to profit and power while reserving sainthood to heroic and obedient figures, Castillo shows that every longsuffering, hard-working woman is already a saint, and that a community's verdict is more important than the official blessing of church authorities.

---

[7]For instance, Catherine of Siena insisted that pope Gregory XI return from Avignon to Rome.

One of the most important points raised by Sauer (2000, p. 72) is that the New Testament regards every baptized person a saint (*hagios*), thus making sainthood a normative condition of all believers. She asserts, however, that after the Constantinian shift, when Christianity became the dominant religion, a community's opinion of a person's goodness and respectability was additionally required to confer sainthood. But when in 1234 the papacy officially assumed full control of the canonizing process, this was a far more sinister transformation of a once democratic and participatory movement. It should be added that also Christian women, once performing important functions in their communities of faith, were being removed from positions of authority until the Church became thoroughly colonized by militant, patriarchal orthodoxy. Castillo, as Sauer asserts (p. 72), seeks to restore the ancient ideal of an egalitarian community of faith by incorporating the community's voice, especially as vested in the women, in bestowing sainthood. In *So Far from God*, it is the people themselves who declare La Loca a saint (Santa) against an explicit warning of Father Jerome, who fears the girl is the devil's messenger. Likewise, it is the people who seek Caridad's blessings and ask her for miracles, even though her lesbian desire has re-articulated the concept of sainthood as inclusive not only of female sensuality (neither Caridad nor other female saints in the novel, including Sofi, embrace virginity), but of an alternative sexuality to boost (Sauer, 2000, p. 84).

6   Colonized Versus Empowering Spirituality: Two Good Fridays

Castillo's narrative of redemptive suffering, framed as it is in syncretic spirituality, juxtaposes two distinct celebrations of Good Friday, the day which commemorates Christ's sacrificial death on the cross. Traditionanlly, the faithful are supposed to draw consolation from meditating on Christ's suffering, as the Cross triumphs over death, the instrument of torture becomes a sign of humankind's reconciliation with God, and the promise of eternal life beyond suffering is made accessible to everyone. In the novel, the first Good Friday celebration takes the form of the traditional Way of the Cross as inherited from the Spanish colonizers. In this hyperrealistic reenactment of Christ's suffering, a man chosen for his piety (Franesco el Penitente) carries a life-size wooden cross on his bare back while a crowd of penitents follows him along the highway to the important Catholic sanctuary of Chimayó, the merciless sun beating down on the procession. This spectacle is rooted in medieval Christianity's harsh, ascetic practices foregrounding the inimitable suffering of God's Son as interpreted by the hierarchical, patriarchal Church.

The Good Friday celebrated the following year, after Fe's death and Sofi's assumption of her leadership role, however, casts the suffering people in the role of the crucified Christ. The composite figure of the Suffering Servant is made immediately relevant to the participants, the procession being present-oriented, community-centered, and egalitarian. In this other procession religion is decolonized: there is no heroic, male Christ-substitute overburdened with a heavy cross and no exceptional mother figure meets her son on the Way. Instead, the faithful carry "photographs of their loved ones who died of toxic exposure" (Castillo, 1994, p. 241) and each station of the cross is dedicated to a contemporary crime against the collective body of Christ: men, women, and children. Rather than to abstractions, the litany of crimes refers to specific acts of violence against justice and each crime is denounced by spokespersons that come from different gender, racial, or ethnic groups. What crucifies God's people at the end of the second millennium, the gathered faithful suggest, are: the dumping of radioactive waste into sewers, unemployment and starvation among native and Hispano families, death of exposure to toxic materials, contamination of the Navajo land ("Our Mother") with uranium and the subsequent birth defects in children, air and water pollution, the spread of AIDS among the poorest, pesticide-contaminated foodstuffs, the threat posed by nuclear plants, and the absurd Gulf War waged to secure US economic interests in the oil-rich area, a war in which innocent civilians die along combatants.

The rare public appearance of La Loca, enfeebled by AIDS and riding her favorite horse in the procession, makes the spontaneously built community of justice a metaphor of intergenerational, interracial, and even interspecies inclusivity. Wearing Esperanza's blue bathrobe—and as such reminiscent of the Blue Lady Guadalupe Tonanzin—the unkempt animal-loving channeler and sociophobic recluse seems to fit in, for the first time, with the crowd. One finds it hard not to think about this Good Friday procession in terms of a grassroots activists' march for justice and tolerance, and a truly Sophianic intuition of an all-inclusive, mercy-centered spirituality, which is the male guardians of orthodoxy's worst nightmare.

7 Living in the House of Wisdom

Matriarchy, as Castillo argued in *Massacre of the dreamers*, is not and has never been simply reversed patriarchy. The feminine principle that needs to be rediscovered and reinserted into human consciousness (as both males and females have been alienated from it) is, in the author's words, "concerned with preservation, protection—especially of the young and less fortunate—and affiliations of communities for the common good" (Castillo, 1995, p. 88). This feminine principle is our inner goddess (the inner Sophia/Guadalupe Tonanzin) which we need to re-appropriate to be capable of "unconditional compassion and acceptance" (Castillo, 1995, p. 88). Consequently, as Castillo's novel suggests, a world governed by a goddess or a motherly God would be a world of peace and justice for all, a world "where death does not come to us in the form of one more violent and unjust act committed against our right to live" (p. 149). This is so because "in this world of the glorification of material wealth, whiteness, and phallic worship" women are "holders of knowledge that could transform this world into a place where the quality of life for all living things on this planet is the utmost priority ..." (Castillo, 1995, p. 149).

Dying unnatural deaths, Sofi's daughters have been declared martyrs (Fe, Esperanza) and saints (La Loca, Caridad). To redeem their deaths, Sofi founds M.O. M.A.S. (Mothers of Martyrs and Saints), an organization open to all mothers mourning their disappeared, tortured and otherwise prematurely dead daughters, as well as, increasingly, also their martyred sons. M.O.M.A.S. annual meetings become bonding, empowering occasions. Believing in the unity of spirit and matter and in the enduring ties of love, the mothers celebrate unity with each other and with their departed children, who, not surprisingly, as becomes saints and martyrs, make ectoplasmic appearances and deliver messages to their parents and the world. The reunion of the living and the dead is presided over by male and female clergy, of both the celibate and the married kind. Coffee and cookies are shared and there is a good deal of laughter. If occasionally a man slips in disguised as a blessed mother, nobody is likely to be bothered and the saint and martyred *jitos* "all seem pretty happy to be there with everybody no matter what their story in this life had been" (Castillo, 1994, p. 251). M.O.M.A.S. grows under Sofi's presidency well into the 21st century and, to the best of my understanding, provides the coordinates of a truly intercultural community.

8   Conclusion

As an antidote to the politics of retaliation and exclusion which has come to define the modern nation-state (the Fortress metaphor) and which keeps minorities in the condition of virtual enslavement, Castillo imagines a post-national, decolonial community based on the spiritual principles of inclusivity, compassion, and equality. In *So Far from God*, such a community comes into existence due to the concerted efforts of community organizers and conscienticized female activists, who, like the saintly Sofi, an embodiment of Hagia Sophia, the female aspect of the Christian God, manifest the "hidden wholeness" and mysterious integrity of all life, even life after death. The Chicana Sofi, her mestiza comrades, and other members of the economic collective, like the "dark but lovely" woman of the wisdom books of the bible, are closer to life-giving, healing knowledge and—as with La Loca, Caridad, the *curandera* Doña Felicia, or the Acoma Pueblo women—privy to ancient wisdom, the wisdom of the Mother (Earth). Channeling spiritual energies which bind the House of Wisdom together, they are motivated by the common good rather than self-interest, accept all life as sacred, and feel responsible even for their former oppressors, thus transforming the relations of power into (eventually and hopefully) family relations. Their struggle, like that of the Zapatista women, is for all life and against every injustice; it is a struggle for a world in which many worlds fit.

References

Anzaldúa, G. (1999). *Borderlands/La frontera* (2nd ed.). San Francisco: Aunt Lute Books.

Castillo, A. (1994). *So far from God*. New York: Plume.

Castillo, A. (1995). *Massacre of the dreamers: Essays on Chicanisma*. New York: Plume.

Cunningham, L. S. (Ed.). (1996). *A search for solitude: The journals of Thomas Merton* (Vol. 3). New York: Harper Collins.

Daggy, R. (Ed.). (1998). *Dancing in the water of life. The journals of Thomas Merton* (Vol. 5). San Francisco: HarperCollins.

Leatham, M. (1989). Indigenista hermeneutics and the historical meaning of Our Lady of Guadalupe of Mexico. Retrieved (02.02.2016) from https://scholarworks.iu.edu/dspace/bitstream/handle/2022/2068/22(1,2)%2027-39.pdf?sequence=1

Livingstone, D. (2008 Christmas). Tonanzin Guadalupe—Our Mother. *Sofia*, 90. *Sea of Faith Network*. Retrieved (02.02.2016) from http://www.sofn.org.uk/sofia/90livingstone.html

Maldonado-Torres, N. (2008). *Against war: Views from the underside of modernity*. Durham & London: Duke University Press.

Merton, T. (1977). *"Hagia Sophia" The collected poems of Thomas Merton*. New York: New Directions.

Mignolo, W. (2011). *The dark side of western modernity: Global futures, decolonial options*. Durham & London: Duke University Press.

Mintz, S., McNeil, S. (2016). Overview of the first Americans. *Digital history*. Retrieved (02.02.2016) from http://www.digitalhistory.uh.edu/era.cfm?eraid=1&smtid=1

Romero, Ch. (2012). *Activism in the American novel: Religion and resistance in fiction by women of color*. Charlottesville & London: University of Virginia Press.

Sauer, M. (2000). 'Saint-making' in Ana Castillo's *So far from God*: Medieval mysticism as predecessor for an authoritative Chicana spirituality. *Mester, 29*(1). Retrieved (02.02.2016) from http://escholarship.org/uc/item/84w613zv

Spurgeon, S. (2005). *Exploding the western: Myths of empire on the postmodern frontier*. Texas: Texas A&M University Press.

Walsh, C. (2012). "Other" knowledges, "other" critiques: Reflections on the politics and practices of philosophy and decoloniality in the "other" America. *Transmodernity: Journal of Peripheral Cultural Production of the Luso-Hispanic World, 1*(3), 11–27.

Author Biography

Małgorzata Poks, PhD, is assistant professor in the Institute of English Cultures and Literatures, University of Silesia, Poland. Her main interests concern spirituality, civil disobedience, Christian anarchism, contemporary US literature, US-Mexican border writing, and Animal and Environmental Studies. She is a recipient of several international fellowships and has published widely in Poland and abroad. Her monograph *Thomas Merton and Latin America: A Consonance of Voices* was awarded "the Louie" by the International Thomas Merton Society.

Literary Presentations of Polish Immigrants in England: Where the Devil Can't Go by Anya Lipska and Madame Mephisto by A.M. Bakalar

Barbara Poważa-Kurko

Abstract The paper examines the identity of two Polish immigrants living in London: Janusz Kiszka and Magda Rodziewicz. The former is the protagonist of Anya Lipska's novel *Where the Devil Can't Go* (2013), the latter is the narrator and heroine, or rather villain, of *Madame Mephisto* (2012) written by A.M. Bakalar. Whereas Anya Lipska only has a Polish connection as she is married to a Pole, A. M. Bakalar is Polish herself. Moreover, she is the first Polish author to have written a novel in English after Poland joined the European Union. Both wrote novels whose protagonists struggle to find their feet in the new, self-imposed cultural context as well as to relate to their roots. The present paper analyses the following aspects of the protagonists identity: their attitude to language, family, religion, work and politics, as well as the status of the immigrant/emigrant in order to ascertain which facets of their personality and lives are crucial for their Polish identity. Furthermore, the authorial treatments of the above-mentioned components of the protagonist's identity in both novels are analysed and compared. The use of Polish in the narrative and the dialogue is also discussed. Some tentative questions are asked concerning the possible authorial agenda that might be hidden in the way Poland is presented in each novel.

Keywords Immigrant · Polish · Bakalar · Lipska

1 Introduction

The aim of this paper is to examine how Polish immigrants are presented in two novels written in English and published in England after Poland joined the EU in 2004. The Polish motifs they contain are the only points of similarity between them, and they certainly have a very different take on the various aspects of Polishness. *Madame Mephisto,* which is incidentally the first novel written by a Polish author in

B. Poważa-Kurko (✉)
Witold Pilecki State School of Higher Education, Oświęcim, Poland
e-mail: barbapow@o2.pl

© Springer International Publishing AG 2017   71
J. Mydla et al. (eds.), *Multiculturalism, Multilingualism and the Self: Literature and Culture Studies*, Issues in Literature and Culture,
DOI 10.1007/978-3-319-61049-8_6

English after 1989, is a psychological analysis which presents the point of view of a young, educated, emancipated woman, who leaves Poland in an attempt to liberate herself from the norms and traditions she finds suffocating. The protagonist's reckoning with her past, her family and a number of Polish sanctities overshadows the plot, which consists mainly of accounts of her subsequent failures at the various jobs she takes in London and her equally disastrous meetings with her family in Poland. The only tension in the novel results from Magda's inability to find peace, as she vacillates between the UK and Poland. Judging from the author's own words, the novel has autobiographical elements, which may account for it being so emotion-charged (Raczyńska, 2012).

Suspense being the crucial element in a crime novel, Anaya Lipska is obligated to concern herself primarily with the plot of her novel. The political and cultural background serves as a setting for the plot, which combines crime and an improbable version of a political plot. She relies on the knowledge she acquired, among others, from her Polish husband (Jędrysik, 2014). Lipska employs the third-person narrative, so it is the choice of the Polish references she makes to illustrate her characters as well as the protagonists' conversations that can be analysed in terms of attitude, as there is no authorial attitude to Poland as such.

Apart from the obvious difference resulting from the choice of narrative strategies, what may strike the readers even before they start reading the novels is the different provenance of the epigraphs. Whereas Lipska chooses a quote from General Jaruzelski's speech declaring martial law in Poland in 1981 and juxtaposes it with a *Solidarność* graffito, which comments on that speech, Bakalar's epigraphs come from Misha Glenny's *McMafia, Crime Without Frontiers* and Maryam Huley's poem "The Sticky Dream of a Banished Butterfly," which was published in *The Forbidden: Poems from Iran and its Exiles.* Lipska plunges at once into the most well-known clichés about the Polish struggle against Communism, whereas Bakalar has chosen words which refer to her protagonist's (and by extension, arguably, her own) life and choices made outside her native country which she detests.

2   The Protagonists

Janusz Kiszka, the protagonist of *Where the Devil Can't Go,* belongs to the wave of immigration which landed on England after the Solidarity movement was suppressed. Once a student of philosophy and an opposition activist in Poland, later in England a simple, unskilled builder, he has secured himself a special position within the Polish community in London. Even if his main income seems to derive from smuggling alcohol and cigarettes, he has the reputation of a "fixer." It is to him that father Piotr Pietruski turns for help when a Polish waitress goes missing, allegedly in very bad company. Neither he nor the reader has any idea at that stage that his investigation would entangle him in the nets of political intrigue.

Magda Rodziewicz, a graduate of the English department, seems quite successful in Poland, as she gets a job as a translator in a bank, but she gladly rejects the prospects of a successful life in Poland and leaves for England, where she takes on a succession of cover jobs, focusing instead on her true passion: the cannabis business. She grows marijuana at home and sells it to intermediaries in the UK and Poland, Jerome and Piotrek, who later sell it on to their clients. "A liar" and "two people": these are the names she uses to introduce herself to the mysterious addressee of her confessions and disquisitions (Bakalar, 2012, p. 3).

Keeping in mind this crucial difference between Janusz Kiszka, who is the protagonist but not the narrator, an actor rather than a commentator, and Magda Rodziewicz, who is both the protagonist and the narrator, and a commentator more than a participant of some intricate plot, I would like to analyze the treatment of politics, religion and family in both novels.

3   Politics, Religion and Family

Bakalar starts with a definition of Poland: "Urban dictionary on Poland: A nation that is unaware of its own collective backwardness, to its utter tragedy. It works efficiently only under occupation and dictatorship. Xenophobic and nationalistic" (Bakalar, 2012, p. 1). She does not provide a reference, but she drew on a real entry in the online urban dictionary ("Polak," urban dictionary). However, the narrator seems to enjoy flaunting this definition before the readers' eyes. She tops it with her own remarks: "You don't believe me? It gets better. Have you heard of a country where twin brothers rule, one the president, the other the prime minister? No? How about this one: the president dies in a plane crash, for which he was most probably responsible because he forced the pilot to land, killing himself, his wife, and ninety-four other people? Did I hear you right? You say it's a conspiracy theory? Not so fast" (Bakalar, 2012, p. 1). The Smolensk plane crash, which took place in 2010, helps to establish the time of action in the novel quite precisely between 2010 and 2012, the year when it was published. Interestingly, Magda, the narrator, opens her portrayal of Poland with political issues. Her anger is visible here, as her description of Poland goes beyond a mere presentation of facts. First of all, the institutional conservatism of the PIS-PSL government had already become a thing of the past; the more liberal Civic Platform took over in 2007 after Kaczyński's government resigned. Yet Magda talks about the Kaczyński brothers as if they still ruled Poland, at the same time blaming one of them for the Smolensk plane crash. Because the time of the right-wing Law and Justice government corresponds more with the image of Poland as a conservative, closed county the frustrated narrator criticises, she does not mention the more liberal Poland of the time she is really describing.

Politics comes first on the list of Polish sins according to Magda Rodziewicz. This is, however, closely tied up with the Polish perception of family and religion. They are so intertwined that it would require a very artificial categorization to discuss them separately. For Magda Rodziewicz they are all responsible for creating the stifling atmosphere in which she was not able to breathe.

Politics did influence Janusz Kiszka's life to a great extent as well. Once an opposition activist, he was imprisoned several times, interrogated in a violent way and intimidated in the notorious Cracow prison, at Montelupich. One of the most painful memories connected with these interrogations was the humiliation of becoming an informant. Despite the fact that his friend was only guilty of a minor misdemeanour, the friend's father was sacked after Janusz's denunciation. Janusz learnt the bitter reverse of the myth of Poland's allegedly indomitable opposition movement. The other incident which tainted his heroism was the death of his beloved Iza, who was trampled to death during a demonstration in Gdańsk, when the protesters were pushed into a corner by the advancing troops. He feels guilty for encouraging her to participate in anti-government demonstrations.

His subsequent unhappy marriage with Marta can also be seen as a consequence of his political involvement. Marta, his late fiancée's best friend, seemed the obvious choice, as they offered mutual consolation in their bereavement. This kind of motivation did not work out in the long run, which they discovered too late, when they already had a son, Bobek.

Janusz has bitter memories of Communist Poland, yet he does not seem induced to come back after the downfall of the regime in 1989. He is in touch with his wife, tries to participate in raising their son, yet it is Great Britain that has become his home now. So politics, even though it did affect his personal life very painfully, is not a crucial factor in his decision to stay away from Poland. He has organized his life in England surprisingly well. Detective Kershaw, who contacts him about the death of another Polish woman, Justyna Kozłowska, is astonished to hear that he owns rather than rents his flat.

It is not his personal ambition, however, that is the *spiritus movens* of the plot but a political intrigue. At first Janusz does not realize that the task he was entrusted with has any political dimension. Nor is he aware of the full extent of that danger. He believes Piotr Pietruski when he tells him that all he needs to do is to find a good, pious Polish girl who has eloped with a rascal. He appears to have been commissioned on behalf of Weronika's worried mother and Mrs. Tosik, who employed Weronika in her restaurant. The intrigue he is unaware of takes him back to Poland and also back in time, as it turns out a group of ex-communists is trying to push Poland back in the direction of Russia.

The intrigue seems to be constructed as a reversal of a common stereotype of Polish resistance and heroism in the face of totalitarianism, for it reveals that the one-time opposition leader, now the most important runner for President and the leader of the *Renesans* party, used to be an informer and a paedophile, who was rewarded for his services not with money but with children from an orphanage. Two factors attenuate the potential provocation this vision of Polish politics entails. First of all, it is very improbable, especially the vision of the pro-Russia lobby that needs the compromising documents in order to keep the apparently liberal Zamorski on a leash lest he try to be too independent. Secondly, all the characters involved in the intrigue are fictitious and, apart from the very general references to their communist past, there are no hints that the novel may be a *roman à clef*. Even historical characters have been veiled in a new identity. Father Kuba, alias Papieżek, whom Zamorski gave away, can remind the reader of Jerzy Popiełuszko (the priest murdered by the secret service in 1984), but it seems that, even if the novelist, Anya Lipska, took great care to use the dramatic potential of Poland's political past and present to build the plot of her novel, she does not really make any statements about real Polish politics. What is more, to forestall any possible accusations, she finally kills Zamorski in the epilogue, thus making sure this suspect, even if fictitious, chapter in Polish history, is irrevocably closed. On the other hand the improbability of the intrigue has been noted by Jędrysik (2014) as a weak point of the novel, which "loses credibility the closer it gets to the denouement" (my translation). On the other hand, one of the readers reviewing the novel on the website for fans of crime fiction praises the novel for being "a diverting read that gives some insight into the close-knit Polish Catholic community in London, and intriguing glimpses into Polish history and consequences" (Peckham, 2013). So the conspiracy presented in the novel might be taken by western readers at its face value and treated seriously. Still a little knowledge helps to see its exaggeration and improbability.

In contrast, in Bakalar's novel the threat of absurd political conservatism is never over. The protagonist might notice some signs of a more liberal approach to life, yet she treats them with suspicion as exceptions rather than new trends. Seeing two girls kissing in the street in Warsaw, she thinks such behaviour is only possible in the capital. Discussing IVF with her sister and brother-in-law, Magda never seems to realize Alicja and Krzysiek are not the only couple in Poland who treat IVF as a legitimate medical treatment for infertility. Instead they all take a very critical view of Poland, in which it is impossible to carry out the procedure. Alicja takes it for granted she has to go to Switzerland, even if she may have to pay much more for the treatment than in Poland. In their criticism of Poland they treat themselves as outliers in a reality dominated by absurd conservatives.

It is this fear of being suppressed as an individual by the three-headed beast of conservative politics, religion and family that accounts for the feeling of alienation Magda experiences while in Poland: "I cannot but feel slightly unnerved when I visit Poland. It has become a voyeuristic experiment, observing my own kind, keeping them at arm's length, so that I can get a better picture of the country I left behind... It was, and still is, a love-hate relationship" (Bakalar, 2012, p. 65). She does not have any friends, apart from her partner in the cannabis business. Her strong attachment to her sister is strained due to two factors: her careless affair with her brother-in-law, Krzysiek, and Alicja's acceptance of the social standards she rejects.

Bakalar shapes her protagonist in strict opposition to all Polish norms. Magda's aggressive defiance of those norms makes her unable to gain total freedom. Motivated by her Catholic faith, her mother constantly nags her about getting married. She regards her as unhappy and solitary in an alien world. When she visits her daughter in England, she shows no interest in sightseeing, apart from the London Eye, and spends her time cooking and cleaning, and dragging Magda to the

Polish Centre in order to marry her off to some God-fearing, well-off Włodzimierz or Kazimierz.

In terms of family and relationship, Magda's identity is created in stark opposition to her mother's narrow-minded ideal. If her mother is a caricature of Catholic family values, so too is Magda a cliché with her total rejection of anything which might confine her to that stereotype. Hence her sexual permissiveness, her lack of qualms about the abortion she had at the age of seventeen, and her very rude behaviour towards the man she meets in the Polish Centre.

Janusz Kiszka is not an ideal *pater familias* either. His telephone conversations with his former wife resemble verbal skirmishes. He is in love with another Polish immigrant, Kasia, who is married to a lazy and violent man, and who works as a dancer and stripper at a peep-show instead of pursuing her career as a graduate of the famous Łódź film academy. Yet their relationship is far from the adulterous adventure Magda Rodziewicz so casually embarks upon. It resembles youthful infatuation and has a chivalric element to it, as Janusz teaches Kasia's violent husband a lesson to be remembered.

Marta does not make any claims on her ex-husband; she only wants him to help with the raising of her son. Janusz's parents are dead, and even when still alive, they did not try to influence their son's decisions. So he is free and responsible for his decisions, whereas Magda, though far away from home, still struggles to gain full independence. In some sense she is still a rebellious teenager.

In both novels Catholicism constitutes an important part of Polish identity. For Janusz Kiszka it seems to be a natural part of his life, whereas for Magda Rodziewicz it is one of the bonds she needs to break to realise her freedom. Kiszka, whom we see at the beginning of the novel as a kind of gangster, violently reminding another Pole that his debts need settling, is still a humble Catholic, coming to confession and acknowledging the moral authority of father Pietruski. When his life is in danger, he resorts to prayer.

Nowhere in *Where the Devil Can't Go* is the Catholic Church criticized or shown as a corrupt institution even if its members and representatives might err. Father Pietruski gets involved in the political intrigue quite unwittingly, not understanding its full scope. He believes the presidential candidate wants to protect his illegitimate daughter from a bad man and is stunned as he learns the real import of the whole affair. Monsignore Zielinski, the principal of a Catholic theology college in London, even though he contributes to the death of one of his students, is not a cold-blooded murderer, but a weak man, who cannot face the consequences of his breach of celibacy. When his lover, Elzbieta Wronska, commits suicide, he disposes of her body because he is overwhelmed by fear her pregnancy might lead to questions and a scandal.

The protagonist of *Madame Mephisto* is the reverse of the stereotypical Polish Catholic. It is the part of her identity which she would most willingly shake off. She rebelled early, in primary school, challenging the virgin birth of Jesus and thus incurring the wrath of the nun who taught her class religious instruction.

As an adult, she rejects her mother's ideals but seems to share her passion. If her mother insists that she marry a Catholic, a Catholic cannot be even taken into consideration. Her hatred of the Catholic Church is stoked by her family, who are the only people, apart from Piotrek, another drug dealer, she keeps in touch with in Poland. Her narrow-minded mother manages to dominate the whole family. Her father and her sister, even if they do not share her mother's beliefs, are too weak to oppose the overbearing matriarchy.

Magda's Catholic upbringing and imposed identity proves such a burden for her that she decides to officially withdraw from the church. In order to do that she needs two witnesses who would testify she was of sound mind when she made this decision. Her father, who shows much more understanding for her choices, agrees at first, but later succumbs to his wife's emotional blackmail. Her sister also resorts to blackmail. Remaining a member of the Catholic Church is the condition on which Alicja might forgive her the affair with her husband, Krzysiek. Alicja, just like her mother, wants to keep up appearances. This is, Bakalar seems to be claiming, how Polish Catholic identity is upheld: through blackmail and intimidation. Interestingly, Magda's mother admits she herself wanted to escape, but she did not, because "Life is not about doing everything you want" (Bakalar, 2012, p. 120).

It is the acknowledgement of boundaries that is a crucial component of the Polish identity which is so constricting for Magda. Even her sister, whom she truly loves, expresses a harsh opinion about her uncompromising search for freedom: "You are simply insensitive sometimes. And you know no boundaries. You hurt people around you. You know that. You hurt me and mother. You destroy everything and everybody. You destroy people who care about you. If you keep doing it there will be nobody left. Perhaps somebody should stop you from destroying yourself" (Bakalar, 2012, p. 208). By accepting her sister's conditional forgiveness, she also accepts the fact she will never be loved unconditionally.

Only Marianna, her niece and ward, gives her an opportunity to be herself. The whole book is a confession she is making in front of the child. Emotionally, for her it means turning a new leaf. For the young girl, however, it might mean an oppressive upbringing with a different set of values. After all, Magda is not prepared to change anything now she looks after Marianna. She gave up the idea of a new cover job and instructs the child in all the Polish ills and vices instead.

4 The Protagonists' Attitudes to the British

The crime story uses the exotic identity of the protagonist to enhance the mystery. Hence there is no need to make him struggle with it, assess and revalue it. In the more psychological novel, in contrast, the Polish identity is the key theme, the plot being to a great extent an outward representation of the inner conflict. "Too British in Poland, too Polish in Britain" (Bakalar, 2012, p. 165)—these words best encapsulate Magda's sense of incomplete identity. On the one hand, she feels quite insecure in England because of her "imperfect command of English with a dominant Polish accent, my unprivileged non-Western education, and my lack of work experience" (Bakalar, 2012, p. 5); on the other hand, she is very harsh in her criticism of the English and her belligerent, uncompromising behavior gets her into trouble. She loses four jobs as a result of her insensitivity to what her friend and colleague, Percy Janties, calls "cultural inconsistencies" (Bakalar, 2012, pp. 12–13). Bakalar's narrator is lashing out at Polish backwardness, but she is equally censorious about the British. Patrick Webb, whom she meets in her second job, is the first person who "knew where Poland was located on the map" (Bakalar, 2012, p. 43). The reader is clearly offered an indication here that the protagonist's censorious attitude is exaggerated and unreliable as she has only just complained about her lack of privileged Western education.

Apart from ignorance, the English are accused of cowardice as nobody complains about anything, even if it means acceptance of hopeless public services (Bakalar, 2012, p. 39). Hypocrisy is also high on the list of English sins. In this egalitarian society a woman has to respect the Orthodox Jews' rules and must not speak to them, even if she is one of the organizers of the business event, as it might jeopardize the deal. There are also strict, though unwritten, rules about whom one is supposed to socialize with at a Christmas party and whom one should not approach. Hypocrisy combined with political correctness leads to the acceptance of a complaint about sexual harassment lodged by a man against the woman he was having an affair with. Of course, Magda does not mince words expressing her disapproval of his behaviour. In her third job she encounters fraud, and the last job involves skirmishes with the Human Resources manager, who bombards her with probing questions about her wellbeing, as well as bitter quarrels with the bossy, unkind Lotta Lejuene.

Janusz Kiszka partially shares Magda's disparaging attitude to the English, as he has no respect for detective Natalie Kershaw. It is one of his thoughts about Kershaw that serves as the title of the novel. "Where the devil can't go, he sends a woman" is a Polish proverb which refers to women's resourcefulness with a mixture of admiration and irony. It reflects Kiszka's patronizing and slightly mocking attitude to the woman detective. He is never too happy to see her, except for at the very end, when he is actually saved by her. Silently, he calls her very bad names in Polish, all of which centre on her gender rather than competence or its absence.

Just as Kiszka's stereotype of the woman gets shattered when he is helped by Kershaw, so is Kershaw's stereotype of the Pole undermined thanks to her encounter with Kiszka. To some extent he does reinforce her stereotype: "Fortyish, with dark brown hair, longish—a style that went out of fashion in the nineties—and peppered with grey. Not bad looking, if you went in for the caveman look" (Lipska, 2013, p. 141). There are some elements, however, which Kershaw cannot reconcile with the caveman: his perfect, even posh English, the damson plums cooking on his stove, the *New Scientist* magazines lying on the table, and the fact of his home ownership.

It seems paradoxical that Bakalar's psychological novel in fact reinforces stereotypes, whereas Lipska's crime novel presents characters who move beyond the stereotypical. The latter may provide a negative vision of Polish politics, but it is a fictitious intrigue, which after all comes to nothing, whereas the characters of Kershaw and Kiszka (despite his mismatched name) endure.

5 The Use of the Polish Language

Both novelists emphasize the nationality of the protagonists by interspersing some Polish words throughout the narration and the dialogues. In *Where the Devil Can't Go,* apart from words referring to specifically Polish phenomena, such as "Solidarnosc," they are almost all swear words or taboo words, which are used in the proper forms according to the rules of declension. They are supposedly used to add ethnic authenticity to the novel. For a Polish reader the effect is rather comical, but then the novel is not meant for the Polish reader. The meaning of these words is pretty clear as they are used in anger, to denigrate somebody. Some Polish also appears in the formal ways of addressing people. Bakalar uses Polish much more sparingly. She resorts to Polish when there does not seem to be a good English equivalent. In *Madame Mephisto* the use of Polish emphasizes the cultural alienation Magda suffers from, unable to make her transition from one culture to the other seamlessly.

6 The Narrators

The reliability of the narrator in *Madame Mephisto* can be questioned. The very title might suggest it, although there is at least one more candidate for the title of "Madame Mephisto," namely Mrs. Rodziewicz. Magda Raczyńska (2012) notices the ambiguity of the title and Bakalar does not make it less equivocal in her answer. The unreliability of the narrator has been also noted by Max Liu, who wrote a review of *Madame Mephisto* in *The Times Literary Supplement.* He also points out that the narrator "elicits sympathy but never affection" (Liu, 2012). On the one hand she is a well-educated, astute young cosmopolitan, who is not overwhelmed by the wonders of the West but has the temerity to assess it harshly, choosing only what she deems right. On the other hand, her judgment seems clouded by the extreme emotions with which she encounters both the Polish and the English culture. Her constant need to oppose, defy, and find fault makes her appear somewhat immature. Even though such narrative unreliability might take the edge off her severe criticism of Poland, the choice of the mysterious addressee, whose identity is not revealed until the end of the novel, does not reinforce that strategy. Magda's interlocutor turns out to be her niece, of whom she receives custody after the car incident in which her sister dies and her brother-in-law is seriously incapacitated. But it is later in the novel that the reader realizes the "you" is a child and that it is a particular person who is sleepy at one moment (Bakalar, 2012, p. 91), was collected by the narrator somewhere she had to fly (Bakalar, 2012, pp. 120–121), and was assumed to be her daughter by a woman in a ticket office (Bakalar, 2012, p. 181). Only at the end does it become clear that it is her niece. At the beginning of the novel, where her criticism of Poland is at its harshest, where she generalizes and provides information about her backward motherland, it seems that the addressee is the English reading public. This seems to have happened accidentally and yet it might have had an impact on the reception of the book by Polish readers, which, Bakalar herself admits, was quite critical (Zagrodna).

She may be referring more to conversations she has had with her readers and acquaintances as the Polish reviews are few and far between. Even though her criticism of Poland is very harsh, it is in fact easy to discount it as a very peculiar point of view of one Polish émigré with a pretty eccentric family and even more eccentric aspirations. The lack of any further perspective, of a a greater panorama of Polish life, makes it pretty innocuous as serious criticism. The novel resembles satire, in which proportions do not have to be kept, and whose power depends on simplicity. Yet Bakalar's satire lacks any positive part. If both the tedious, old-fashioned, oppressive Polish mentality is discarded, and the modern, politically-correct British project questioned, what then is the ideal she strives for? The total freedom of a criminal until she is caught? It is hardly convincing, especially in view of the fact that the drug dealing motif was absent from the first draft of the book. The protagonist first became a drug dealer when the author's partner found the novel "a bit dull, another story of an immigrant" (Staňková, 2014, p. 77). Thus the element of her "career" was added, making the protagonist's choices as unexpected as improbable. This is what one of the readers nominating the book for the Guardian First Book Award pointed out as its most serious flaw. The reviewer also "felt the book promised more that it delivered" (GetOver99, 2012). The author may have made her protagonist choose drug dealing rather than a decent, legal job as a means of earning a living for herself and her niece at the end of the book to avoid a sentimental happy ending. Otherwise Magda may have seemed a reformed sinner who finally amends her ways and finds the meaning of life in fulfilling her role of carer, thus embracing, at least partially, the stereotype her mother wishes her to live by.

Lipska does not have to fear she will fall into the traps of woman's literature. Hers is a more journalistic, historical knowledge of Poland. The insights the reader gets into the principal protagonist's private life do not make him vulnerable but more attractive: the macho man is, after all, capable of feeling and loving. The external factors that complicated his private life resulted from an imposed, oppressive political system, not some intrinsic harmfulness of Polish mores and tradition. There is a big divide between common Poles and the top echelons of society, which have always been to a great extent corrupt. England provides a refuge, a land to escape from the past, even if its shadow sometimes follows one there.

England is no sanctuary for Magda, for the divide runs right through her soul and she is very confused about what she chooses, having rejected almost all the values she was brought up with as well as those immigrants look for abroad. Though the protagonist's dilemma seems to be very serious for her, Popescu (2012) notices something comic in the novel, calling it "a darkly-comic account of a Polish immigrant's experiences in London."

Whereas Magda's greatest opponent is her mother, and her struggle is psychological, Janusz faces real gangsters when he gets involved in a plot which is far beyond his understanding and as a result his very life, not just his identity, is at risk. The most important "other" he has to face in psychological terms is detective Natalie Kershaw. His dislike of her goes far beyond the possible conflict between her official investigation and his private one. He seems to dislike the fact she is a woman put in a position of authority reserved for men. Just as the feminist agenda is quite prominent in Bakalar's novel so are patriarchal prejudices in Lipska's presentation of the protagonist.

Janusz Kiszka simply does not dwell on his own identity, on its possible hybridity, on the clash of cultures. For him the most painful is the confrontation with the past and the menacing resurrection of the monsters of the communist past. Interestingly, Magda does not seem to show much interest in the past, unless it is connected with her private life. There is no celebration of the country's recently regained sovereignty, which enabled her not only to start a career in England but also to move between the two countries. The focus is on Poland's conservatism, backwardness, oppressiveness.

7   A Positive Message?

In both novels it is the child that brings hope and makes the future appear more bearable. At the end of the novel Janusz Kiszka is awaiting his son, Bobek, who is at last coming to see him in London. Magda has her niece to look after. For Janusz, Bobek's visit means a symbolic reconciliation with the past. For Magda, the role of a carer is much more ambiguous as it may mean a new beginning or another human life sacrificed at the altar of ideology. What Magda can offer her ward is a reversal of Polish conservatism, a life in a kind of limbo, where they would dwell until perhaps it is time for the girl to go to school.

A.M. Bakalar considers herself "an intellectual immigrant" (Staňková, 2014, p. 77), which fact must have influenced the creation of her protagonist. *Madame Mephisto* is certainly a novel which, for better or for worse, can serve as a kind of manual of Polish mentality. Whether it will reinforce the stereotype quoted at the beginning from the *Urban Dictionary* or whether the young independent protagonist's indomitable will to gain total freedom will leave a more lasting impression on the English reader is uncertain. Janusz Kiszka is merely an exotic character, whose un-English identity is created by means of references to well-known historical events. Both characters are interesting additions to migrant literature, though I am not sure they would understand each other well, should they meet as real people.

8   Conclusion: Different Models of Acculturation

The difference between the two literary characters I have discussed can be also considered within Berry's model of acculturation (Ward and Deuba, 1999, 423). Berry distinguishes four acculturation strategies on the basis of the immigrant's willingness to maintain one's own cultural heritage and participate in the host culture.

A balanced appreciation and participation in both cultures results in integration, more emphasis put on belonging to the new society than on maintaining one's connection to the roots leads to assimilation, more concern with one's own heritage than the need to adjust is characteristic of a separatist approach, and lack of interest in either is tantamount to marginalization.

Janusz Kiszka seems closer to integration than Magda, whose radical denigration of many aspects of both cultures corroborates the classification of her strategy as 'marginalization'. Such placement of the protagonists within Berry's model is indeed surprising as Magda seems to have mastered all the necessary tools to fully integrate in the British society, especially compared to Janusz Kiszka, who, although also intelligent and educated, has to work below his qualifications.

Kiszka's emigration was not fully his personal choice, but a result of the complicated political and personal situation, so his ties to Polish culture are stronger as he seeks solace and guidance from Polish figures of authority, especially priests. His attitude is closer to that of the post-war Polish immigrants as compared to those who arrived after the EU accession (Bielewska, 2011).

Magda Rodziewicz, who is one of the beneficiaries of that accession, sticks to her original choice and chooses Great Britain as a place to live and bring up her niece. In view of the latter, some degree of participation in the British culture seems indispensable, even if she makes a choice to give up a regular job and withdraw into the cannabis underworld.

Word and Kennedy's model as discussed by Ward and Deuba (1999, p. 424) may be more appropriate to measure the protagonists' respective degree of integration as it posits two levels of adjustment. Both protagonists show high degrees of sociocultural adjustment, that is they manage to organize their lives within the new cultural context. When the psychological adjustment is considered, however, the protagonist of *Madame Mephisto* seems much less capable than Lipska's main character. Janusz seeks happiness in a relationship with a Polish woman and is at the beginning overtly hostile to the young English woman detective, but his is not an attitude of scorching criticism towards anything English or British.

Literary characters are fictional; they need not be discussed as real people. Yet their acculturation strategies certainly resemble some of those chosen by Polish immigrants. The older immigrants' forbearing attitude is contrasted with a kind of nonchalant defiance shown by a member of the privileged post-accession immigration wave, who takes her opportunities for granted and feels entitled to full citizenship, including the right to criticize.

References

Bakalar, A. M. (2012). *Madame Mephisto*. London: Stork Press.

Bielewska, A. (2011). National identities of Poles in Manchester: Modern and postmodern geographies. *Sage*. Retrieved from http://journals.sagepub.com/doi/pdf/10.1177/1468796811 427086

GetOver99. (2012). Guardian first book award reader nominations: Madame mephisto by A.M. Bakalar. Books blog. *Guardian*. Retrieved from https://www.theguardian.com/books/ booksblog/2012/jul/24/first-book-award-madame-mephisto?newsfeed=true

Jędrysik, M. (2014). Anya Lipska, "Toń." *culture.pl*. Retrieved from http://culture.pl/pl/dzielo/ anya-lipska-ton

Lipska, A. (2013). *Where the devil can't go*. London: The Friday Project.

Liu, M. (2012). A.M. Bakalar. *Madame Mephisto*. *The Times Literary Supplement*. Retrieved from http://www.the-tls.co.uk/

Peckham, M. (2013). Lipska, Anya—Where the devil can't go, a review. *Euro Crime*. Retrieved from http://www.eurocrime.co.uk/reviews/Where_the_Devil_Cant_Go.html

Polak. Urban dictionary. Retrieved from http://www.urbandictionary.com/define.php?term= polak&defid=1904687

Popescu, L. (2012, December 9). Supporting independent publishers. *The Haffington Post*. Retrieved from http://www.huffingtonpost.co.uk/lucy-popescu/supporting-independent-publis hers_b_2251256.html

Raczyńska. (2012, 7/3). M.A. Bakalar: profesjonalna kłamczucha. *Wysokie Obcasy*. Retrieved from www.wysokieobcasy.pl

Staňková, A. (2014). *Depiction of Polish migrants in the British press*. *Pilsen*. University of West Bohemia. Retrieved from https://otik.uk.zcu.cz/bitstream/handle/11025/15121/Bakalarska% 20prace%20Aleksandra%20Stankova.pdf?sequence=1

Tonkin, B. (2014, March 30). Anya Lipska: A tortured past brought to life in crime fiction. *Independent*. Retrieved from http://www.independent.co.uk

Ward, C., & Rana-Deuba, A. (1999). Acculturation and adaptation revisited. *Journal of Cross-Cultural Psychology, 30,* 422–442. doi:10.1177/0022022199030004003

Zagrodna, K. Madame skandalistka. *Cooltura*. *Moja wyspa. Polska strona w Wielkiej Brytanii*. http://www.mojawyspa.co.uk/artykuly/29143/Madame-skandalistka

Author Biography

Barbara Poważa-Kurko received her PhD from the Jagiellonian University. Her Ph.D. thesis explored the reception and translation of Harold Pinter's plays in Poland. At present she works as a lecturer in the State School of Higher Education in Oświęcim. Her main scholarly interest is in contemporary British literature, especially its cultural dimension.

"Convergence of Different Threads": Tom Stoppard's *Dogg's Hamlet, Cahoot's Macbeth*

Jadwiga Uchman

Abstract Tom Stoppard's varied and rich dramatic output seems to be characterized by some recurrent features, one of these being the intricate weaving together of a number of different motives, intertextual references, as well as literary, cultural, scientific, philosophical and political allusions—a dramatic technique which he himself calls the "convergence of different threads." His double-bill, *Dogg's Hamlet, Cahoot's Macbeth* (1979), is no exception to the rule and most of the literati will immediately recognise Shakespeare's two famous tragedies incorporated within its title. Not many people, however, will be able to reveal the other kernel stones of Stoppard's inspiration. The Dogg in the title happens to be the literary pseudonym of Ed Berman, a naturalized American, who was the founder and director of Almost Free Ambiance Theatre. The word "Dogg" refers both to Berman, a friend of Stoppard, and the imaginary language invented by the playwright. The idea of constructing a language—similar to building a wall—was taken by Stoppard from Ludwig Wittgenstein, a member of the Vienna circle of positivist philosophers. Probably the most difficult word to decode is Cahoot. The imaginary Cahoot, who appears in the play, in a sitting-room production of *Macbeth,* during the normalization period in Czechoslovakia, is a reference to Pavel Kohout and Pavel Landovsky, Czech dissidents who organized the Living Room Theatre in their socialist country. Thus, Stoppard weaves a magnificent carpet by means of combining different threads, starting from people coming from different countries and cultures, as well as a variety of ideas from theatre and culture, to philosophy and politics.

Keywords Stoppard · Drama · Wittgenstein · Berman · Kohout

J. Uchman (✉)
University of Łódź, Łódź, Poland
e-mail: jagodauchman@wp.pl

© Springer International Publishing AG 2017
J. Mydla et al. (eds.), *Multiculturalism, Multilingualism and the Self: Literature and Culture Studies*, Issues in Literature and Culture,
DOI 10.1007/978-3-319-61049-8_7

1   Introduction

Tom Stoppard, one of the most outstanding, creative, gratifying and praised contemporary British playwrights, conceded in one of his interviews that his main objective in writing plays is to "entertain a roomful of people" (Hudson interview 1974, p. 6). At the same time, however, as Taylor argues: "It would be tempting to label Tom Stoppard as the intellectual among our young writers" (Taylor, 1978, p. 94). The majority of Stoppard's pieces are entertaining, enjoyable plays of ideas. It is important to stress here that this artist's uniqueness results from his ability to present serious ideas by means of the comic genre. Stoppard himself has commented on this issue: "What I try to do, is to end up by contriving the perfect marriage between the play of ideas and farce or perhaps even high comedy" (Hudson interview, 1974, p. 8). In another interview, the artist conceded: "there's more than one point of origin for a play, and the only useful metaphor I can think of for the way I think I write my plays is convergences of different threads. Perhaps carpet-making would suggest something similar" (Hayman, 1979, p. 4).

2   Intertextual References

The double-bill *Dogg's Hamlet, Cahoot's Macbeth*, written in 1979, is no exception to the rule as it combines, on the one hand, both entertainment and instruction and, on the other, it weaves an intricate carpet incorporating references to people from the world of literature, theatre, philosophy and politics coming from different times, countries and cultures, namely William Shakespeare, Ed Berman, Pavel Kohout and Ludwig Wittgenstein. Thus, the threads of this wonderful carpet are, among others, the numerous intertextual references to literary and philosophical works, as well as allusions to real life people who are evoked by the fictitious characters appearing in the plays.

The most obvious intertextual reference which may be deduced from the very title is obviously to William Shakespeare, whose two great tragedies become an integral part of Stoppard's drama. This playwright is undoubtedly fascinated by Shakespeare and has given evidence of this enchantment in a number of ways. He has written some articles about the great Elizabethan (1967, p. 23; 1972, p. 1219; 1982), and at least a single quotation from the bard's ouevre appears in most of his plays, this being a trademark of Stoppard similar to Hitchcock's logo of making an appearance on the screen in most of his feature films. Last but not least, the artist has written four plays employing Shakespeare's famous tragedies and co-written the script of the Oscar winning film—*Shakespeare in Love.*

The choice of *Hamlet* for the first part of the double bill may have arisen for a number of reasons, the first of which is the fact that the play which brought Stoppard fame, *Rosencrantz and Guildenstern Are Dead*, is an intertextual dialogue of the artist with Shakespeare, on the one hand, and Beckett, on the other. Secondly, the playwright used the great tragedy earlier as the backbone for *The (15 min) Dogg's Troupe Hamlet* which, together with *Dogg's Our Pet*, were the predecessors of *Dogg's Hamlet, Cahoot's Macbeth*. All three plays refer to Dogg, which brings us to another, and double at that, thread of Stoppard's intricate carpet.

The first reference contained in the word "Dogg" is to Ed Berman, a man of the theatre, a naturalized American, and one of the most prominent figures in Inter-Action, a group characterised by off-beat taste, improvisatory techniques and energetic community involvement. It was to celebrate the opening of Ed Berman's new drama centre, called The Almost Free Theatre, in December 1971, that Stoppard wrote *Dogg's Our Pet* introducing, firstly, the imaginary Dogg language and, secondly, celebrating the figure of Berman, known also as the author of children's poems published under the pseudonym Prof. R. L. Dogg (Berman 1979, pp. X–XI). The first part of the double bill is "dedicated to Professor Dogg and The Dogg's Troupe of Inter Action" (p. 144).

The second part of the double bill, *Cahoot's Macbeth* introduces yet another prominent figure of theatre life, but, in this case, not in England but in Czechoslovakia. In the "Introduction" to the printed text, Stoppard writes:

> *Cahoot's Macbeth* is dedicated to the Czechoslovakian playwright Pavel Kohout ... During a short visit to Prague in 1977 I met Kohout and Pavel Landovsky, a well known actor who had been banned from working for years since falling foul of the authorities. (It was Landovsky who was driving the car on the fateful day of January 1977 when the police stopped him and his friends and seized the first known copies of the document that became known as Charter 77.) ... A year later Kohout wrote to me: "As you know, many Czech theatre-people are not allowed to work in the theatre during the last years. As one of them who cannot live without theatre I was searching for a possibility to do theatre in spite of the circumstances. Now I am glad to tell you that in a few days after eight weeks rehearsals – a Living-Room Theatre is opening, with nothing smaller but Macbeth (p. 142.)

Even though Stoppard argues slightly later on that "Cahoot is not Kohout" (p. 143), it may be reasonably justified to argue that both the title characters of the double-bill, Dogg and Cohoot, bear many similarities to real life theatre people just as the dramatic events of the play are a fictionalized reflection of actual happenings.

Yet another intertextual reference is to a different sphere, namely philosophy. Stoppard was familiar with Ludwig Wittgenstein's *Philosophical Investigations*, which seemed to him to be "about the correspondence between language and reality," and the book evoked an image in his mind of a man building, first a wall of bricks, and then steps, "the whole thing [being] a kind of opening ceremony" (*Yes*, 1971, p. 10). The initial stage image for *Dogg's Our Pet* thus developed. It includes the two basic components of the play—Wittgenstein's language-game and the opening of Ed Berman's new drama centre called The Almost Free Theatre in December 1971. The imaginary language, invented by Stoppard under the influence of Wittgenstein, is called Dogg language.

Ludwig Wittgenstein's early work *Tractatus Logico-Philosophicus*, dealing with the picture theory of language presents the opinion that there must be a correlation between the structures of a reality and the language describing it. The philosopher puts forward a pragmatic conception of language, "use" being the key term in his investigations. In his works he tries to set limits to language, to make it a logical and consistent tool for describing reality. Accordingly, *Tractatus* specifies precisely what can, and what cannot be said. Thus, it imposes logical limitations upon language as a tool for describing reality.

Tractatus was often criticised, and Ludwig Wittgenstein himself started to be dissatisfied with it and set out to write a second work on language, namely *Philosophical Investigations*, a treatise first published only two years after the great philosopher's death. It begins with a quotation from St. Augustine's *Confessions* which suggests that a child acquires language when a grown-up points to an object and states its name, that is by means of an ostensive definition. Wittgenstein argues that Augustine's premise—assuming that "every word has a meaning. This meaning is correlated with the word. It is the object for which the word stands" (p. 2e)—could only be true of very primitive language forms:

> Let us imagine a language for which the description given by Augustine is right. The language is meant to serve for communication between a builder A and an assistant B. A is building with building stones: there are blocks, pillars, slabs and beams. B has to pass the stones, and that in the order in which A needs them. For this purpose they use a language consisting of the words "block," "pillar," "slab," "beam." A calls them out;—B brings the stone which he has learnt to bring at such-and-such a call.—Conceive this as a complete primitive language (p. 3.)

In his double-bill Stoppard makes direct use of the above fragment from Wittgenstein, but takes it a step further, arguing in the "Introduction" that "this is not the only interpretation":

> Suppose, for example, the thrower knows in advance which pieces the builder needs, and in what order. In such a case there would be no need for the builder to name the pieces he wants but only to indicate when he is ready for the next one. So the calls might translate thus:
>
> Plank = Ready   Block = Next
>
> Slab = Okay   Cube = Thank you (p. 141)

The assumption behind the opening scene of *Dogg's Our Pet,* presenting the building of a platform, is that Charlie is using one language—English, in which words describe the pieces of wood, while his helper, Brick, uses the invented, imaginary Dogg language. Thus the two speakers use the same word (phonemic signifier) to indicate different meanings. If the action of the play were limited to the building of the platform only, they might never discover they are using different languages.

3 Constructing a Language and a Platform

While Stoppard was working on the double-bill, he slightly reworked the two short plays written earlier for Ed Berman, yet he preserved their two basic components. When the drama starts, we are in the world of Dogg language, and the schoolboys and Professor Dogg use it while playing football, counting flags, telling the time, and listening to the football scores announced on the radio, also given in Dogg. Easy, who has come to erect a platform for the school ceremony, just like the audience in the theatre, gradually acquires a knowledge of this foreign language. The building of the platform is parallel to the construction of a language, which, using the same phonemic signifiers as English, reflects different meanings. To make the reference between the erection of the platform and the construction of the language more obvious, Stoppard introduces building blocks, some of which "*have got apparently random letters printed on them* (p. 157). As the construction progresses, inscriptions become visible. The following labels appear in vertical arrangement, each word occupying one level: MATHS OLD EGG (p. 158), MEG SHOT GLAD (159), GOD SLAG THEM (p. 161). Being dissatisfied with the successive messages, Dogg gets irritated at Easy and knocks him through the wall, which disintegrates every time. Finally, however, the required caption is achieved: "DOGGS HAM LET" (p. 163) and the inner play starts. Shakespeare appears in propria persona, bows and utters the Prologue:

For this relief, much thanks.

Though I am native here, and to the manner born,

It is a custom more honoured in the breach

Than in the observance

Well.

Something is rotten in the state of Denmark.

To be or not to be, that is the question.

There are more things in heaven and earth

Than are dreamt of in your philosophy–

There's a divinity that shapes our ends,

Rough hew them how we will

Though this be madness, yet there is a method in it.

I must be cruel only to be kind;

Hold, as t'were, the mirror up to nature.

A countenance more in sorrow than in anger.

(LADY *in audience shouts "Marmalade"*)

The lady doth protest too much.

Cat will mew, and Dogg will have his day! (p. 163–164)

Shakespeare's speech is a compilation of lines which belong to different characters of the drama (mainly *Hamlet*) and are repeated by them in their proper places as the play progresses. The interruption of the lady, in which the word "marmalade" expresses "pleasure and approval" (p. 156) and Shakespeare's answer to it deserve special attention. It could be presumed that the sentences uttered by him to her do not belong to the great play but are added on the spot to suit the circumstances—they are an answer to her protest and refer to Ed Berman (the latter could be supported by the fact that the word "Dogg" is spelled in such a way). Later on, however, they are repeated in the original context of their Shakespearean drama as, in fact, they do appear in the bard's original play (pp. 164, 167,171, *Hamlet* III, iii, lines 124–125 and V, i, line 286). Before the curtain goes down, Easy says to the audience "Cube ..." (p. 174). He has learnt the lesson and knows how to say "Thank you" in Dogg. Hopefully the audience have also learnt their lesson, are familiar with Dogg, and will be able to decode its meanings in the second part of the double-bill.

4   Czechoslovakia in the Normalization Period

Even though both parts use Dogg language, its function in them is different. In *Dogg's Hamlet* it is the language of the majority and both Easy and the audience have to pick it up by exercising their intellect and getting the meaning contained in non-verbal communication. In *Cahoot's Macbeth* the same method of learning Dogg is described verbatim by Cahoot when he tells the astonished Inspector: "You don't learn it, you catch it" (p. 206). Yet, in this play Dogg becomes the language of a minority revolt, a metaphor for subversion, something that is accessible to the dissidents and unattainable for their oppressors.

Cahoot's Macbeth starts with the beginning of the bard's famous tragedy. Again, the choice of tragedy does not seem to be coincidental as this Shakespearean drama is especially relevant for the situation in Czechoslovakia during the period of "normalization." The initial lines of Shakespeare's *Macbeth* are uttered in English and the audience tend to accept the illusion of reality created in front of their eyes. Then, however, after the exit of the witches the lights go up "*to reveal a living room*" (p. 180). The sounds of a bell, owls and crickets—so important for the murder scene, are evoked verbally and also aurally (pp. 183–184). Macbeth enters, carrying two blood-stained daggers and the following scene occurs:

> MACBETH: I have done the deed. Didst thou not hear a noise?
>
> LADY MACBETH: I heard the owl scream and the crickets cry.
>
> (*A police siren is heard approaching the house. During the following dialogue the car arrives and the car doors are heard to slam.*) (p. 52)

The above lines, uttered by the two characters, are taken from Shakespeare's original. So are the references to the knocking, yet the aural image identified thrice by the stage directions is slightly different—it is

Sharp rapping (p. 184.)

They leave. The knocking off-stage continues. A door, off-stage, opens and closes. The door into the room opens and the INSPECTOR *enters an empty room. He seems surprised to find himself where he is. He affects a sarcastic politeness* (p. 185.)

The audience soon discover that two realities start to overlap: a play within a play, *Macbeth*, is produced in Czechoslovakia in the period of "normalisation" by the Living-Room Theatre, of which two of the actual, historical participants, Landovsky and Kohout, are soon mentioned. The outer play is a representation of the concrete situation in Czechoslovakia in the 1970s, and bears much resemblance to the situation presented in *Macbeth*, a fact which is initially indicated by Stoppard, who indirectly compares the Inspector to the forces of darkness and evil by using aural images.

Commenting on the Inspector's behaviour, Roger Sales writes: "Stoppard suggests that totalitarianism is a form of overacting. The Inspector attempts to steal the show, metaphorically as well as literally" (p. 132). The Inspector, concentrating on keeping up the pose, is strongly contrasted with the actors who, after his entrance, maintain a sharp distinction between themselves and their roles. Not wanting to accept the rules imposed on them by his game, they step out of their roles and speak in *propriis personis*.

The distinction between real life and theatrical illusion is blurred by the Inspector, who side by side enumerates Landovsky's job as a concrete individual, and the occupations of several characters impersonated by him in theatre productions. The division into real life and theatrical fiction is also distorted when the words "rough night," said by him, "*operate as a cue for the entrance of the actor playing* MACDUFF" and he appears in the room/on the stage, uttering the appropriate lines from *Macbeth* (p. 187). Soon the other actors enter the stage, yet they are "*unco-operative*," reluctant to go on performing in front of the Inspector, who is now seated among the audience, waiting for the show to begin. This leads to the latter's outburst and threat made directly to Macbeth/Landovsky:

Now listen, you stupid bastard, you'd better get rid of the idea that there's a special *Macbeth* which you do when I'm not around, and some other *Macbeth* for when I *am* around which isn't worth doing. You've only got one *Macbeth* (p. 188.)

Speaking as a representative of the regime, of the one-party system, he does not seem to realise that *Macbeth* can be understood by the dissidents in a way that is different from his. For them, the great play of Shakespeare is an adequate description of what tyranny can do, be it the tyranny of the fictitious Macbeth or of a real-life totalitarian regime. Also for the theatre audience, the production of the piece by the actors explicitly demonstrates the analogy between Macbeth's usurpation and the "normalisation" in Czechoslovakia. Shakespeare's masterpiece is so universal that it can be perceived as an adequate description of what is happening in a modern totalitarian state.

The performance is resumed again. The Inspector, who highly appreciated the scene of Macbeth's coronation, arguing it is "so nice to have a play with a happy ending" (p. 190), is dissatisfied with what happens to Shakespeare's monarch afterwards. In a lengthy exchange of views, which takes place in the outer play now, the Inspector argues that "this performance of yours goes against the spirit of normalization" (p. 194) and, just before leaving, he says: "Things are normalizing nicely. I expect this place will be back to normal in five minutes ..." (p. 195). Before this happens, however, Landovsky attempts to make references to the constitution and argues that producing *Macbeth* is not against it (p. 193). Cahoot pokes fun at the Inspector by reacting in a literal way to his "metaphorical" argument that, due to their own actions, "intellectuals" are now "in the doghouse": "BANQUO, *henceforth* CAHOOT, *howls like a dog, barks, falls silent on his hands and knees*" (p. 193). Being a case of verbal humour, and an act of changing the metaphorical into the literal, this scene abounds in varied allusions. No doubt it is a reference to Cahoot's status as an underdog, a non-person for the totalitarian authorities, an idea which is underlined by the Inspector's phrase "Nice dog," uttered just before his departure (p. 195). Thomas Whitaker has noticed: "Cahoot's howling and barking repeats the lucidly lunatic behaviour of Kohout's own *Hamlet* actor, Kerzhentsev, in *Poor Murderer* (1972), who says: 'Why should a human being without conventional scruples—that is, a normal human being—if he suffers like a dog, not howl like a dog?'" (1986, p. 157). Furthermore, it may also evoke a reference to "dog drama," a 19th century type of drama in which dogs appeared on stage as part of the cast.[1] Finally, the dissidents will soon perform their own underdog/Dogg version of *Macbeth*.

After the departure of the Inspector, the actors continue their performance of Shakespeare's play, yet the theatrical illusion, a characteristic of the beginning of the drama, is absent. Now the audience know that they are watching a production of the inner play performed by the Living-Room Theatre. Furthermore, the performance keeps being interrupted by the repeated appearances of Easy, a lorry driver. His first appearance, in the scene presenting the two murderers of Banquo, seems to place him in the position of the missing third murderer. His sudden intrusion into the world of the production of *Macbeth* naturally causes some bewilderment on the stage and the hostess (Lady Macbeth) leads him off (p. 198). He soon re-enters, however, accompanying the first Murderer only to exit with him a few moments later. During the banquet scene Easy's five appearances either at the window or at the stage door produce confusion among the actors' described in the stage directions (pp. 198–200), and finally he disrupts the production of the play. Then it is resumed again, after a short exchange in which Easy uses Dogg and the actors use English. Upon Macduff's words, "Bleed, bleed, poor country." "*Police siren is heard in distance*" and soon afterwards the Inspector again interrupts the

---

[1]Thomas Whitaker writes: "A popular entertainment in the nineteenth-century England was the 'dog-drama,' for which plays of all kinds were adapted to include canine protagonists. There was even a dog-*Hamlet*', in which Hamlet's dog, always at his side, listens to the ghost, observes the king, watches the duel with Laertes, and at Hamlet's dying command leaps at Claudius' throat and kills him" (1986, p. 160).

performance (p. 204). Once more, the reality of totalitarian Czechoslovakia is adequately described by the words taken from Shakespeare's masterpiece.

The Inspector's appearance not only disrupts the theatrical illusion of the inner play, but also that of the outer play. A similar direct address to the audience could have been noticed earlier, when, on his first appearance, the Inspector initially apologised for interrupting the performance (p. 188). Later on he started being threatening and, acting his part of a regime functionary, he said: "Please don't leave the building. You may use the lavatory but leave the door open" (190). Now he starts pointing his torch at different people in the audience and his orders become more threatening: "Stay where you are and nobody use the lavatory ..." (p. 204). Getting more and more bewildered with the situation, which he cannot comprehend as both the actors and Easy have started communicating in Dogg (which he is not able to grasp), the Inspector, who is incapable of controlling them again directs his commands to the theatre audience: "Put your hands on your heads. Put your— placay manos—per capita ... nix toiletto!" (p. 207). The fact, that he has started using foreign phrases, indicative of his putting on a pose adequate for a repre- sentative of the authorities, adds to the general language confusion. It is charac- teristic of the scene that certain words are often used in their Dogg and English meanings simultaneously.

In the meantime, the production of *Macbeth* resumes, the actors now uttering their lines in Dogg. In the general confusion, the performance progresses. The Inspector keeps consulting his superiors on the phone. With Easy's help, the Czech dissidents start building a platform on the stage. When the Inspector says down the phone: "How the hell do I know? But if it's not free expression, I don't know what is!" (p. 207), he specifies in verbal terms what we can see happening on the stage. Despite the strict regulations of the totalitarian regime people can still communicate and express their dissatisfaction with the situation by means of their own language. Its construction is visually represented by the construction of the platform.

This facility, however, is short-lived. Nearly in panic, the Inspector wants to speak to the chief, yet when he gets through to him, he does not tell him what is happening: "Yes, chief! I think everything's more or less under control, chief ..." (p. 209). It could be guessed that, wanting to keep up the pose of an efficient police inspector, and being unwilling to let his superior know about his helplessness, he has in the meantime found his own solution to the problem. He then calls his two helpers, Maurice and Boris, and with their help starts erecting a wall round the actors, a wall which blocks up the proscenium behind which the Living Room Theatre actors disappear.

The end of the play can be interpreted in two different ways. It may be argued that the play ends pessimistically, victory belonging to the police who now occupy the acting space (Kelly, 1991, p. 133). A similar opinion has been voiced by Phyllis Ruskin and John H. Lutterbie who also remark that Stoppard "directed one of the actors to place a bunch of flowers on the wall, so that the final tableau was a theatrical image of the well-known picture of flowers on the Berlin wall" (1983, p. 553). It seems, however, that even though the ending is pessimistic to quite an extent, there is still some hope left. It can be found in Easy's last words, which close the play: "Well, it's been a funny sort of week. But I should be back by Tuesday" (p. 211). His words seem to indicate that he might be willing to teach yet another lesson in Dogg as a means of free expression.

5 Conclusion

Even though *Cahoot's Macbeth* deals with the grave subject of the suppression of basic kinds of freedom in Czechoslovakia during the period of normalisation, the play often evokes a smile or even laughter, weaving a carpet in which both the comic and tragic elements are intrinsically bound. Many critics have noticed this aspect of the artist's writing and Whitaker (1986, p. 2) has argued that one of Stoppard's main contributions to modern drama is his "ability to shape intellectual debate into a dazzling three-ring circus." In this double-bill, just like in his whole ouevre, Tom Stoppard manages to achieve the two ultimate aims of poetry according to Horace's *Ars Poetica*—he teaches and delights at the same time.

References

Hayman, R. (1979). *Tom Stoppard*. London: Heinemann.
Hudson, R., Itzin, C., & Trussler, S. (1974). Ambushes for the audience: Towards a high comedy of ideas. Interview with Tom Stoppard. *Theatre Quarterly, 4*(14), 3–17.
Kelly, K. E. (1991). *Tom Stoppard and the craft of comedy. Medium and genre at play*. Ann Arbor: The University of Michigan Press.
Ruskin, P., & Lutterbie, J. H. (1983). Balancing the equation. *Modern Drama, 6*(4), 543–554.
Sales, R. (1988). *Tom Stoppard. Rosencrantz and Guildenstern are dead. Penguin critical studies*. London: Penguin Books.
Shakespeare, W. (1968). *Hamlet. Complete works of Shakespeare* (pp. 1028–1072). London and Glasgow: Collins.
Stoppard, T. (1967). Footnote to the Bard. *Observer*, 23.
Stoppard, T. (1971). Yes, we have no banana. *Guardian*, 10.
Stoppard, T. (1972). Playwrights and professors. *The Times Literary Supplement*, 1219.
Stoppard, T. (1979). The (15 Minute) Dogg's troupe Hamlet. In Ed Berman (Ed.), *Ten of the best British short plays* (pp. 137–152). London: Ambiance/Almost Free Playscripts 3, Inter Action Imprint.
Stoppard, T. (1982). Is it true what they say about Shakespeare? *International Shakespeare Association occasional paper* no. 2. Oxford: University Press.
Stoppard, T. (1993). Dogg's Hamlet, Cahoot's Macbeth. *Tom Stoppard: Plays one*. London: Faber and Faber. 139–211.
Taylor, J. R. (1978). *The second wave. British drama in the sixties*. London: Eyre Methuen.
Whitaker, T. R. (1986). *Tom Stoppard*. London: Macmillan.
Wittgenstein, L. (1974). *Philosophical investigations* (G. E. M. Anscombe, Trans.) Oxford: Basil Blackwell.

Author Biography

Jadwiga Uchman is the head of the Department of Studies in Drama and pre-18th Century British Literature, University of Łódź. She specializes in modern English Drama, especially poetic drama, the Theatre of the Absurd, T.S. Eliot, Samuel Beckett, Harold Pinter and Tom Stoppard. She is the author of numerous articles and three books: *The Problem of Time in the Plays of Samuel Beckett. Folia Litteria* 1987. *Reality, Illusion, Theatricality: A Study of Tom Stoppard.* Łódź: 1998 and *Playwrights and Directors: Samuel Beckett, Tom Stoppard and Harold Pinter* 2011.

The Matter of Cosmopolis. Multi-Cultural Motifs in Geoffrey Chaucer's Work (With a Special Emphasis on *The Shipman's Tale* and the Character of the Shipman)

Andrzej Wicher

Abstract C. David Benson says that: "Perhaps the most extreme disjunction of teller and tale is the contrast between the rough, murderous Shipman of the *General Prologue* and the cool, sophisticated art of the *Shipman's Tale*." The author of the present article hopes to be able to show that there is a link between the character of the Shipman and the nature of the tale told by him, and that this link is provided by, among other things, the medieval understanding of cosmopolitanism. The problem of cosmopolitanism was no doubt important for Chaucer, who himself may be thought of as embodying this social phenomenon, being a well-traveled man, like several of the pilgrims he shows in *The Canterbury Tales*, and being a man who was deeply influenced by at least three foreign cultures and languages, while showing little interest in his native English tradition. Naturally, I do not intend to subscribe to the view that Chaucer was a typical, rootless cosmopolitan. On the other hand, the matter of the so called worldliness, in the context of Chaucer's work, seems to offer many shades of meaning, ranging from appreciation to condemnation.

Keywords Cosmopolitanism · Morality · Sexuality · Medieval culture · Folktales

1 Introduction—the Character of Chaucer's Shipman

Is it legitimate to connect Chaucer's Shipman with the topic of cosmopolitanism? He is just one of Chaucer's famous, or notorious, gadabouts, such as the Knight, the Wife of Bath, the Clerk of Oxford, or the Pardoner, whose descriptions in *The General Prologue* are provided with particularly impressive lists of geographical names. The characters described in *The General Prologue* to *The Canterbury Tales*

A. Wicher (✉)
University of Łódź, Łódź, Poland
e-mail: andwich@wp.pl

© Springer International Publishing AG 2017   97
J. Mydla et al. (eds.), *Multiculturalism, Multilingualism and the Self: Literature and Culture Studies*, Issues in Literature and Culture,
DOI 10.1007/978-3-319-61049-8_8

are already, to some extent, cosmopolitan by virtue of being pilgrims, that is people on the move. And yet there are no foreigners among them.

It is the Shipman who seems to come the closest to being a foreigner because his job, that of a sea captain, and probably also a pirate, keeps him constantly on the move, so it is possible that his lifestyle is more consistently, and radically, nomadic that that of other pilgrims. He is on the move between various, usually foreign, or even exotic, places. The vast range of his voyages[1] extends from Gottland, that is an island in the Baltic, which today belongs to Sweden, to Carthage, an ancient, and very famous, city the ruins of which can be found nowadays on the African coast near the city of Tunis,[2] the capital of Tunisia. The choice of most of the geo-graphical places mentioned in the description of the Shipman: Gottland, Bordeaux, Hull, Carthage, is clearly appropriate. They were, or had been, important sea ports and commercial centres. The fact that Carthage no longer had this importance in Chaucer's times may be misleading, it is quite possible that Chaucer used the name Carthage to denote Tunis, which was a very important sea port and a big city in the 14th century. Most of his readers would probably know that these two places are, in fact, one. The name Gottland probably stands for the Hansaetic town of Visby, an important sea port, and the biggest town on the island of Gottland, which played a great role in the North European trade until the end of the 14th c. The expressions "from Hulle to Cartage" and "from Gootlond to the Cape of Fynystere" (Cawley, 1976, p. 13 [ll. 404, 408]) refer to the range of the Shipman's voyages, but they are probably also symbolical, the former one seems to refer to the North-South dimension, Hull being in Northern England and Carthage in Africa, and the latter to the East-West dimension, Gottland lying already in Eastern Europe, not far from the Latvian port of Riga, and Finisterre standing for the westernmost point of the main body of the European continent, it is in fact a promontory that marks the western end of the Spanish Galicia (or the French Brittany). Thus, the Shipman's travelling, and perhaps also his criminal activities, extend over almost the whole of the world as it was known to Geoffrey Chaucer.

Also the Shipman's being a native of Dartmouth in Devon contributes to the effect of this character's foreignness because, as has been emphasized by John Cunningham (cf. Cunningham, 95), places like Devon or Cornwall, even though technically lying in England, were perceived as rather exotic from a 14th century Londoner's, that is Chaucer's, point of view. Dartmouth was, in Chaucer's times, a centre of privateering, which is usually taken as allusion to the Shipman's being a pirate himself. It seems also significant enough that Dartmouth was in those times a

---

[1]J. Cunningham writes about Chaucer's Knight the following: "The other great point of interest … is the very extensive journeys he had made: only one other pilgrim is recorded as having covered anything like this sort of distance—the Wife of Bath!" (Cunningham, 1989, p. 45). It is remarkable that he does not take the Shipman's travelling into account, perhaps because the Shipman hardly ever travels on land, and maybe also because he is such an off-putting character that one can hardly think of him as a pilgrim.

[2]In fact, the modern Carthage is an important enough suburb of the big city of Tunis, but in Chaucer's times it seems to have been no more than a fishing village, not far from Tunis.

place situated near the linguistic border between the English and the Cornish speaking area. Like most geographic names in Devon, Dartmouth is a Celtic name, or rather the river Dart, from which the name of the town is derived, is a Celtic name, which apparently means "river where oak trees grow" (River Dart).[3] Thus the Shipman comes from an English locality which, however, is, at the same time, not quite English, and even could be perceived by some English people as distinctly un-English.

The mention of Bordeaux, as a centre of wine production and wine trade, could be a clue allowing us to link the Shipman with Chaucer himself. It is well known that Chaucer's family came originally from Bordeaux, and it was a family of wine merchants. Just as in the case of the Shipman's coming from Dartmouth, Chaucer's having links with Bordeaux, even though he himself was a Londoner born and bred, is a little similar to the Shipman's being from Dartmouth. Chaucer's family, inasmuch as it was French, was at the same time foreign, and not really foreign, considering that Bordeaux and the adjacent part of France was an English possession. At the time Chaucer was born it was in fact the only English possession in France, and it remained the most important one until it was lost and reunited with France in 1453. The following lines:

Ful many a draughte of wyn had he ydrawe

Fro Burdeux-ward, whil that the chapman sleep.

Of nyce conscience took he no keep (Cawley, 1976, p. 12 [ll. 398–400].)

show that men such as the Shipman, that is the thieves of wine, could be the bane of the Bordelais wine merchants. If then Chaucer's ancestral trade created a valuable economical link between England and the continent, the Shipman represented the underside of that profession. As a pirate, he is of course a professional and quite shameless thief and as a captain of a merchant ship, he is an opportunist thief masquerading as an honest businessman. His wide ranging activities are essentially those of a parasite who makes trade less profitable and more dangerous. Additionally, he is represented as a dangerous troublemaker, or perhaps even a hired assassin, who frequently kills the man he quarrels with and gets rid of him by throwing him overboard. But it may also be said that he is the obverse of the rather positive image of the cosmopolitan represented by Chaucer's Knight, the Wife of Bath, and naturally Chaucer himself.

---

[3]The Cornish word for "oak" may be indeed "dar," or "derwen," like in Welsh, which seems to be related to the Slavic word represented by the Russian "derevo," or the Polish "drzewo," and also to the English word "tree," that is, to words that denote trees in general.

2   Chaucer's Patriotism Versus His Cosmopolitanism

At this point it would be natural to ask ourselves about the nature of that (alleged?) cosmopolitanism and the problems that it represents. Certainly Chaucer could be called a cosmopolitan, in a sense, if we consider that he had a very polyglot education, and most probably was a polyglot himself, being able to speak at least French and Italian, apart of course from his native English, and having an extensive, even if perhaps only passive, knowledge of Latin. But naturally a polyglot is not necessarily a cosmopolitan.[4] Chaucer is often called the father of English literature, or even the father of English language, and his *Canterbury Tales* is, or at least used to be, often described as a celebration of the so called merry England.[5] So it would be perhaps unfair to think of him as a cosmopolitan. On the other hand, we cannot quote any lines from Chaucer that would be openly patriotic in their sense or sentiment (or openly cosmopolitan for that matter). This is a little strange because his good friend John Gower did write such a line,[6] even though, or perhaps exactly because, he was much more polyglot in his writing career, having written books of poetry not only in English, but also in French and Latin, whereas Chaucer, remarkably enough, only translated some poetry from the French, but it seems he never actually wrote anything in a language other than English. On the other hand, it is also remarkable that Chaucer never seems to refer to or to draw on any literature written in English either before him, or by his contemporaries. His quite a considerable poetic output reveals many influences from other writers, and contains numerous direct allusions to some of them and their works, but it so happens that they are all foreign writers. In this respect *The Canterbury Tales* is not even a little bit more English than Chaucer's works belonging to the so called French and Italian periods of his artistic career. As A.C. Baugh has succinctly put it: "[Chaucer] is remarkably indifferent to English writings, but the *Roman de la Rose* and the poems of Machaut are his missal and breviary; in Latin Ovid is his bible" (Baugh, 1967, p. 252). Thus, we have, in Chaucer, to do with an almost ideal balance of facts that seem to point to his patriotism, and of other facts that seem to point in the opposite direction.

It is perhaps this state of affairs that Emile Legouis had in mind when he wrote:

> It is Chaucer's distinction that he turned impartial, eager, and clear-sighted eyes not only on the past, which his books discovered to him, but also on all society of his time, on foreign countries, and on every class in his own country. His work reflects his century not in

---

[4]For example, the Polish leader of the so called National Democracy, Roman Dmowski (1864–1939), a man with very patriotic, or even nationalistic, views, was renowned for his excellent command of French and English.

[5]Cf. G. G. Coulton's statement: "...Chaucer, with incurable optimism, sees chiefly a Merry England to which the horrors of the Hundred Years' War and the Black Death, and Tyler's revolt are but a foil" (Coulton, 1993, p. 11).

[6]I mean the line "O gentile Engletere, a toi j'escrits" [O gentle England, it is to you that I write], quoted by G. G. Coulton (p. 5). The line comes from Gower's French poem *Mirour de l'Omme*, and it is probably significant that Gower is at his most patriotic when he writes in French.

fragments, but completely. More than this, he is often able to discern permanent features beneath the garments of a day, to penetrate to the everlasting springs of human action. His truthful pictures of his age and country contain a truth which is of all time and all countries (Legouis, Cazamian, & Las Vergnas, 1964, p. 129.)

If this is true, then the dilemma: was Chaucer a patriot, or a cosmopolitan, becomes pointless because he, apparently, contrived to be both, being, as it were, a man for all places, a universal writer, very much in the spirit of John Dryden's famous verdict about *The Canterbury Tales*: "here's God's plenty."

This assessment of Chaucer's attitude seems, however, a trifle too quietistic. Instead of appropriating Chaucer for the, essentially nationalistic, ideology of merry England, we are now, apparently, appropriating him for some kind of unproblematic Europeanism in which one's local loyalties merge imperceptibly and harmoniously with more universal and international ones. I do not think this is very adequate.

3   Chaucer's Knight, Squire and Prioress as Icons of Cosmopolitanism

If we look, for example, at the relationship between the Knight and his son, the Squire in *The Canterbury Tales*, we easily discover that they differed from each other, among other things, in that the Knight appears to be an internationalist, taking part in many military campaigns in the area of the Mediterranean and Baltic sea, that is in the two opposite ends of Europe, while his son is happy to serve his own English king and takes part only in military expeditions authorized by that king. It would be natural, for this reason, to describe the Knight as a cosmopolitan, and the Squire as a patriot. Such a conclusion would have been, however, a little paradoxical because cosmopolitanism is often associated with a liberal stance on religion, or even with an unreligious outlook, while patriotism is associated with a rather puritanical and conservative social behaviour. In the case of the Knight and Squire, such associations would be completely inappropriate and wide of the mark. The Knight is a stern religious believer, by modern standards perhaps even a fanatic, while the Squire is a dedicated follower of fashion and a ladies' man who apparently has had already many erotic encounters.

It is, I think, debatable whether Chaucer wanted, in this way, to challenge some clichés, or perhaps those clichés, or stereotypes, did not exist in his times. Another, and, in my opinion, the most likely, possibility is that the 14th century Europeanism was quite a conservative idea founded upon the identification between Europe and Christianity. Thus the Knight traverses Europe, concentrating on its borderline areas, that is, the areas where Christianity comes into contact with paganism, or Islam, in fact the Knight would probably, just like Chaucer, call all non-Christians pagans, and he "fights for our faith," that is takes part in a holy war. His peculiar brand of cosmopolitanism is then undistinguishable from a worldview which, by the post-modern standards of our age, would qualify as religious fanaticism. The patriotism of his son is also, apparently, very unmodern, it does not resemble at all any enthusiastic identification with one's ethnic group, its content seems purely political and consists in the loyal service to the king: "he'd seen some service with the cavalry" (Coghill, 1977, p. 21). The Squire is perhaps too worldly to be bothered about the rather old fashioned crusading ideology of his father. The thinking in terms of nation-states must have seemed cold and cynical in comparison with religiously tinged cosmopolitanism of a Europe united, however imperfectly and incompletely, by Latin Christendom.

It is certainly the Prioress that represents the brand of cosmopolitanism that we might call modern. She is not only a great stickler for elegance and good manners, in this respect she is not probably very different from the Squire, even though her accomplishments, unlike his, are of a stereotypically feminine kind. But she also affects airs of being a fluent speaker of French, the language of the international and rather aristocratic elite, though perhaps not so much in Chaucer's times as in, for example, the 18th century. The name she uses, Eglantine, is also rather pretentious and it definitely sounds French.[7] Such touches of cosmopolitan snobbery are absent in the description of the Squire. It should, however, be stressed that the Prioress is hardly a cosmopolitan in the usual sense of being "a citizen of the world" who parades his or her rootlessness, that is, lack of tribal or local loyalties. She rather, as we might suppose, envisages herself as a citizen of the city which she considers the centre and compendium of the world, that is the city of Paris. This is visible also in her habit of swearing "By St Loy" (Coghill, 1977, p. 22), considering that St Loy, known also as St Eloi, or St Eligius, was a typically French saint. Therefore, in my opinion, Chaucer's comment on the Prioress "French in the Paris style she did not know" (Coghill, 1977, p. 22) is of a particularly biting kind. This is certainly not what she would like to hear, it would be naïve, I think, to imagine that she would be satisfied with the status of a speaker of provincial French, this was not, in all probability, the reason why she took an interest in that language.

4   The Shipman's Tale as a Reflection of the Shipman's Character

This brings us back to the Shipman, or rather to *The Shipman's Tale*, the action of which happens to take place in Saint-Denis, a town situated just north of Paris, and today part the Parisian agglomeration associated with a particularly high rate of

---

[7]It denotes the sweet briar, or sweetbriar rose, in itself perhaps not a very elegant flower, it often grows wild. Considering that there was no well known saint Eglantine, and the word "eglantine," etymologically speaking, means "thorny, prickly," the name seems rather inappropriate for a nun.

criminality. In the Middle Ages it was the centre of the cult of St Denis, the patron saint of France, and a destination of popular pilgrimages, comparable to Canterbury. St Denis was a bishop of Paris beheaded around the year 250 probably on the hill of Montmartre, which means the mountain of martyrs. After his decapitation he is believed to have picked up his head and walked for ten kilometres till he reached the place where he finally died a real death, and this is where St Denis Basilica was constructed which in due time became the burial place for the kings of France.

Of such matters we learn nothing from *The Shipman's Tale*, but the distance between St Denis and Paris appears to be symbolically significant there. The plot of Chaucer's tale apparently is just another version of the so called eternal triangle, very much in the spirit of the fabliau, but the tale shows some signs of its French background, mainly owing to its use of the short French phrase "qui là" (who's there) which the merchant employs in a conversation with his wife, and some references to the French cultural context, such as the names of French saints: saint Denis, saint Martin and saint Ives. There are also references to continental geography, the gullible merchant with his lustful wife live in Saint-Denis, the wife's worldly wise lover is an inhabitant of Paris, and the merchant goes on business to Bruges.[8]

The Shipman's Tale opens with what might be called a cynical and rather unconventional prologue apparently spoken by a woman[9] who maintains that "the sely housbonde, algate he moot paye" (Cawley, 1976, p. 361 [l. 11]) for his wife's expensive clothes if he wants to uphold his reputation:"al for his owene worshipe" (Cawley, 1976, p. 361 [l. 13]). Later the wife, who is the tale's protagonist, will complain to her monkish lover, known as "daun John" ("sir John") (Cawley, 1976, p. 362 [l. 43]), that her husband is so miserly that she cannot dress "for his honour" (Cawley, 1976, p. 366 [l. 179]). On the one hand, then, she is putting forward some rather radical, quasi-feminist, ideas, demanding that the husband should be "buxom unto his wyf" (obedient to his wife) (Cawley, 1976, p. 365 [l. 177]), on the other hand, however, she is quite prepared to play the essentially decorative role of a wife whose outward appearance is part and parcel of her husband's material possessions that bear witness to his high social position.[10] It is perhaps significant that, when the question of the wife's expensive clothes is mentioned for the first time, a native English word "worshipe" is used to denote the moral value which those clothes are supposed to represent, but, when the matter is broached for the second time, the

---

[8]Bruges is a Flemish city in today's Belgium, but in Chaucer's times it was part of the County of Flanders which, in theory, belonged to France, even though in practice it was almost independent. Bruges was also one of the most important centres of the international trade in the late medieval Europe.

[9]This gave rise to the hypothesis that *The Shipman's Tale* was originally intended for the Wife of Bath, who does represent quasi-feminist views (cf. Cawley, 1976, p. 361 n.).

[10]It is also significant that she is afraid of her husband's anger should he discover that his wife is short of money: "And if myn housbonde eek it myght espye, I nere but lost;" (Cawley, 1976, p. 366 [ll. 184–185]).

wife, in her conversation with the young monk, uses the French word "honour." It is, in this context, more appropriate, though in an ironical and paradoxical way, as she is going son to dishonour her husband and to lose her own wifely honour, as an adulteress.

The merchant, that is the cuckold husband in the tale, is generally shown as too busy with his professional affairs to pay much attention to his wife. It is very likely that he neglects not only her material needs, but also her sexual desires. Thus, her request for a loan of one hundred franks from the monk is combined with a sexual overture, as can be seen from the following lines in which the wife promises a reward to the monk:

> For at a certeyn day I wol yow paye,
>
> And don to yow what plesance and service
>
> That I may doon, right as yow list devise. (Cawley, 1976, p. 366 [ll. 190–192])

Finally, the wife endorses her promise to repay the monk by invoking Ganelon, the famous traitor who betrayed Roland and Oliver in the epic French poem *The Song of Roland*:

> And but I do, God take on me vengeance,
>
> As foul as evere hadde Ganylon of France. (Cawley, 1976, p. 366 [193–194])

This is of course deeply ironical, the wife in effect betrays her husband pretending that she would have been the worst of traitors if she had not betrayed him. Ganelon is eventually cruelly punished for his treason, the wife theoretically agrees to pay as much as did Ganelon if she were untrue, but in reality she is not punished at all. From her point of view, she did not deserve a punishment because she was not untrue to her creditor, she paid him as much as he wanted, she repaid the sum with sex because this was what he wanted. Naturally the wife, by treating her body as a saleable commodity, becomes no better than a prostitute. In her own eyes, however, and also in those of her husband's, she remains virtuous. The irony is naturally deepened by the fact that it is in reality the husband, that is the merchant, who pays the monk for the pleasure of having sex with the merchant's wife. Unlike those husbands who derived some profit from offering their wives to powerful people, he, unwittingly, offers her to a person who cannot and does not help him in any way, and he also loses a considerable sum of money in the process.

Boccaccio's analogous tale from the *Decameron* is called Gulfardo and Guasparruolo; Eighth Day 1, which in the original version of the *Decameron* appears just as "Giornata Ottava. Novella Prima." It follows basically the same pattern, the wife is called Madonna Ambruogia, the lover is Gulfardo and the husband is Guasparruolo. What makes the story remarkable is that the wife is actually called a punk there,[11] and that Gulfardo is presented as a foreigner, specifically a German mercenary, who is "very loyal to those with whom he took

---

[11]In fact only in Johan Payne's English translation, the original Italian uses the euphemistic "cattiva femina"—bad woman (Giavardi, 1972, p. 503).

service; a quality most uncommon in Germans" (Payne)—"il che rade volte suole de' Tedeschi avvenire" (Giavardi, 1972, p. 502). Naturally Gulfardo proves disloyal to the merchant, which, in the eyes of Boccaccio, confirms the endemic disloyalty of the Germans among whom Gulfardo is no exception even though, technically, he shows himself as loyal, having repaid the loan he took from the merchant to the merchant's wife. Also the second story of the Eighth Day is an analogue to *The Shipman's Tale*, and it is not essentially different from the first story. The adulterous wife's lover is here a lecherous priest, and the tale's narrator, Panfilo, open's his story with a short diatribe against the priestly class: "Fair ladies, it ocurreth to me to tell you a little story against those who continually offend against us, without being open to retaliation on our part, to wit, the clergy, who have proclaimed a crusade against our wives ..." (Payne), "li quali sopre le nostre mogli hanno bandita la croce" (Giavardi, 1972, p. 504).

5 Conclusion

There seems to be a common denominator between the monk in *The Shipman's Tale*, the German mercenary, and the priest in Boccaccio's stories. They all represent what might be called the cosmopolitan principle, that is, one of them is a foreigner, another is an inhabitant of the capital city known for its mixture of peoples and races, and the third one is a priest who is a well known gadabout visiting assiduously all attractive women in the vicinity, and carrying small presents for them, very much in the manner of Chaucer's Friar, described in *The General Prologue*. Among folktales we find a bundle of types belonging to the class of Tales of the Stupid Ogre, AT 100-1029, known as "Labor Contract" or "Anger Bargain" where the protagonist is a trickster, usually a vagrant of some type, who knows how to take advantage of a usually well established figure, such as a merchant, whose wife he seduces and gets away with it (cf. Thompson, 1977, p. 203). *The Shipman's Tale* and related ones constitute a subgroup of such tales known, by their principal motif, as "The Lover's Gift Regained." They are clearly related to the tales about a supernatural husband, who usually is a rather unpredictable figure, a shape shifter, who can turn himself into an animal, or is simply a devil.

The statement of C. David Benson that: "Perhaps the most extreme disjunction of teller and tale is the contrast between the rough, murderous Shipman of the *General Prologue* and the cool, sophisticated art of the *Shipman's Tale*" (Benson, 1986, p. 103) may then be qualified. The disjunction is no doubt there, but there are also significant, though not always obvious, conjunctions, or rather parallels, between the character of the Shipman and the story that Chaucer has put into his mouth. It is obvious enough that *The Canterbury Tales* offers us many types of medieval cosmopolitanism represented by various figures, appearing both as the narrators, or characters within the tales. The Shipman is certainly the most disquieting among those figures and his tale, in which the sacrament of marriage becomes a matter of sordid financial transactions, confirms this impression.

References

Baugh, A. C. (Gen. ed.). (1967). *Literary history of England* (Vol. 1). London: Routledge and Kegan Paul Ltd.

Benson, C. D. (1986). *The Canterbury tales*: Personal drama or experiments in poetic variety? In P. Boitani & J. Mann (Eds.), *The Cambridge Chaucer companion* (pp. 93–108). Cambridge et al.: Cambridge University Press.

Cawley, A. C. (Ed.). (1976). *Geoffrey Chaucer–Canterbury tales*. London: J. M. Dent & Sons Ltd and New York: E. P. Dutton.

Coghill, N. (Transl.). (1977). *Geoffrey Chaucer–The Canterbury tales*. London: Penguin

Coulton, G. G. (1993). *Chaucer and his England*. London: Bracken Books.

Cunningham, J. E. (1989). *Chaucer–The prologue to the Canterbury tales. Incorporating Chaucer's text*. Harmondsworth, Middlesex, England: Penguin Books.

Giavardi, L. (Ed.). (1972). *G. Boccaccio–Il Decamerone*. Milano: Editoriale Lucchi.

Legouis, E., Cazamian, L., & Las Vergnas, R. (1964). *A history of English literature*. London: J. M. Dent & Sons Ltd.

Payne, J. (1906). *The Decameron* (Trans.). London. Retrieved from http://sites.fas.harvard.edu/~chaucer/special/authors/boccaccio/boc-8-1.html

Thompson, S. (1977). *The folktale*. Berkeley, Los Angeles, London: University of California Press.

Author Biography

Andrzej Wicher is Professor of English literature and theory of literature in the Institute of English Studies of Łódź University. He published, apart from numerous articles, a book entitled *Archaeology of the Sublime. Studies in Late—Medieval English Writings* (Katowice 1995) and two more: *Shakespeare's Parting Wondertales—a Study of the Elements of the Tale of Magic* in William Shakespeare's Late Plays (Łódź 2003), and *Selected Medieval and Religious Themes in the Works* of C.S. Lewis and J.R.R. Tolkien, which appeared in 2013. He also published a volume of Polish translations of *Middle English literary works*, including Sir Gawain and the Green Knight, and Pearl. His professional interests include Medieval and Renaissance studies, cultural studies, and modern fantasy literature, with a special emphasis on the presence of folktale motifs in works of literature.

Finessing the Multilingual World in Commercial English Cinema

Anthony David Barker

Abstract As a highly capitalised business, the film industry cannot afford to confuse its target audience with the plethora of communicative difficulties that exist in the world. Narrative exegesis demands that we get down to what is important or appealing expeditiously. A series of conventions have therefore grown up to simplify linguistic diversity, many of them obvious and scarcely claiming our attention. The most notable of these is the Hollywood convention that everyone, from everywhere, with or without a foreign accent, speaks English. Before the coming of sound cinema, it made little sense to talk of national cinemas and language communities. Since sound arrived, these have become dominant forms for categorising film content, and dominant ways that films are marketed and consumed. This article will start by focusing on the period 1927–1930 to see exactly what ground rules established themselves for representing the world. It will then look at the (often serio-comic) conventions of the Hollywood studio era, in such classic movies as *Casablanca* (1942) and *Bridge on the River Kwai* (1957), before turning to the emergence of a tentative self-aware internationalist cinema in the 1960s and 70s. Finally, I will review some recent developments in cinema and speculate on what a truly multilingual cinema might look like, what commercial realities would still be brought to bear but also see what possibilities might exist for its wider dissemination.

Keywords Film · Cinema · Hollywood · Multilingualism

1 Introduction

The account of the building of the Tower of Babel provides us with a powerful metaphor for the development of commercial cinema. According to the Bible, the impetus to construct the tower came from humankind's realization that they had powerful new technologies they could bring to bear:

A.D. Barker (✉)
University of Aveiro, Aveiro, Portugal
e-mail: abarker@ua.pt

© Springer International Publishing AG 2017   109
J. Mydla et al. (eds.), *Multiculturalism, Multilingualism and the Self: Literature and Culture Studies*, Issues in Literature and Culture,
DOI 10.1007/978-3-319-61049-8_9

Now the whole world had one language and a common speech. As men moved eastward, they found a plain in Shinar and settled there.

They said to each other, "Come, let's make bricks and bake them thoroughly." They used brick instead of stone, and tar for mortar. Then they said, "Come, let us build ourselves a city, with a tower that reaches to the heavens, so that we may make a name for ourselves and not be scattered over the face of the whole earth."

But the Lord came down to see the city and the tower that the men were building. The Lord said: "If as one people speaking the same language they have begun to do this, then nothing they plan to do will be impossible for them. Come, let us go down and confuse their language so they will not understand each other."

So the Lord scattered them from there over all the earth, and they stopped building the city... (*Holy Bible* 1984, Genesis 11, 1–7)

In this myth, we have the divine forestalling of urban life and the foreshadowing of the nation state founded on a single language community and divided off from all other linguistic groupings. The "bricks and tar" that led to the babelisation of cinema was of course the adoption of the optical sound track developed by Western Electric and showcased by Warner Bros in the 1927 film *The Jazz Singer*. Hitherto, it was possible to believe in cinema as a kind of universal language crossing national frontiers and speaking with almost equal clarity to the peoples of the world. For example, when the German expressionist classic *The Cabinet of Dr Caligari* was released in Los Angeles in 1921, there were strikes and riots in protest against the film in anticipation that it would sweep America and cost jobs and livelihoods in Hollywood (Skal, 1993: 37–40). There has scarcely been a comparable scare since, as the American film industry post-World War One went on to achieve in reverse more or less what this panic feared, the domination of many if not all domestic markets. American film-makers' capacity to generate product through the types of industrial practice pioneered by Henry Ford in the manufacturing sector put the US in the dominating position that it still holds to this day. The size of the American domestic market dictates that costs can be recovered in the US alone, so all success in foreign markets just adds to the profitability of commercial film-making. This is barely an opportunity open to any other nation. However, the hegemony that American film was exercising in 1926, although registered with chagrin by many national governments concerned about revenues exiting their countries, was not felt much by foreign audiences until actors began to open their mouths and speak and/or sing. Then national and cultural differences became a matter of some general concern.

Without spoken language, in a world of inter-titles, intelligibility was guaranteed. To be sure, people registered national differences; the slick high-rise America of the Jazz Age did not resemble anywhere you might find in Europe. And, equally clearly, Hollywood was not constrained to represent just local or contemporary realities. Questions of foreignness and ethnicity could be addressed in casting, costume, and set design. But as soon as words were pronounced, vexing issues of verisimilitude came to the fore. Put simply, why was *everyone* speaking English, including those declaring themselves to be foreign or in places where English was largely unknown? There were also issues about the types of emotional engagement people could have following the passing of a world of mime. This is how Alexander Walker saw the problem:

> Movie-goers were experiencing another kind of loss than simply that of silence: the loss of wonder. Characters on the screen had no vocal identities; they were assumed to be leading the emotional life that audiences, of greater or lesser sophistication, chose to project onto their mimed feelings. But with the talkies, they were having to declare themselves in speech, define their relationships much more precisely to each other – and, by extension, to the spectator. Being a filmgoer at the talkies offered far less choice in the matter of emotions. (Walker 1979, p. 99)

That greater definition and precision would extend to whether characters up on the screen either were or were not "like us."

2 The Coming of the Talkies

Of course, talkies were not a problem to language communities which only purported to talk amongst themselves. At the end of the 1920s, truly national cinemas were born amongst filmmakers happy to produce films for and about the countries and peoples of their place of making. But it was not long before national cinemas aspired to be seen and admired beyond their frontiers. The problem was particularly acute for the USA, which had a dominant position in international film production and distribution and aspired to be de facto "world cinema." In 1928/9, the American film industry borrowed upwards of 300 million dollars to build sound stages, develop optical soundtrack technology and to wire thousands of cinemas for sound equipment. The vulnerability of this level of indebtedness led to a frenzy of amalgamations and attempted buyouts, with new studios and electronics giants (Western Electric and RCA/RKO) entering the field of movie-making. The appointment of 6–8 bankers and electrical company executives to the boards of all the major film-making studios (RKO had 19 banking interests represented on its board) increased concern for the industry's profitability going forward. All those bankers in 1929 started worrying about the risk to international distribution and exhibition of all these now markedly *English language* films. At this time, export markets represented 20–25% of American movie revenues. For the first 10 years or so of the talkies, synchronised dubbing was not technically feasible. So, ironically and somewhat counter-intuitively for a wonderful new resource, studios came under pressure to keep talking to a minimum. Singing was the safer strategy and a surprisingly large number of films of the time were either musicals or had scenes showcasing music.

Meanwhile, Hollywood was looking for ways to press the technological advantage it enjoyed over its European competitors. This mainly consisted of plans to wire European cinemas for sound. Big-city large-attendance profitable cinemas in Europe enthusiastically embraced talkies and were quickly "wired." The smaller local cinemas could not afford the capital investment and went out of business. Many of these were locally-owned, whereas the city picture palaces were partly US-owned. In general, cinema attendance did not decline with the talkies—indeed the late thirties are the high-watermark of cinema attendance. As for film distribution, Europe's "quota systems" for blocking American imports did nothing to prevent prestige talking pictures from arriving and actively helped to impede sales of lower quality, less profitable films to smaller poorer "unwired" exhibitors.

By 1929, America was producing enough talkies to begin a full-scale invasion of principal export markets in Europe and South America. Film production competitors like Britain, Germany, and France feebly attempted to defend their domestic film industries. Only Mussolini's Italy, however, and for plainly nationalistic reasons, passed legislation in 1929 that prohibited the screening of films in any other language than Italian. France altered its authorised ratio of film imports to home-produced films from 7:1 to 3:1. America immediately retaliated by withdrawing from the French market in protest, accompanied by market-leader US wiring and recording companies. After 6 months of boycotting the French market, under pressure largely from French exhibitors who were starved of commercial product, the 7:1 ratio was restored.

Other initiatives were in the offing. The commonest of these was to make a Spanish-language version of popular prestige productions by night on the same sets and with the same set-ups as had been used by day with the English-language versions. Whenever necessary, whole films would be recast with Spanish-speaking actors. Thompson (1985, p. 92) estimates the additional cost of reshooting a picture on the same sets in another language was between 30,000 and 40,000 dollars per picture, a perfectly acceptable additional expense to satisfy South American and Iberian markets. Extraordinarily, Hollywood also considered selling "how to make" packages or "kits" of their latest English films to foreign studios, complete with set-ups, lighting schemes, camera positions, etc., before later abandoning the idea. In November 1929, MGM announced a 2 million-dollar programme of French, German, and Spanish language versions of their major films. Paramount established a studio at Joinville outside Paris in early 1930 exclusively to make multiple-language productions. In its first year, it made 66 features in 12 different languages (Vasey, 1997, p. 92).

As these commercial efforts gathered pace, it became clear that the language spoken in movies was something of a minefield. Some foreign markets were just too small to attract the resource needed to produce other language versions. Three divisions of nations were created, based upon a calculation on potential commercial returns. Only French, Spanish and German markets were considered profitable enough for reshooting, along with the Italian market, which attracted special treatment for the political reason given above. But into what language would one reshoot or dub? South American audiences were frequently bemused and offended in equal measure by Castilian Spanish. A similar sort of political tension existed between Brazilian and European Portuguese language forms. These issues came to a head in various films of the 1930s. I am indebted to Vasey (1997, p. 93–94) for the following example. First National (shortly to merge with Warner Bros) released a picture in 1930 called *The Bad Man* starring Walter Huston as a Mexican gang leader. In the film, an American family is terrorised by the gang—the family speaks conventional American English and the Mexicans speak a kind of pidgin broken English. This is classical actor Huston as Pancho Lopez:

> "I make ze love to you myself — personal... What? Because you are marry you do not wish to spik of love! Leesen Lady — eef Pancho Lopez want woman, he take her, damn queek!" (cited on the imdb.com webpage for *The Bad Man*)

Such stereotyping went largely unnoticed by indigenous audiences at this time. However, when the film was rendered into *El Hombre Malo* (1930), the family spoke Castilian and the bandits Mexican Spanish. Mexican audiences were alerted to this status distinction by disgruntled members of the cast and in anticipation of the film's release revolted against it. Their Embassy in Washington protested the stereotyping of Mexicans. But, such are the cross-currents of identity politics, Mexican sensibilities were also offended that a Spanish-born actor was cast in the role of Lopez and not a Mexican. The constellation of Spanish language forms and accents in South America was so diverse that subtitling was eventually to emerge as the preferred form of release there for US films.

3   Studio Era Language Conventions Established

Mixing and synchronised dubbing was perfected with the introduction of the Moviola machine in the late 1930s, but language dilemmas did not stop there. It was quickly discovered that dubbing was both culturally and semantically inflexible. In the first instance, audiences found it somewhat discordant to hear their own language perfectly expressed by professional actors grafted onto comportment and social mannerisms that were markedly American. On the other hand, the cheaper subtitling process (1) was technically easier to achieve (2) left space for local inflections and (3) accommodated audience's abilities to engage imaginatively with the action without this dissonance. Different countries chose to react differently to the babelisation of cinema phenomena but economic realities always underpinned these preferences. Larger language communities, used to hearing their own language and taking pride in its diffusion, preferred dubbing. Smaller nations, where the money was not there to make multiple language versions, opted for sub-titling and took pride in their greater openness to the foreign. The Polish compromise of the foreign language version talked over by a narrator/translator seems to accord with a market where the source language could be swiftly and cheaply both naturalised and censored in translation.

Once the sound and language conventions had reached a level of technical sophistication and freedom (sound recording had very much cramped the style of studio-bound film-making, as one can see in the comic reconstructions of the hit musical *Singin' in the Rain* (1952)), we begin to see Hollywood's version of the world taking shape. Essentially, this can be understood as bringing the whole world within a Los Angeles studio. For example, in 1938 independent producer Walter Wanger and United Artists released a film called *Algiers*. This was a transcultur-ation of the French movie classic *Pépé Le Moko* (1937), directed by Julien Duvivier. It was as if Wanger had bought a kit of the French film. The dialogue was the same and the actors performed their roles with a precise familiarity with the original. It was only that Jean Gabin and Mireille Balin spoke French in *Pépé* and Charles Boyer, Hedy Lamar and everyone else spoke heavily-accented English in *Algiers*. Casting foreign actors in roles approximating to their native languages was the way ahead, and those parts of the world where those languages were spoken became absorbed into this conventional system. Perhaps the clearest and best known exposition of this strategy is *Casablanca* (1942), directed by Michael Curtiz.

As might be expected in war-torn 1942, no one left California to visit or otherwise recreate the city of Casablanca. There are virtually no people of North-African descent in the film, and only two Americans, Rick (Humphrey Bogart) and his side-kick Sam (Dooley Wilson). The various nationalities of cos-mopolitan Casablanca are represented by Hollywood's "foreign legion" of émigrés —the majority of whom came from the disintegrating Austro-Hungarian empire, like director Mihály Kertész. Many of Hollywood's German Jews were obliged to play Nazis to make a living. The case of the villain Conrad Veidt is instructive. Having a Jewish wife, he was a refugee from Hitler's Germany. Like Peter Lorre, also one of Germany's greatest film stars, he eked out a living as a character actor playing heavies. Here, Casablanca the place and *Casablanca* the film are metonyms for the linguistic practices I am discussing in this article. Rick's is the *lingua franca* café, Casablanca the place where the conceit is made flesh.

It would be too much to expect at this time any anti-colonial sentiment and so Arabic is nowhere seen or heard; more surprisingly, French hardly puts in an appearance either, even though the plot requires that what it means to be French is constantly before us. France and "Frenchness" is mostly expressed by music ("La Marseillaise") and clichéd Gallic attitudes. Of the supporting cast, only Madeleine Lebeau ("Yvonne") is French. Claude Rains occupies the position of the most prominent French character and he makes no stab at the language or the accent; his Frenchness consists of sly hypocrisy and a way with the ladies. Yet the convention that this is a French-speaking country requires visual support. The signs, like the famous poster of Marshall Pétain articulating the slogans of Vichy France are in French, as are the public signs ("Défense de stationner" or "DÉFENSE ABSOLUE DE FUMER" found in the aircraft hangar at the film's climax). In this way, the Frenchness of Casablanca is reduced to the set-dresser's art. However, when the information is important to the narrative, it appears in English: "Closed by Order of the Prefect of Police," it says on the door of Rick's café.

The use of spoken French and German is reserved for scenes of symbolic rather than functional import, like a brief flair-up between French and German officers in the café. Mostly French is confined to the flashback sequence in Paris. One scene uses a loud-speaker announcement in French that the German invasion is imminent (sub-titled in English); a follow-up announcement in German then shows that it has taken place. It matters little what is said because the language switch is the point, and the sequence is only background to Rick and Ilse's separation and departure. The reverse side of the coin is also addressed in the film. An elderly couple of German Jews *en route* for America sit at a table in Rick's and practice their nascent English: "What clock is it?... It is three clocks" in a parody of what it is to speak a foreign language maladroitly (ignoring the context in which a cast of foreigners are all speaking it perfectly, as scripted by the Epstein brothers). However much a film flags up its exotic location, like Hitchcock's *Notorious* (1946) set in the Brazil of post-war fugitive Nazis, that place remained for all practical purposes a Los Angeles film set and both its locals and its émigrés tended to speak English.

4 Internationalisation

By the 1950s, production norms were beginning to shift. After the war, millions of dollars of film revenues were tied up in Europe as a result of European currency restrictions. It made sense to come to Europe to make films. It also served to undercut expensive unionised labour costs in the domestic industry. The so-called "runaway production" was born, where an essentially American film was shot on location and in the studio facilities of cash-strapped Europe. Another reason why this mode of production took root was of course the arrival of international air travel in the post-war period. Not only could personnel move quickly and relatively cheaply between America and Europe but these routes also opened up for the expansion of large-scale tourism. Many of the films in question were also show-cases for these countries as tourist destinations. I would argue that filming these productions out of the States in countries where foreign languages held sway, as well as the increased contact that travelling Americans had with those cultures, necessarily brought about changes in the filmic representation of the world. These are some of the more notable runaway productions of the 1950s: *Pandora and the Flying Dutchman* (1950) dir. Albert Lewin; *Roman Holiday* (1952) dir. Wiliam Wyler; *To Catch a Thief* (1955) dir. Alfred Hitchcock; *An Affair to Remember* (1957) dir. Leo McCarey; *Bonjour Tristesse* (1958) dir. Otto Preminger. But perhaps the film which best captures the production *zeitgeist* is Mike Todd's lavish version of *Around the World in 80 Days* (1956), which showcases widescreen location Technicolor photography in his own Todd-AO 70 mm format and which acknowledges the help of 19 different airlines in its making, taking the cast and crew to 7 principal foreign locations as well as multiple outdoor locations in the USA. To be sure, these films privilege English and English-speakers, but there is a sense that misunderstandings and culture shocks are possible for American visitors there. Strangely, the many sword and sandal epics, like William Wyler's *Ben Hur* (1959), which were also mostly made on location and in Europe, were exempt from this realization of linguistic diversity. It was as if by casting them in the historical past, we could return to a pre-Babelian time.

There were however films of the 50s where the conventions of the day create serious cultural dissonance. David Lean's *Bridge on the River Kwai* (1957) was a multiple Oscar-winning picture from the time, ostensibly about culture clash. Based on the French novel by Pierre Boulle, the text purports to expose the outdatedness of colonial attitudes in an era of frank and rapid decolonisation. However, the film's need to dramatise its plot intelligibly distorts the likely nature of power relations in Occupied Burma during the War. This dissonance is largely registered in linguistic issues; the Japanese are constrained to speak English by the commercial logic of the film, putting them at a communicative disadvantage. The narrative logic of the film is that they have the whip hand. By casting Sessue Hayakawa, a non-English-speaking actor opposite Alec Guinness, his apparently abject adversary, the Japanese seem to lose the authority and confidence of their position. Lean's reported bullying and humiliating of actor Sessue Hayakawa as he schooled him in the phonetic delivery of his lines [see Brownlow's (1977: 345–92) detailed account of the making of this film on location in Ceylon—now Sri Lanka] adds to the sense that language diversity is needed even to approximate to a convincing version of cultural relations. For, on the other hand, Nicholson's (Guinness) delusional self-importance (so central to the source text's anti-British, anti-imperialist critique) is clouded by his linguistic assurance. One sees just how conventionally arranged power and linguistic relations are in the film if you contrast it with the 1983 film *Merry Christmas Mr Lawrence*, directed by Nagisa Oshima. Here, the Japanese language prevails in the camp (although prisoners speak their own language when alone together). The Japanese sergeant, who has tyrannised the inmates, only speaks his first phrase of English when the camp is liberated and he himself becomes a prisoner.

I would argue that the 1960s and early 1970s were a watershed for the increased internationalisation of cinema. European directors moved back and forth between their homelands and America and American directors, like Kubrick and Losey, based themselves in Europe. A production like Daryl F. Zanuck's Normandy landing tribute *The Longest Day* (1962) makes extensive use of German and French, as well as English, as it attempts to relate the events of that day from the points of view of attackers, defenders, and bystanders. Zanuck said that he used German "because he wanted the German military to be seen as real people, and not as Nazi caricatures of Fox war films" (Custen, 1997: 362), that is, the films Zanuck himself had made 20 years earlier. Following the 60s, mixed nationality casts started to be put together for thrillers in European settings, often with lone or partly isolated North American protagonists. A certain disorientation and deracination were the moods required for these thriller and important elements in this were the specific communication difficulties of English monoglots. Tension is ramped up by the inability to negotiate local ways and local bureaucracies. Two films by Nicolas Roeg, *Don't Look Now* (1973) and *Bad Timing* (1979), are representative of the Anglophone protagonist (Donald Sutherland and Art Garfunkel respectively) cut adrift in a sinister and decadent Europe, heavy with unintelligible history and folk belief. These figures are the 70s sour response to the Gene Kellys and Gregory Pecks of the 50s, who had breezed their way around European capitals and who were greeted in their own tongue as welcome liberators and the bearers of much-needed dollars.

Perhaps the best version of this updated post-70s take upon an American in Paris is Roman Polanski's aptly-named *Frantic* (1988). A doctor arrives with his wife for a medical conference in Paris. There is a mix-up with their luggage and his wife is abducted. Harrison Ford (as Dr Richard Walker) has to unravel the mystery of her abduction in a context where he does not speak the language and can hardly depend upon the authorities. The first hour (which the critics liked) is a taut thriller; the second (which they did not) is a fascinating exercise in cultural deracination. Ford loses focus as he becomes beguiled by a *louche* criminal underworld and the attentions of a 19-year old French girl. Climbing over the rooftops of Paris, he loses his bearings (in the particular form of his shoes) and has to become something more feral to cope with this cultural jungle. There is a scene where he (ambiguously) invites a hotel receptionist to his room just so he can interpret an incoming call from the kidnappers. Everywhere, spoken clues fall on deaf ears, written messages can't get through. The girl increasingly becomes his only means of subsistence and she is dubiously loyal and killed off at the end. Once again, non-English-speaking Emmanuelle Seigner in her first film role had to be schooled by Polanski in the delivery of her lines (Parker, 1993, p. 256–259). English here is confined to those tourist and professional settings that Walker and his wife have safely come to inhabit; instead they are propelled into a hostile francophone world where their linguistic and cultural assumptions do not apply. Part of the problem is that films where cultural confusion is the subject must to some extent sacrifice easy narrative coherence; no film that takes on this subject can expect to be widely popular, to say nothing of the fact that mixing languages and rendering major parts of films in sub-titles is a high-risk strategy.

A film-maker who has not taken risks with multilingual contexts is Woody Allen. Following his personal difficulties in America in the 1990s, Allen decamped to make more and more of his movies in Europe. These films are perhaps knowing and partly ironic throw-backs to the days of Gene Kelly and *An American in Paris*. Because they are comedies and marked as Woody Allen films, there is a sense in which they opt to deal with the "foreignness" of Europe through a series of filters. One of these filters is prior representations of European cities on film and in the other arts, as seen from the perspective of an educated American. *To Rome with Love* (2012) has more to do with Fellini than with *Roman Holiday*. His *Paris by Moonlight* (2011) is an imaginative engagement with the Paris of the Modernist period and, obviously, *Vicky Cristina Barcelona* (2008) is Picasso's Barcelona, to the extent that it is somewhere where one can create and fall in love without the trammels of bourgeois morality. They are places with distinctive cultures, places where art is taken seriously, but largely without a linguistic character of their own. This is evidenced by the ubiquity of English but also, strangely, by Javier Bardem's poet father in *Vicky Cristina Barcelona*—a man whose artistic calling is so high that he refuses to have his work translated. This is taken as a mark of integrity, as a rejection of the purely commercial, but it also leaves us with a man, an artist, who is a poet only in name. All attempts in these films to show the work and commitment of "real artists" ring a little hollow. The appeal to past (and dead) artists also has a valuable retrograde appeal; it does not have to confront social change, or deal with the real (non-privileged) character of these cities. In that sense, they are constructs like the films of the 50s, playground for Americans in love. It's worth observing that they are also paid-for travelogues, since Allen took public money (Campo, Brea, & Muniz, 2011, p. 137–154) for his productions from these cities to make his films there and that they are clearly cost-effective marketing targeted at the English-speaking tourist.

5   The Road to Multilingualism

There are no easy explanations for the changes in language policy across an international industry like that of commercial cinema. But it is possible to see how far we have come if we compare an (essentially) long-running 60s franchise like the James Bond films (itself a runaway production series mostly shot in Pinewood Studios, West London), with a more recent update of the spy thriller, the Jason Bourne movies (2002, 2004, 2007, 2012, 2016). The Bond movies see the world as a playground for the licensed mayhem of its elegant and well-funded protagonist. As well as featuring many of the globe's beauty spots and holiday venues, an unending series of intermediaries and flunkies anglicise the world for Bond so that his intercultural competence is never put to the test. Villains and potential sexual partners, always marked as exotically foreign, invariably address him in English. This carries with it a sense of entitlement which is at odds with Britain's con-temporaneous imperial decline but which is to some extent intended to assuage it. It does so partly by merging with a new reality, that of English spoken ubiquitously as *lingua franca*, based upon America's power around the world. Jason Bourne, on the other hand, is the agent gone feral and gone native. Living in opposition to the intelligence institutions which have created and trained him, he can only subsist by blending in. For this, he needs and possesses local knowledge and competence in foreign languages. The plots of both agents glide easily between countries but those countries are markedly different. In Bond, we see the world as homogenised, made up of an international jet-set predicated on cartoonish characterisation and larger-than-life criminal plots. In Bourne, we find treachery closer to home, in the covert operations of government organisations gone rogue. But here each country is different, posing different challenges. We see Bourne hastening to, through, and away from crowded public spaces, moving as inconspicuously as possible. The pattern is replicated in the Luc Besson-produced *Taken* series (2008, 2012, 2014) starring Liam Neeson. In these, and in the Bourne films, French, German, Russian, Albanian, Turkish and Arabic are spoken in significant amounts.

One of the reasons the Bourne films have a greater feel of authenticity is that three of them were directed by British documentary film-maker Paul Greengrass. Greengrass is largely responsible for introducing a strong accent of documentary realism into the action-adventure film. On the technical level, this has entailed a lot of hand-held camera work, location-shooting, fast editing and background sound work—but it also implies a radically different attitude to the circumambient world. His cross-over to action-adventure began with documentary reconstruction of real-life events, notably a film version of the controversial confrontation in Northern Ireland known as *Bloody Sunday* (2002). In a similar vein, he went on to direct the 9/11 reconstruction, *United 93* (2006), containing all its opening scenes in Arabic, the Iraq drama *Green Zone* (2010), also using Arabic, and more recently the Horn of Africa piracy thriller *Captain Phillips* (2013), which makes extensive use of the Somali language. In perhaps a less commercial vein, another British documentarist, Nick Bloomfield made the film *Battle for Haditha* (2008). Like Greengrass's work, Bloomfield tries to represent the occupation of Iraq in even-handed terms through documentary techniques. This involves immersion in the local culture and language, engaging with the victims of atrocity but also including the experience of the insurgents, who are humanised. This has the effect of making sense of the total disorientation of American forces operating there. *Haditha* shows that the fog of war is primarily a fog of cultures and languages, as US marines, living in protective compounds, are totally unable to discriminate between friendlies, hostiles and neutrals. In microcosm, it shows why regime change and nation-building from without is doomed to ignominious failure.

At some distance from the open violence of warfare and espionage, the multi-ethnic multi-layered narrative of culture clash was also developing. Sophia Coppola's *Lost in Translation* (2003) offers a view of mutually uncomprehending cultures but baulks at trans-linguistic contact because the distance between English and Japanese in the film is so great. Instead, *anomie* and alienation in the great high-tech urban landscape of Tokyo are foregrounded. Alejandro Iñárritu and his writer Guillermo Arriaga's invention of the many-sided convergent narrative form in *21 Grams* (2003) was a breakthrough in the representation of a linguistic-cultural interface, the ones between Mexico and the United States and between Spanish and English. The idea was greatly enlarged for and then transferred to trans-cultural and trans-linguistic contexts in the international success *Babel* (2006). Here the theme is cross-cultural misunderstanding but it takes place across the wide world, informed by the idea that something that happens in one place can have far-reaching consequences in another time-zone. In this case, it is that a rifle given as a gift to a Japanese businessman can be passed on to a north African tribesman who then loans it to a son who accidentally shoots an American tourist, whose injuries on holiday cause a Mexican nanny to be unable to attend a family wedding. When she perhaps unwisely attempts to take US kids with her to the wedding over the nearby border, she falls foul of US immigration and several lives are put in jeopardy. Treacherous language interfaces are discovered at the North African site of the shooting, as well as on the US-Mexican border, and show that communication difficulties collude with other factors in the generation of racial and ethnic prejudices. The hand-over of the rifle in an act of gratitude is not a site of misunderstanding although it subsequently proves to be an error. The Japanese segment is the least well-integrated element in the *Babel* mosaic, precisely because the language (if not the culture) gap is too wide to present an interface. The result is a monoglot section concerning a distressed Japanese schoolgirl which is more enigmatic than meaningful. It is an incidental observation but productions which attempt an international dimension can often work out a little unfocussed because it is difficult to master all the specific cultural contexts they wish to capture. Contrast the intimacy of Iñárritu's Mexico-US border with the neon burn-out and generalised alienation (à la *Lost in Translation*) of the Tokyo scenes.

So, in conclusion, what would a commercial multi-lingual cinema look like? Well, it might look like that of South Africa, a country of 11 official languages. It might dramatise the lives of Sowetans, for example—living in a 1.3 million person township where English and all 9 black African languages are spoken. It might be like Oliver Schmitz's apartheid-era *Mapantzulu* (1987), for example, which moves between English, Afrikaans, Zulu, and Southern Sotho. Or it might be like Schmitz's more recent *Hijack Stories* (2001), which has constant language switching between English and two different African languages, subtitling as and when needed. In a place where 98.5% of the residents are black, it would make little sense to show them all chatting away in the colonial language. At the same time, it would make no sense at all to show them avoiding English altogether—in a place where no tribal language is wholly dominant and where English has both expressive force and utility as a *lingua franca*. And to offer any kind of understanding of the texture of life in Soweto, that heady brew of cultures and languages are necessary elements. To attempt to render Soweto through the dominant conventions of commercial cinema would be to admit to its packaging as a locus which shows less potential for conflict but which is significantly less culturally rich.

A parallel example exists within Portuguese cinema. Portuguese experience since the 1950s has been marked by the fact of economic migration; before that, there was colonial experience based largely on the eastern and western flanks of southern Africa (Mozambique and Angola). These significant movements of population from a mainland home to a place of settlement are central to many people's understanding of their lives and with them have come an intimate knowledge of other lands, their languages and cultures. Until this year, the most commercially successful Portuguese film was a comedy called *A Gaiola Dourada* (2013) [*The Golden Cage*]. It is also known as *La Cage Dorée* because most of it was shot in France and the predominant language of the film is French (although about 40% of it is in Portuguese). It concerns a family of Portuguese immigrants living in France who are so popular locally that their neighbours will resort to any stratagem to prevent them returning to their homeland when they inherit a country house there. People flocked to see this film because it spoke directly either to their positive immigrant experience in France or to that of people they knew well. At the other end of the scale of popularity, we have Manoel de Oliveira's self-conscious art film *Um Filme Falado/Un Film Parle/A Talking Picture* (2003), in which an international cast including John Malkovich, Catherine Deneuve, Irene Papas, Stefania Sandrelli and Luis Miguel Cintra speak to each other in their 5 different native languages and it is pretended that there is universal understanding. The film has a serious purpose in that the characters discuss what European culture means to them as they travel by cruise ship from Lisbon, across the Mediterranean, through the Suez Canal and into the Indian Ocean. A Portuguese-French-Italian co-production subsidised by Eurimages—an EU support fund for European Cinema, *Um Filme Falado* made a miserable 13,000 dollars on its US release and did little better in Europe. This was an effort in linguistic gymnastics too far for all but the most ardent of cinephiles.

Naturally, it is beyond the power of this paper to propose a solution to the problems created in *Genesis* by God's aversion to tall buildings. Hollywood has been famously characterised as "an excessively obvious cinema" (Bordwell, Staiger, & Thompson, 1988: 3–11), one prepared to sacrifice almost anything to narrative clarity and coherence, and excessive obviousness, if it becomes an industry standard, will lead to the impression that any other cultural prioritisation is courting difficulty and/or sowing confusion. This is not the case. Films for children are now dubbed pretty well everywhere, as the cost of doing so is not prohibitive and the risk of stretching the as yet under-educated does not seem worth taking. But, in adult contexts, a degree of difficulty is a reasonable price we should be prepared to pay for encountering the world in *some* of its diversity. Wholly sub-titled movies in their original language(s) will continue to enjoy a following from what are largely educated elites; but partly sub-titled films can expect to receive a greater degree of acceptance as the world becomes increasingly more "wired" and this thing called globalisation marches on. The North Africa of *Casablanca* is clearly a studio mock-up compared to, say, the North Africa of *Raiders of the Lost Ark* (1981)—product "par excellence [of] the new style of the New Hollywood blockbuster" (Chapman & Cull, 2009, p. 169). But look at the distance that cinema has come from that adventure cartoon of the Kasbah to, say, the North Africa of *Babel*.

On the positive side, this new openness is not just about a seamless processing of the world for the monoglot hard of understanding. Bilingual and multilingual films do and will speak frankly to the communities that generate them and are so represented in them. These communities were formerly under-represented in national cinemas, but with the migration of peoples across the world it is becoming increasingly difficult to ignore the diversity in our midst. So, those of us who would like to see a more linguistically diverse cinema are merely asking and expecting cinema to register and reflect existing language interfaces, as *A Gaiola Dourada* and *Hijack Stories* do. This should not be commercial suicide. When justifying the unconscionable quantity of dollars thrown at the screen in respect of the so-called "realistic" CGI effects which are anything but, we are told film audiences increasingly need to see things they can believe in. What better way to do this than by showing our (often painfully shared) cultural and linguistic diversity as a theme. As *United 93*, *Battle for Haditha* and *Captain Phillips* show, it is much harder for damaging stereotypes to take root if you are frank about the form and nature of our differences.

References

Bordwell, D., Staiger, J., & Thompson, K. (1988). *The classical hollywood cinema: Film style and mode of production to 1960*. London: Routledge.

Brownlow, K. (1977). *David Lean*. London: Faber and Faber.

Campo, L. R., Brea, J. A. F., & Muniz, D. R. T. (2011). Tourist destination image formed by the cinema: Barcelona positioning through the feature film *Vicky Cristina Barcelona.*" *European Journal of Tourism, Hospitality and Recreation, 2*(1), 137–154.

Chapman, J., & Cull, N. J. (2009). *Projecting empire: Imperialism and popular cinema*. London: I.B. Taurus.

Custen, G. F. (1997). *Twentieth century's fox*. New York: Basic Books.

Holy Bible – International Version. (1984). East Brunswick. N.J.: International Bible Society.

Parker, J. (1993). *Polanski*. London: Victor Gollanc.

Skal, D. J. (1993). *The monster show: A cultural history of horror*. London: Plexus.

Thompson, K. (1985). *Exporting entertainment: America in the world film market 1907–1934*. London: British Film Institute.

Vasey, Ruth. (1997). *The world according to hollywood (1918–39)*. Taunton: University of Exeter Press.

Walker, Alexander. (1979). *The shattered silents: How the talkies came to stay*. New York: William Morrow and Co.

Author Biography

Anthony David Barker is an Associate Professor in the Department of Languages and Cultures at the University of Aveiro and the Coordinator of a Cultural Studies research group. He obtained a D.Phil at Oxford University in 18th-century literature and was Munby Fellow in Bibliography at Cambridge University. He was director of the Master course on Languages and Business and is director of the Doctoral Programme in Cultural Studies. He now teaches film, literary and cultural disciplines and publishes in these areas. Publications include collections on *Europe: Fact and Fictions* (2003) and *Stereotyping (2005)*, and articles on televisualising the 50s, Henry James on Film, the American and the British road movie, and British film and television comedy. He has edited a volume on *Television, Aesthetics and Reality* (2007) and another on *Success and Failure* (2009). Recent works include articles on zany film and television comedy, ultra-violence in the cinema of the 1970s and a book on *Identity and Cultural Exchange in Travel and Tourism* (2015). He is currently editing a volume of essays on the First World War.

Spaceflight as the (Trans)National Spectacle: Transforming Technological Sublime and Panoramic Realism in Early IMAX Space Films

Kornelia Boczkowska

Abstract In this paper I present and discuss the relationship between the techno-logical sublime, panoramic realism and American identity, as represented in some of the most remarkable space films produced by IMAX: *Hail Columbia* (1982), *The Dream Is Alive* (1985) and *Destiny in Space* (1994). While continuing the U.S. science documentary traditions of visualizing space-related concepts, the produc-tions depict the missions of NASA's Space Shuttle programme and its memorable moments, such as the first launch of Discovery or the crews' stay on the shuttle. Their form, best exemplified by the late 1970s and 1980s space science docu-mentaries, relied on a stunningly realist format and a mediated experience of the astronomical as well as technological and dynamic sublime, largely present in the U.S. and global space imagery. Particularly the latter concept, as developed by Marx (1964), Kasson (1976) or Nye (1994), is defined as a distinctively American formation and "an essentially religious feeling," which has become "self-justifying parts of a national destiny, just as the natural sublime once undergirded the rhetoric of manifest destiny" (Nye, 1994, pp. 13, 282). Simultaneously, however, whilst imbued with some typically American space-related values and conventions, including the frontier myth or White's Overview Effect, the IMAX films tend to perpetuate an intrinsically transnational and multicultural image of spaceflight through demythisizing the concept of American transcendental state centered around the idea of exceptionalism and destiny in space (Sage, 2014).

Keywords IMAX space films · Sublime · Technological sublime · Panoramic realism

K. Boczkowska (✉)
Wydział Anglistyki UAM, Adam Mickiewicz University, Al. Niepodległości 4, 61 874 Poznań, Poland
e-mail: kboczkowska@wa.amu.edu.pl

© Springer International Publishing AG 2017
J. Mydla et al. (eds.), *Multiculturalism, Multilingualism and the Self: Literature and Culture Studies*, Issues in Literature and Culture,
DOI 10.1007/978-3-319-61049-8_10

123

1   Introduction

The IMAX Corporation is widely credited with producing one of the first documentary films which literally brought the space shuttle experience down to Earth to millions of viewers through combining the dynamic sublime with the mundane routine. An in-depth coverage of spaceflight was plausible due to the use and convergence of new technologies, including the large-format projection, surround-sound system and 70 mm film cameras, some of which were accommodated inside the space shuttle during its mission. Similarly to other motion pictures, IMAX space films utilize a wide range of formal and stylistic traits, including an enlarged field of vision, mobility and steady camera movement, authenticity of mise-en-scene, shot scale, and voice-over narration (Margithazi, 2012, p. 150), which reintroduce "a technologically mediated form of tourist gaze" (Acland, 1998, p. 430). As a result, the footage yields a high-resolution as well as remarkably sharp, vivid and highly detailed imagery of unprecedented quality capable of stimulating an almost lifelike experience of space travel. Not surprisingly then, *The New York Times* film critic Canby (1987) called IMAX productions "the most viscerally exciting, mind-expanding movies being made today—the kind that provide windows on worlds previously undreamed of."

Hail Columbia (Ferguson, 1982), *The Dream Is Alive* (Ferguson, 1985) and *Destiny in Space* (Burtt and Ferguson, 1994), often referred to as early IMAX space films, originated from the cooperation between Michael Collins, the National Air and Space Museum's director, and founders of the company, who in 1976 provided an IMAX theatre for the newly opened museum. Being one of only six such venues in the United States, the theatre immediately became a popular tourist attraction in Washington D.C., where all major space films were premiered, including the aforementioned pictures, *Blue Planet* (Burtt, 1990), *Mission to Mir* (Galin, 1997), *Space Station 3D* (Myers, 2002), *Roving Mars* (Butler, 2006) or *Hubble 3D* (Myers, 2010). *Hail Columbia*, the first IMAX picture to feature the space shuttle mission, contained sequences filmed mostly on the ground, "culminating in a thunderous, bodyrattling launch shown repeatedly from various angles for maximum effect" (Neal, 2013, p. 150). Due to the unquestionable success of the documentary, the production of its successors, *The Dream Is Alive* and *Destiny in Space*, involved the collaboration between NASM, IMAX and NASA, the latter of which, despite not having interfered in the films' factual content, provided the fights and technical support in installing the IMAX equipment on board the shuttle. The organizations' joint efforts were committed to making the films an uplifting educational and artistic endeavour through introducing elements of "visual splendor, scenic beauty, humor, visceral excitement, … [and] excellent music" in an attempt to "optimize public enjoyment and the success of the film"[1] (as cited in Neal, 2013, p. 151).

---

[1]The latter citation originally comes from "A General Statement of Conditions and Proposed Letter of Agreement," SIA, Record Unit 338, Box 23, *Dream Is Alive* file.

2 The Sublime in American Space Imagery and IMAX Space Films

There is no denying that the majority of IMAX productions, known for utilizing the unique projection technology as well as the largest commercial film format in the history of motion pictures, are capable of filling the audience's peripheral vision (Cox, 2006, p. 616). The effect might extend and reinforce their experience of the cosmic and technological sublime, particularly when displaying interactions between an overwhelming man-made technology and an awe-inspiring extraterrestrial environment. The original concept of the sublime, as formulated by Burke ([1757] 1990), Kant ([1764] 2003), Schopenhauer (1909) or Gilpin (1792),[2] was successfully adopted in 20th century American space imagery, including space art, astrophotography, Hubble's deep space images or science documentary, which commonly envisioned the infinite and immense magnitude of the universe, reducing the viewer to a metaphysical dissolution and bringing a sudden realization of an inevitable transience of their own existence (Schopenhauer, 1909, p. 266). In one of her recent works, *Picturing the Cosmos: Hubble Space Telescope Images and the Astronomical Sublime*, Kessler (2012) comments more broadly on 20th century practices of representing space subjects in the U.S. culture where scientists and artists often utilize the mode of the sublime when translating complex data into a number of popular images depicting galaxies, nebulae or star fields. More specifically, she argues that rather than coming up with an entirely novel system of visualizing space, they have extended an existing one, inseparable with the idea of exploration and settlement, to subsequent stages of space exploration. This mode, used extensively in the last few decades, is that of the mythisized American frontier which has "functioned as the framework through which a new frontier was seen"

---

[2]A distinctively American tradition of depicting sublime qualities of grand and largely uncivilized natural scenery goes back to the 19th century Hudson River School movement. Some official landscape painters, including Thomas Moran, Frederick Church or Alfred Bierstadt, are all credited with creating vast canvas depicting yet undiscovered territories of the Niagara Falls, Yellowstone or Yosemite and thus familiarizing the American public with the magnificent views they were unable to eyewitness. The artists' practices were mostly in accordance with the main principles of American romanticism, which gave rise to the nationwide appreciation of deistic wilderness recognized as one of the principal constituents of national self-esteem (Nash, 1982, pp. 67–68). Therefore, among the most prominent characteristics of the movement was its preoccupation with the notion of romantic landscape, which stands in opposition to scientific empiricism and secularism of Western Europe and attempts to rediscover the presence of God and spirituality in nature. The two principal strands, which evolved in the course of the school's development, are pastoral elegiac and scientific exoticism, also inseparably connected with visualizing the sublime and the picturesque (Allen, 1992, p. 27). The depiction of the former aesthetic concept would often involve elements later identified with Romanticism, whose aim was to evoke the feelings of uncertainty, fear, horror and terror brought about by visualizing conditions, such as vastness and infinity, darkness and danger or solitude and pain. These and similarly boundless, horrifying or violent qualities of nature tend to agreeably terrorize the beholder and render them fearful, helpless, yet at the same time astonished and highly inspired by the power of nature (Arensberg, 1986, pp. 3–4).

(Kessler, 2012, p. 8). A similar view is expressed by Sage (2014) who, in the introduction to his recently published book, *How Outer Space Made America: Geography, Organization and the Cosmic Sublime*, investigates the way and reasons why the U.S. space programme reproduced the nation's geographical, cultural and political imagination by appealing to the image of America as the transcendental and sublime state. Sage (2014) claims that audiences exposed to the visions of outer space and space exploration, whether generated by space telescoped or popular media, are always confronted with a strong sense of sublime vastness and infinity:

> Those passionate about outer space have long been in awe of its apparent "spacelessness," outer space appears unbounded, infinite, sublime. When we see or think through Space, whether by looking at images produced by a powerful space telescope or enjoying a science-fiction film, we can journey in an instant to the most distant reaches of the universe, and simultaneously billions of years back in time, or into a barely imaginable future, far beyond the possibility of human life (p. 1.)

Meanwhile, in the wake of earlier scholarly discussions on the cosmic sublime, Lyotard (1994, pp. 53–54) suggests that the sublime of transcendence is sometimes replaced by the sublime of immanence. More specifically, he argues that humans' capability of feeling and imagining the cosmos constitutes the cause for sorrow as they realize the constraints of their own physical condition. In this way, the scholar challenges a largely positive vision of the sublime, stemming mostly from the vastness of space and limitless possibilities created by new space technologies, by noting that modern astrophysics also draws on evoking a negative sublime feeling by providing their audiences with painful and finite outer space experiences. Akin emotions may be evoked by the technological sublime, which transferred a sense of "awe and wonder often tinged with an element of terror" (Nye, 1994, p. xvi) from the natural environment to the technological achievements of the industrial revolution.

3   Technological Sublime

Originally proposed in Marx's famous work, *The Machine in the Garden* (1964), the concept of the technological sublime was ideally supposed to strive for the "middle landscape" through reconciling the machine with the pristine and pastoral wilderness. One of its earliest descriptions, however, was proposed by Charles Caldwell in the 1832 issue of the *New England Magazine* (as cited in Marx 1964):

> Objects of exalted power and grandeur elevate the mind that seriously dwells on them, and impart to it greater compass and strength. Alpine scenery and an embattled ocean deepen contemplation, and give their own sublimity to the conception of beholders. The same will be true of our system of Railroads. Its vastness and magnificence will prove communicable, and add to the standard of the intellect of the country (p. 195.)

Some more recent analyses of the technological sublime, the most notable of which include Nye's monograph, define the notion as a distinctively American formation and "an essentially religious feeling, aroused by the confrontation with impressive objects," which has become "self-justifying parts of a national destiny, just as the natural sublime once undergirded the rhetoric of manifest destiny" (Nye, 1994, pp. 13, 282). Both Nye (1994) and Noble (1999) suggest that the concept, seen in a close relation to a sense of national identity, is often indicative of a religious quest for morality, fulfillment, transcendence as well as scientific and spiritual development. Similarly, Serres and Latour (1995, p. 141) emphasize a quasi-religious dimension of the human relationship with technology: "Our god is the machine, the technical object, which stresses our mastery of our surroundings." In the context of space-related imagery, the technological sublime, often investigated through the lens of space launching sites, space rockets or supersonic space travel, seems to be founded on the idea that American national identity is intrinsically related to technological progress, in particular nuclear prowess and aerospace industry. As pointed out by Conway (2005),

> ... aerospace technology, as it did in Germany between the wars, has, and aided by the culture of nuclear fear that waxed and waned throughout the cold war, its promoters have relied heavily on the discursive strategy of linking aerospace technology to national defense and thus to national greatness. Aerospace technology is part of the "American technological sublime." Space-related accidents, the Apollo 204 fire, explosion of the Space Shuttle Challenger, and disintegration of the Space Shuttle Columbia, provoke periods of national mourning because they are highly public failures of one thing most Americans accept as part of the nation's identity (and destiny): its absolute superiority in aerospace technology (p. 13.)

Sage (2014) contributes to the discussion by stating that space and computing technologies instill faith in the U.S. leadership in 20th century space exploration ventures: "Project Apollo, NASA's technocratic triumph, was always bound up with something beyond itself: transcendental spaces and times which are far from calculable in technical abstractions—sublime mythologies of American exceptionalism." (p. 72) On the other hand, Simon (2003, p. 26) pinpoints that such majestic forms do indeed foster a sense of national unity, yet in most cases they appear to be not only largely incomprehensible or irrelevant for the masses, but also temporary, namely lasting for the duration of the spectacle itself. What is more, events or experiences associated with NASA's institutional, secular and technocratic culture should not be merely associated with gigantism, showiness and communal feelings, but also with privacy and individualistic values. Such an impression is to a large extent created in the analyzed material where, as put by Nye (1994, p. 77), technology does not "displace or conquer" the cosmic environment but rather intensifies its sublime qualities, functioning akin to electrification. Even through the very titles, the documentaries seem to draw on the nationwide conception of American transcendental state centered around the idea of exceptionalism and destiny in space. However, not only is the evocation and consumption of the technological sublime imbued with some typically American space-related values and conventions, including the frontier myth, but also it gives rise to a more personal experience of space travel through its numerous references to White's Overview Effect. Undoubtedly, all the productions are somewhat likely to reinforce Turner's frontier thesis[3] by depicting space exploration as a continuation of the Wild West expansion and Manifest Destiny[4] (Spiller, 2013):

> The space-age version of Turner's storyline became colloquial once again as NASA depicted the shuttle as a frontier workhorse and its future space station as a frontier outpost, a valuable scientific platform, gravity-free manufacturing center, and transit point for piloted missions to the moon and Mars. These depictions appeared across popular media and carried over into many new science and technology museums. The dream of home-steading that frontier was alive, the movie implied, because "some of our children will live in space, and their children may even be born there" (p. 68.)

On the other hand, the pictures' narrative and visual content seem to counteract an idealized image of the Apollo astronaut, commonly portrayed as a revered hero as well as a heroic, hard-working and non-conformist frontiersman (Kauffman, 1994, pp. 31–36). Largely in contrast to the astronaut myth, they successfully deliver and perpetuate a different representation of spacefarers, presented as living and working in Earth's orbit, as well as emphasize the value of teamwork over individual courage. Audiences are given the opportunity to witness a wide range of behind-the-scene activities and listen to astronauts' personal reflections on

---

[3]Originally formulated by Turner in his 1893 paper, "The Significance of the Frontier in American History" delivered to the American Historical Association in Chicago, the frontier thesis postulated that a distinctive character of American national identity and democracy was shaped by the frontier experience. The process of westward expansion had a considerable impact on the pioneers and settles whose personal qualities, including individualism, egalitarianism, determination, strength, independence, innovation, pragmatism, resourcefulness or inclination to use violence, evolved in the course of discovering and taming largely unknown and unexplored lands. Turner also elaborated on the U.S. frontier tradition as one of the most important factors which helped establish a new form of liberty distinct from the European, old, eroding and often dysfunctional socio-political system, and traced the birth of American democracy and institutions to social and economic conditions provided by frontier life of early pioneers. Predominantly, however, Turner's thesis is seen as an evolutionary model accounting for the impact of geographical space of the U.S. uncultivated and vast land on some unique characteristics of the American national identity formed precisely at the juncture between the uncivilized, savage wilderness and the civilized human settlements: "[T]he frontier is the outer edge of the wave—the meeting point between savagery and civilization" (Turner, 1893, p. 3).

[4]Originally coined by John O'Sullivan in 1845 to denote and advocate the U.S. annexation of Texas and the Oregon Country, the concept of manifest destiny refers to the nationwide ideology, which implied that American settlers were destined to explore and expand across the Western and North American territories. As proposed by historians (see e.g. Hietala, 1985; Merk and Merk, 1963; Tuveson, 1980; Weeks, 1996; Weinberg, 1935), the three basic themes pertaining to the idea are as follows: "(1) The special virtues of the American people and their institutions; (2) America's mission to redeem and remake the world in the image of America; and, (3) A divine destiny under God's direction to accomplish this wonderful task" (Miller, 2006, p. 120). Some of the chief social, political and cultural principles and movements underlying manifest destiny included American exceptionalism, Romantic nationalism, Turner's frontier thesis and Jacksonian democracy. Later, the phrase became associated with the U.S. territorial expansion between 1812 and 1860, also known as "the age of manifest destiny," during which the American nation succeeded to expand to the Pacific Ocean and thus largely define the present-day borders of the contiguous United States.

spaceflight dealing with the burdens of everyday routine. Some of these impressions referred to the Overview Effect, coined by White (1998, p. 4) and denoting "the predicted experience of astronauts and space settlers, who would have a different philosophical point of view as a result of having a physical perspective." The concept, usually seen as an intense and profound personal experience, captures the most essential qualities of space travel, which encompasses physiological, physical and psychological impact on human beings and whose practice might eventually lead to the emergence of global space ethos or development of deep ecological movement as well as transhumanist and bioethical thought. White (1998, pp. 15–26) argues that spaceflight experience should serve primarily awareness-increasing functions and provide the opportunity for an individual's spiritual development, the emergence of cosmic consciousness as well as a major transformation in global belief systems. The main idea behind the Overview Effect, now proliferating in space-related popular culture and often used in the promotion of space tourism, is to provide a sense of grand purpose of humanity's future space efforts and to mark the new beginning after the Challenger explosion (Bjornvig, 2013, p. 6). In line with such an ideology, IMAX films, two of which were produced before the disaster, appear to draw on the imagery strongly associated with the New Age[5] and environmentalism movements, which implied a holistic understanding of the world. For instance, the global rendering of Apollo 17's *Whole Earth*, defined as "an environmentalist conception that appeals to the organic and spiritual unity of terrestrial life" (Cosgrove, 1994, pp. 289–290) has been often employed in documentary films on space exploration and still tends to prevail in the popular mind. In IMAX pictures, the message is additionally reinforced by special techniques associated with cinematic spectacle and realist aesthetics based on a frequent use of aerial photography and camera-induced kinesis, which skillfully combine fact and sensation by providing an "optic onto the world and a roller-coaster ride for audiences" (Klinger, 2016, p. 992).

4 Some Sublime Cinematic Conventions in IMAX Space Films

In an attempt to enhance the aforementioned effect, *Hail Columbia*, *The Dream Is Alive* and *Destiny in Space* tend to draw on Bazin's myth of total cinema (1967) by employing an immersive aesthetics as well as a set of cinematic conventions based on gigantism and exaggerated realism. Images of launching sites, the crew working on the shuttle and outer space landscapes seem to utilize the sublime mode of

---

[5]The term New Age, often defined as a form of Western esotericism, denotes a broad cultural, philosophical and religious movement, which developed in Western nations in the 1960s and 1970s. Its practitioners held the belief in the coming of the Age of Aquarius, connoting either the present-day or upcoming astrological era that marked the beginning of a new spiritual awareness and collective consciousness (New Age, 2016).

representation and expose their audiences to both illuminating and terrifying experiences of the infinite universe and bewildering technology. Wasson (2007, p. 88) claims that by enacting a drama of scale, most IMAX productions make use of "extreme realism to emulate a full-body immersion rife with the anxiety integral to its enormity." Indeed, large-scale space technologies, including the rocket thrust or Shuttle launches capable of immense speeds, clearly draw on the Kantian dynamic and mathematical sublime in their sensual terror (Nye, 1994, p. 287). It may be further argued that through relying on the construction of cinema as travel (Acland, 1998; Acland & Wasson, 2011; Bruno, 2002), they tend to focus more on the spectacle of outer space and state-of-the-art technology as well as expose the experiential rather than narrational aspects of the actual plot (Bukatman, 2006, p. 77). In the era of "proliferating screens" (Straw, 2000), the screen itself functions both as an abstract and physical concept which links the spectator to the spectacle (Wasson, 2007, p. 99) and features the tropes of spectacular space travel, accentuated by slow, sweeping pans and atmospheric scores. The car window acts in a similar manner, exposing the viewers to wide, dynamic and two-dimensional panoramic views as well as providing them with a genuinely cinematic experience (Piek et al., 2011, p. 265). Acland (1998, p. 430) notes that through its wide use of travelling camera shots as well as strict adherence to a powerful form of film realism, "it is easy to mistake the IMAX screen for a wonderful, varying window on to real and imagined worlds." This theoretical approach has been broadly discussed within epistemology of the panoramic view, which examines the relation between travel and representation in the history of motion pictures (Crary, 1990; Friedberg, 1993; Shivelbusch, 1979; Baudrillard, 1988, etc.).

5 Panoramic Realism

In the context of IMAX widescreen cinema, the concept of panorama seems to be one of the most crucial factors, which determines, reformulates and facilitates the viewing experience in the medium associated primarily with the realistic effect of immersion. The term itself, denoting a wide-angle view or representation of a given physical space, stems from the Greek words "pan" (all) and "orama" (sight). Originally known as "La nature a coup d'oeil" (nature at a glance), the panorama was invented by the English painter Robert Barker to describe his panoramic canvasses of Edinburgh and London exhibited on a cylindrical surface. Meanwhile, the name itself was first used in 1791 in reference to circular panoramic paintings, which gave the illusion of unrestricted perspective and enabled the spectator to experience an almost infinite field of vision (Verhoeff, 2012, p. 36). Barker's invention, often considered the forerunner to the moving panorama and early cinema's phantom rides, did not only become one of the first commercially successful forms of visual entertainment and a predominant model for 19th and 20th century landscape representations, but it also gave rise to some key concepts and conventions used in more contemporary media. Some of them referred to the new modes of viewing, termed monologic (perspective, voyeuristic and panoptic gaze) and dialogic, the latter of which is usually defined as a more immersive, engaged and bodily way of looking (Verhoeff, 2012, pp. 42–44). It is particularly the panoptic gaze, however, that is seen as deriving from and alleviating the widespread use of the major framing devices in IMAX, namely the natural and technological sublime as well as the idea of virtual travel (Griffiths, 2013):

> The panoptic gaze, made prominent by Michel Foucault in *Discipline and Punish* (1975), is another variety of monologic viewing that implies appropriation. Here, with regard to the corporeal, the spectator remains less bodily engaged than in voyeurism. However, this gaze demands—just as with panoramic painting—a mobility of the body (turning around), albeit not for the looker's own exhilaration, as with voyeurism, but to exercise a restrictive power over the objects seen (p. 43.)

The monologic gaze is quite evidently interrelated with other early and contemporary film genres and conventions, often exploiting the panoramic representations through various forms of tourist or mobilized virtual gaze (Friedberg, 1993). As argued by Griffiths (2013, p. 95), IMAX can be described as "an eclectic derivative of a cluster of pre-cinematic entertainments," such as Gothic cathedrals, medieval tapestries, panoramic landscape paintings, moving panoramas, planetarium, Cinerama and CinemaScope or the present-day 360° Internet-distributed technologies, which all provide their viewers with haptic and highly immersive travel experiences. These and related generic inspirations not only attest to IMAX's complex legacy, but they also situate it within an ongoing discussion of cinema seen through the lens of virtual travel and armchair tourism, whose aesthetic agenda may be reminiscent of travelogue conventions traditionally associated with phantom rides. In line with some of this early genre's visual tropes, many productions are based on the viewer-as-passenger schema (Musser, 1991), which intensifies sensual illusions produced by an almost palpable spectacle of motion and dramatizes the act of visual appreciation by evoking "the uncanny effect of ghostly movement" (Gunning, 2010, p. 55). Similarly, the analyzed space films' use of the travelogue format, which lies at the core of numerous IMAX productions (Beeton, 2015: 50), is also more of a contemplative nature, which might be partly attributed to their employment of panoramic realism, defined by Acland (1998, p. 430) as the spectatorial mode of perception enacted by IMAX audiences, who become immersed into cinematic space or, more literally, the panoptic field of the screen. Hence, rather than of the hyper-real "ride-film" (cf. Acland, 1998; Rabinovitz, 1998), the conceptualization of travel and simulation of motion appear to heavily rely on the technological sublime, which conveys the sense of both reflective and captivating journey. As pointed out by Wasson (2007, p. 88), IMAX "reenacts the moment of our encounter with Burke's sublime, the threat and promise of overtaking us compels us to look and also to be fearful less of what we will see but how we will feel when we see it." In this sense, the analyzed space films, which quite evidently tend to marvel at the power of technology to dominate and master awe-inspiring and sometimes destructive qualities of nature, can be interpreted not only as an extension of the technological sublime, but also as a source of meditative aesthetic experiences, largely induced by slow pans and likely to give rise to a terrorizing sense of anticipation and dread. Therefore, such an illuminating and terrifying appeal of the natural and manmade elements featured in the pictures, additionally enhanced by the auditory sublime (Supper, 2014), helps create suspenseful, panoramic spectacles rather than challenges the audiences' assimilation abilities.

6 Spaceflight as the (Trans)National Spectacle

As implied above, all the pictures, whether seen on a cinema screen or a computer monitor, are clearly positioned in discourses of virtual tourism, which allow its audiences to encounter breathtaking and authentic-like images of natural and technological wonders. This particular tradition also coincides with IMAX's legacy as a museum-based resource and thus a largely didactic purpose of its production, which has been designed primarily for the educational market (Griffiths, 2013):

> Traditional nature-documentary Imax films are expository texts that, while not conforming exactly to John Grierson's vision of documentary film as an art/propaganda symbiosis which inculcates heightened social awareness and civic responsibility in the viewer, nevertheless contain a didactic element befitting the school-group audience … (p. 96.)

In the analyzed material, the IMAX technologies of visualization, in particular spectatorial primacy seen as a form of knowledge (Acland, 1998, p. 434), promote ideas traditionally associated with space education. More specifically, the films' panoramic realism perpetuates an intrinsically transnational and multicultural image of spaceflight through demythisizing the concept of American transcendental state centered around the idea of exceptionalism and destiny in space (Sage, 2014). Some late 20th century popular culture representations of space endeavours are likely to reinforce and promulgate the recently re-emergent and re-discovered spirit of Cosmism (Harrison, 2013) and space ethos (Harris, 1992), particularly due to the efforts of space advocacy groups, such as the National Space Society or the Planetary Society, which successfully deliver various pro-space messages to the American public. Also the IMAX depiction of a highly profitable Shuttle program, then perceived as a routine, low-cost and low-risk venture, has altered the image of space exploration by encompassing multinational and multicultural perspectives within its narration as well as targeting ordinary audiences. The film company itself, often considered an emblem of transnational culture (Acland, 1998, p. 440), is credited with producing the first realistic, in-depth treatment of the subject of space exploration and featuring astronauts as the actual cinematographers (Neal, 2013):

> The films presented the new norm of men and women, Americans and other nationalities, working together companionably in space. Interesting as their daily routines and challenges were, their own words were even more captivating. … Personalities and perspectives gave audiences new insight into the spaceflight experience and perhaps into commonalities that enabled viewers to think "they could be me." The shuttle era had been heralded as the age

when spaceflight might become possible for ordinary people. Although actual flights of nonastronauts were few, through the IMAX films, millions of ordinary people "went" into space. And still do. Viewers now enjoy the IMAX spacefaring films in the comfort of home on a flat screen television or computer monitor via high-definition DVDs with Dolby digital sound ... (p. 165.)

Also the accompanying computer-generated special effects along with some vivid and highly immersive high-resolution imagery, particularly numerous shots of Earth from space indicative of a moral message of environmentalism-related ideology, contribute to demythisizing the transcendental state, seen as an embodiment of American geopower. Moreover, by giving viewers an illusion of witnessing extraterrestrial scenery and spacecraft technology through the crews' eyes, they create a thrilling sense of proximity to the events featured throughout the film, thus rendering the spaceflight experience personal rather than collective. Again, the effect is achieved by the use of dizzying heights, hyper-presence and sensation of rapid movement (Acland, 1998, p. 435), which only attests to the fact that IMAX's massive screen amplifies a captivating mode of travel and acts as a window through uniting the technological sublime with panoramic realism and the sublime of mobilized landscape (Perry, 1998, p. 168). What is more, the films' ability to stimulate a profoundly palpable impression in the viewers may lay foundations for the so called embodied film spectatorship, also known as haptic visuality (Marks, 2000). The concept, located within the cinema of attractions (Gunning, 1986), is usually defined as a sensual experience or bodily perception of a filmed subject and, as explained by Sobchack (2004, pp. 67–68), is founded on the two related terms, synaesthesia and coenaesthesia. While the former notion stands for an involuntary, immediate, concrete and meaningful cinematic experience strictly dependent on the spectator's perception of a diegetic sound as colour, shape or taste, the latter refers to "the perception of one's whole bodily state as the sum of its somatic perceptions" (Sobchack, 2004, pp. 67–68). Taking such an assumption, it may be argued that the pictures' excessive audiovisual appeal only enhance an active and embodied mode of spectatorship as they invite the audience to sensually follow a projected scene and might even evoke a physical response.

7 Conclusion

The conducted analysis has suggested that IMAX space films' visual and narrative content tends to rely on a hyperrealist format and a mediated experience of the astronomical and technological sublime, largely present in the U.S. and global space imagery. Interestingly, the latter concepts, evoked partly due to IMAX's travelling camera and massive screen, are not only essential in constructing multiple panoramic views based on the concept of total cinema, but they also help portray spaceflight as the (trans)national spectacle. In particular, the sublime mode of representation, although traditionally embedded in the rhetoric of manifest destiny, also reinforces a mundane and multicultural image of space exploration through its explicit or implicit allusions to virtual tourism as well as environmentalism- and cosmism-related ideas. The sublime mythologies of American exceptionalism are thus quite evidently interrelated with or even overshadowed by a highly captivating cinematic experience of panoramic space travel, which enacts large-scale spectacles of extraterrestrial landscapes and engulfing technology and gives global audiences a new insight into commonalities of the spaceflight experience.

References

Acland, Ch. (1998). IMAX technology and the tourist gaze. *Cultural Studies, 12*(3), 429–445. doi:10.1080/095023898335492

Acland, Ch., & Wasson, H. (Eds.). (2011). *Useful cinema.* Durham, NC: Duke University Press.

Aitken, I. (2006). *Encyclopedia of the documentary film 3-volume set.* London, England: Routledge.

Allen, J. (1992). Horizons of the sublime: The invention of the romantic west. *Journal of Historical Geography, 18*(1), 27–40. doi:10.1016/0305-7488(92)90274-D

Arensberg, M. (Ed.). (1986). *American sublime.* New York, NY: State University of New York Press.

Baudrillard, J. (1988). *America* (Ch. Turner, Trans.). New York, NY: Verso.

Bazin, A. (1967). *The myth of total cinema in What is cinema* (A. Bazin & H. Gray, Trans.). (pp. 17–22). London, England: University of California Press.

Beeton, S. (2015). *Travel, tourism and the moving image.* Bristol, England: Channel View Publications.

Bjornvig, T. (2013). Outer space religion and the overview effect: A critical enquiry into a classic of the pro-space movement. *Astropolitics: The International Journal of Space Politics & Policy, 11*(1–2), 4–24. doi:10.1080/14777622.2013.801718

Bruno, G. (2002). *Atlas of emotion: Journeys in art, architecture, and film.* New York, NY: Verso.

Bukatman, S. (2006). Spectacle, attractions and visual pleasure. In W. Strauven (Ed.), *The cinema of attractions reloaded* (pp. 71–81). Amsterdam, Holland: Amsterdam University Press.

Burke, E. (1990). *A philosophical enquiry into the origin of our ideas of the sublime and beautiful.* Oxford, England: Oxford University Press.

Burtt, B. (Director). (1990). *Blue planet* [Motion picture]. United States: Imax.

Burtt, B., & Ferguson, P. (Director). (1994). *Destiny in space* [Motion picture]. United States: Imax.

Butler, G. (Director). (2006). *Roving Mars* [Motion picture]. United States: Imax.

Caldwell, Ch. (1832, April 4). Thoughts on the moral and other indirect influences of rail-roads. *The New-England magazine 2.* Retrieved from http://worldlibrary.org/

Canby, V. (1987, April 19). Big screen takes on new meaning. *New York Times.* Retrieved from http://www.nytimes.com/

Cosgrove, D. (1994). Contested global visions: One world, whole earth and the Apollo space photographs. *Annals of the Association of American Geographers, 84,* 270–294. doi:10.1111/j.1467-8306.1994.tb01738.x

Conway, E. (2005). *High-speed dreams: NASA and the technopolitics of supersonic transportation, 1945–1999.* Baltimore, MD: The Johns Hopkins University Press.

Cox, K. (2006). Imax. In I. Aitken (Ed.), *Encyclopedia of the documentary film 3-volume set* (p. 616). London, England: Routledge.

Crary, J. (1990). *Techniques of the observer. On vision and modernity in the nineteenth century.* Cambridge, MA: MIT Press.

Ferguson, G. (Director). (1982). *Hail Columbia!* [Motion picture]. United States: Imax.

Ferguson, G. (Director). (1985). *The dream is alive* [Motion picture]. United States: Imax.

Foucault, M. (1975). *Surveiller et punir*. Paris: Gallimard.

Friedberg, A. (1993). *Window shopping: Cinema and the postmodern*. Berkeley, CA: University of California Press.

Galin, I. (Director). (1997). *Mission to Mir* [Motion picture]. United States: Imax.

Gilpin, W. (1792). *Three essays: on picturesque beauty; on picturesque travel; and on sketching landscape: to which is added a poem, on landscape painting*. London, England: Printed for R. Blamire.

Griffiths, A. (2013). *Shivers down your spine: Cinema, museums, and the immersive view*. New York, NY: Columbia University Press.

Gunning, T. (1986). The cinema of attractions: Early film, its spectator and the avant-garde. *Wide angle, 8*(3–4), 63–70. Retrieved from http://www.columbia.edu/itc/film/gaines/historiography/Gunning.pdf

Gunning, T. (2010). Landscape and the fantasy of moving pictures: Early cinema's phantom rides. In G. Harper & J. Rayner (Eds.), *Cinema and landscape* (pp. 31–70). Bristol, England: Intellect.

Harris, P. (1992). *Living and working in space: Human behavior, culture and organization*. New York, NY: Ellis Horwood.

Harrison, A. (2013). Russian and American cosmism: religion, national psyche, and spaceflight. *Astropolitics: The International Journal of Space Politics & Policy, 11*(1–2), 25–44. doi:10.1080/14777622.2013.801719

Hietala, T. (1985). *Manifest design: anxious aggrandizement in late Jacksonian America*. Ithaca, NY: Cornell University Press.

Kant, I. (2003). *Observations on the feeling of the beautiful and sublime* (J. T. Goldthwaite, Trans.). Berkeley, CA: University of California Press.

Kasson, J. (1976). *Civilizing the machine: Technology and republican values in America, 1776–1900*. New York, NY: Grossman Publishers.

Kauffman, J. (1994). *Selling outer space: Kennedy, the media, and funding for project apollo, 1961–1963*. Tuscaloosa, AL: University of Alabama Press.

Kessler, E. (2012). *Picturing the cosmos. hubble space telescope images and the astronomical sublime*. Minneapolis, MN: University of Minnesota Press.

Klinger, B. (2016). Cave of forgotten dreams: meditations on 3D. In J. Kahana (Ed.), *The documentary film reader: History, theory, criticism* (pp. 989–996). Oxford, England: Oxford University Press.

Margithazi, B. (2012). See more, think big: The IMAX brand before and after the digital remastering. In Á. Pethő (Ed.), *Film in the post-media age* (pp. 143–160). Cambridge, England: Cambridge Scholars Publishing.

Marks, L. (2000). *The skin of the film: Intercultural cinema, embodiment, and the senses*. Durham, NC: Duke University Press.

Marx, L. (1964). *The machine in the garden: Technology and the pastoral ideal in America*. Oxford, England: Oxford University Press.

Merk, F., & Merk, L. (1963). *Manifest destiny and mission in American history: A reinterpretation*. New York, NY: Knopf.

Miller, R. (2006). *Native America, discovered and conquered: Thomas Jefferson, Lewis & Clark, and manifest destiny*. Westport, CT: Greenwood Publishing Group.

Musser, Ch. (1991). *Before the Nickelodeon: Edwin S. Porter and the edison manufacturing company*. Berkeley, CA: University of California Press.

Myers, T. (Director). (2002). *Space Station 3D* [Motion picture]. United States: Imax.

Myers, T. (Director). (2010). *Hubble 3D* [Motion picture]. United States: Imax.

Nash, R. (1982). *Wilderness and the American mind*. Haven, CT: Yale University Press.

Neal, V. (2013). Bringing spaceflight down to earth: Astronauts and the IMAX experience. In M. J. Neufeld (Ed.), *Spacefarers: Images of astronauts and cosmonauts in the heroic era of spaceflight* (pp. 149–174). Washington DC: Smithsonian Institution Scholarly Press.

New Age. (2016). In *Encyclopaedia Britannica*. Retrieved from http://www.britannica.com/EBchecked/topic/704347/New-Age-movement

Nye, D. (1994). *American technological sublime*. Cambridge, CA: MIT Press.

Noble, D. (1999). *The religion of technology*. New York, NY: Penguin.

Lyotard, J. F. (1994). *Lessons on the analytic of the sublime* (E. Rottenberg, Trans.). Stanford, CA: Stanford University Press.

O'Sullivan, J. (1845). Annexation. *United States Magazine and Democratic Review, 17*(1), 5–11. Retrieved from http://web.grinnell.edu/courses/HIS/f01/HIS202-01/Documents/OSullivan.html

Perry, N. (1998). *Hyperreality and global culture*. New York, NY: Routledge.

Piek, M., Sorel, N., & van Middelkoop, M. (2011). Preserving panoramic views along motorways through policy. In S. Nijhuis, R. van Lammeren, & F. van der Hoeven (Eds.), *Exploring the visual landscape: Advances in physiognomic landscape research in the Netherlands* (pp. 261–302). Amsterdam, Holland: IOS Press.

Rabinovitz, L. (1998). From Hal's tours to star tours: Virtual voyagers and the delirium of the hyper-real. *Iris, 25*, 133–152.

Sage, D. (2014). *How outer space made America: Geography, organization and the cosmic sublime*. Farnham, VA: Ashgate.

Schopenhauer, A. (1909). *The world as will and representation. Vol. 1* (R. B. Haldane & J. Kemp, Trans.). London, England: Kegan Paul, Trench, Trübner & Co.

Shivelbusch, W. (1979). *The railway journey: Trains and travel in the nineteenth century* (A. Hollo, Trans.). New York, NY: Urizen Books.

Serres, M., & Latour, B. (1995). *Conversations on science, culture, and time*. Ann Arbor, MI: University of Michigan Press.

Simon, Z. (2003). *The double-edged sword: The technological sublime in American novels between 1900 and 1940*. Budapest, Hungary: Akademiai Kiado.

Sobchack, V. (2004). *Carnal thoughts: Embodiment and moving image culture*. Berkeley, CA: University of California Press.

Spiller, J. (2013). Nostalgia for the right stuff: Astronauts and public anxiety about a changing nation. In M. J. Neufeld (Ed.), *Spacefarers: Images of astronauts and cosmonauts in the heroic era of spaceflight* (pp. 57–80). Washington, DC: Smithsonian Institution Scholarly Press.

Straw, W. (2000). Proliferating screens. *Screen, 41*(1), 115–119. doi:10.1093/screen/41.1.115

Supper, A. (2014). Sublime frequencies: The construction of sublime listening experiences in the sonification of scientific data. *Social Studies of Science, 44*(1), 34–58. doi:10.1177/0306312713496875

Turner, F. (1893, July 12). *The significance of the frontier in American history*. Paper presented at the American Historical Association, Chicago. Retrieved from http://xroads.virginia.edu/~hyper/turner/chapter1.html

Tuveson, E. (1980). *Redeemer nation: The idea of America's millennial role*. Chicago, IL: University of Chicago Press.

Verhoeff, N. (2012). *Mobile screens. The visual regime of navigation*. Amsterdam, Holland: Amsterdam University Press.

Wasson, H. (2007). The networked screen: Moving images, materiality, and the aesthetics of size. In J. Marchessault & S. Lord (Eds.), *Fluid screens, expanded cinema* (pp. 69–106). Toronto, Canada: University of Toronto Press.

Week, W. (1996). *Building the continental empire: American expansion from the revolution to the civil War*. Chicago, IL: Ivan R. Dee.

Weinberg, A. (1935). *Manifest destiny: A study of nationalist expansionism in American history.* Baltimore, MD: The Johns Hopkins Press.

White, F. (1998). *The overview effect. Space exploration and human evolution.* Reston, VA: American Institute of Aeronautics and Astronautics Inc.

Author Biography

Kornelia Boczkowska is a senior lecturer at the Faculty of English, Adam Mickiewicz University in Poznań. She holds a PhD in English (2015) with a specialization in American culture studies, and an MA in Russian (2010) and English (2011). Her research interests and publications focus on American experimental cinema as well as selected aspects of American and Russian astroculture in the context of visual, popular culture and film studies. Her current research is on the development of space science documentary and the representation of natural and urban landscape in American experimental documentary film.

Multiculturalism in Video Game Studies: An Inquiry into the Current Research and Perspectives for Study

Agnieszka Kliś-Brodowska

Abstract The following chapter surveys a number of ways in which video games may be studied from the perspective of multiculturalism in a way that benefits both video game studies and studies in multiculturalism. It strives to locate the multi-cultural perspective of study with regard to the general field of video games research, stressing the cultural status of video games and the centrality of the notion of multiculturalism to their functioning. It familiarises the reader with an existing model for studying video games with cultural diversity in mind, and provides a brief review of two important sources that provide information on the current state of video game research: *The Routledge Companion to Video Game Studies* and a selection of texts from DiGRA's digital library. In so doing it strives to highlight both the diversity of perspectives already taken on the multicultural aspect of games and their functioning in culture, and the pressing need for further research.

Keywords Video games · Multiculturalism · Diversity · Video game studies

> Stated simply, games are culture. Chutes and Ladders is not just a children's playtime activity, but a cultural document with a rich history, designed to express a religious doctrine of a particular time and place. The Sims is not merely a simulation of suburbia, but a representation of cultural interaction that relies on an ideological reality located beyond the scope of actual game play . . . Just as any game can be framed in terms of their formal or experiential qualities, they can also be framed according to their status as cultural objects. (Salen & Zimmerman, 2004, p. 507)

A. Kliś-Brodowska (✉)
Institute of English Cultures and Literatures, University of Silesia,
ul. Grota-Roweckiego 5, 41-205 Sosnowiec, Poland
e-mail: agnieszka.klis@us.edu.pl

© Springer International Publishing AG 2017
J. Mydla et al. (eds.), *Multiculturalism, Multilingualism and the Self: Literature and Culture Studies*, Issues in Literature and Culture,
DOI 10.1007/978-3-319-61049-8_11

139

1 Introduction

No matter whether they are labeled as serious, indie or commercial,[1] games may and do raise serious questions, that of multiculturalism included. One thinks, for example, of a non-digital games series by Brenda Romero (formerly Brathwaite), *Mechanics is the Message*. The series is a project consisting of six board games, each deigned to engage the player with a difficult cultural topic. Of these, for example *Train* (2009) is dedicated to the atrocities of the Holocaust, while *The New World* (2008) was originally designed to help Romero's daughter, Maezza, grasp the meaning of the Middle Passage (Romero, 2011). Also, there is the series of the *Assassin's Creed* games: each of them begins with a statement that it was developed by "a multicultural team of various religious faiths and beliefs" (see e.g. Ubisoft Montreal, 2007) which, in *Assassin's Creed: Syndicate*, changes into "a multicultural team of various beliefs, sexual orientations and gender identities" (Ubisoft Quebec, 2015). Or, consider Tauriq Moosa's (2015) article "Colourblind," published at Polygon, in which he uses *The Witcher 3: Wild Hunt*, an AAA game, to address the issues of whitewashing in video games and colorblindness in game reviews; or the response written by Dave Bleja (2015), an Australian of Polish origin, posted at *Gamasutra*, in which Bleja argues against Moosa's perspective on the game as lacking diversity by stressing its promotion of Slavic ethnicity and culture.

The following article surveys a variety of ways in which studying video games from the perspective of multiculturalism proves a worthwhile effort. It is, however, by no means to be seen as a comprehensive, conclusive, or in any way complete overview of the field. It started off as an attempt to answer the question about the extent to which games studies address issues that have to do with multiculturalism nowadays, and, as such, constitutes only a preliminary study, which certainly requires—and deserves—further elaboration. The major idea behind choosing the sources was to juxtapose more comprehensive accounts with individual texts of a narrower focus, in order to provide a brief glance at both the general and the particular. Still, the scope of materials can be certainly extended by listing other valuable, perhaps more canonical resources and perspectives. As a result, this article may serve as a possible vantage point for further discussion. While it devotes much attention to game studies, the insight into games research it provides makes it clear that video games constitute a fruitful field of interest for multiculturalism as well.

2 Video Games as Multicultural Phenomena and Video Game Studies

Multiculturalism infuses video games on multiple levels, by no means restricted to their audio-visual contents. In the following section the basic focus is on how cultural contexts impact both internal and external game environments, and how

---

[1]For a discussion of serious games see e.g. Bogost (2007, pp. 54–59).

games as cultural artefacts generate spaces for further influence. In other words, we shall adopt the view that games are inescapably, "indisputably culture," to repeat after Salen and Zimmerman (2004, p. 512), in the sense that culture engulfs and crisscrosses the "magic circle" they provide, and the influences thus created have their further resonance in extra-game spaces.

Salen and Zimmerman make it clear that culture is always at the foundation of games, be they digital or not. As they note, "[g]ames are embedded in lifestyles, media, ideologies, histories, and a range of social contexts" (2004, p. 512). This, however, makes games not simply *cultural* objects. If we take the very basic definition of a multicultural society seen as "a society—a state, a nation, a country, a region or even simply a bounded geographical location ... composed of people who belong to different cultures" (Watson, 2000, pp. 2–3), including those of minorities and underprivileged groups (Watson, 2000, p. 6), then video games may be seen as almost naturally preconditioned to be *multi*cultural. They often constitute and generate delimited (in a physical and non-physical sense) internal as well as external spaces of interaction between various nationalities, races, ethnicities, genders, sexualities, religious beliefs, ages and classes. Sometimes, this variety manifests itself explicitly, with a resulting clash upon facing cultural barriers, as it may happen in Massively Multiplayer Online Games (MMOGs) (see e.g. always_black, 2006); and sometimes implicitly, for example when a game takes us on a journey through gendered spaces (see e.g. Jenkins, 2006). In a way, games' ubiquity and dispersion—even though this dispersion is perhaps more limited than one might imagine—guarantee diversity. Certainly, with their widespread accessibility, ability to go online, global fandom, world-wide marketing, or the adoption of a distributed production model of software (Kerr, 2010, p. 8), video games tend to undo certain boundaries—a matter worth studying as such—as much as lead to encounters. Simultaneously, they are strongly tied to cultural contexts and may testify to existing disparities on various levels. The problems they pose for localization as much as the fact that they often appear strangely uniform as far as representation is concerned are but a proof of that.

To discuss the ways in which studying the intersections between video games and multiculturalism benefits both game studies and multicultural inquiry, it is useful to adopt a particular understanding of video games. The term is used in this chapter in a general sense, following the approach taken by Bogost (2006, p. xiii), and thus encompassing various types of digital artefacts played on and created for different kinds of platforms. There are available more detailed, formal definitions (see e.g. Juul, 2003); still, once we approach games with multiculturalism in mind, a broad definition turns out to be more workable—and revealing. Formal (or formalist) definitions are useful in pinpointing qualities that make games stand out against other media; they also help to illuminate the need for a separate field of study (or research) and more game-specific methodologies (Frasca, 1999; Aarseth, 2001).

Still, they are unavoidably exclusive, and multiculturalism (as much as culture as such) is often tied to what they discard as not inherent in games.[2]

What may or may not count as a "part of" a video game is one vital question that we need to address while approaching video games as multicultural phenomena. The question of the place of multicultural inquiry in the field of game studies is another one. For example, Mäyrä (2008), one of the founding fathers of the Digital Game Research Association (DiGRA), defines the discipline of game studies[3] as the study of video games, players, and the contexts of both (p. 2). The context is further explained as "a more general concept that includes multiple frames of reference, and thus also multiple possible realities" (Mäyrä, 2008, p. 2). Such a framework appears particularly promising for multicultural inquiry. Broadly speaking, multi-culturalism resides in all the areas Mäyrä mentions, which makes it a strikingly central matter. However, as in the case definitions, different frameworks for game studies will locate its relevance differently depending on their aim and on the premises they adopt.

Certain frameworks for game studies appear to be inherently problematic when it comes to extending the scope for research to culture. Taylor (2006), in her study of *EverQuest* MMOG player community,[4] notes a persistent drive to reconstitute a boundary between the game and the real life, rooted in the concept of the "magic circle" derived from the work on play by Johan Huizinga.[5] While she admits that the concept is useful in illuminating some aspects of games, she highlight that it

---

[2]As Frasca (2003a) notes, "[c]ertainly, formal approaches are limited—and ludologists should always keep that in mind—but they are probably the easiest way to uncover the structural differences between stories and games. I personally see this structural approach as a first, necessary step in game studies, which we will definitively outgrow once it helps us to better grasp the basic characteristics of games" (p. 222). For a discussion of the shortcomings of a formalist approach to games see e.g. Jenkins (2006), Warnes (2005), Pearce (2005), or Bogost (2009). For the benefits of narratological approaches, see e.g. Ryan (2001). For a critical overview of the so-called ludology vs narratology debate, see e.g. Bogost (2006, pp. 66–71); Bogost (2006) also discusses what he terms "functionalist separatism" in approaches to studying games, which he views as a result of early attempts at separating video games scholarship from literary studies (pp. 52–54). For a polemical response to those stances, see Aarseth (2014, pp. 185–189). For Fransca's own comment on the debate, see Frasca (2003b).

[3]It is debatable whether the discipline game studies actually exists, has any chances of coming into being, or is, in fact, necessary. This, however, does not prevent multidisciplinary research from flourishing, the result of which is a continuing formation of a body of knowledge. See e.g. Aarseth (2015), or Mäyrä, Van Looy, and Quandt (2013).

[4]Interestingly, Taylor also points to the problematic status of MMOGs viewed from the perspective of game definition, and hence the possibility of viewing her own study as falling outside the limits of games research. However, as he writes, this points to the problems inherent in the definition itself, noting that "[t]here still seems to me something at stake in whether or not we bestow on MMOGs the label 'game'" (p. 153).

[5]Huizinga writes in *Homo Ludens*, published in 1955: "A second characteristic [of play] is … that play is not 'ordinary' or 'real' life. It is rather a stepping out of 'real' life into a temporary sphere of activity with a disposition all of its own. Every child knows perfectly well that he is 'only pretending', or that it was 'only for fun'" (2006, p. 103). For a polemical discussion of video games as only fun, see Bogost (2006, pp. 112–127).

tends to obscure the on-going, messy interplay between the two worlds, real and virtual, and aptly pinpoints the possible implicit agenda behind speaking of games as necessarily removed from everyday reality: "solving the deeper social and regulatory issues that can nag us" (2006, p. 151).

A similar problem might be traced in Mäyrä's aforementioned account. Games culture is here introduced as a key concept. Mäyrä's major focus is, however, the question of how video games generate meaning, and, indeed the definition of culture he adopts is that of "*a system of meaning*" (2008, p. 14). Such a focus allows for linking games with music or dance by stressing the aspect of non-linguistic meaning-making, and serves to better illuminate the specific character of games as residing in interaction and performance (Mäyrä, 2008, p. 14). Placing the stress on what makes video games stand out against related phenomena such as literature or film, Mäyrä (2008) distinguishes between the "core" components of the game, that is rules and gameplay, as opposed to "shell" features, comprising the audio-visual, representative, semiotic layer. Although he stresses that both "core" and "shell" are "the structural key elements of a game" (p. 17), his framework nevertheless introduces a significant hierarchy: video games are "interactive cultural systems," however "with a specific emphasis on *meaning-making through playful action* (*ludosis*), as contrasted with meaning-making as decoding of messages or media representations (*semiosis*), typical for such cultural systems as television shows or contemporary poetry" (p. 19). Mäyrä does stress that meaning can never be entirely absolute, or non-referential, and that games as systems necessarily derive their significance from culture in which they are embedded (2008, pp. 18–19). However, relying on a hierarchical definition of games, his framework risks being significantly limiting. Although cultural values and assumptions are reflected so in the "core" as in the"shell,"[6] representation is in fact crucial to the investigation of many questions that video games raise, including multiculturalism, while introducing the hierarchy of elements more and less inherent in the medium[7] may serve, in extreme cases, as a basis for diminishing the importance of findings.

In the above model, much stress is put on games culture understood as a culture formed around games. Hence, Mäyrä devotes much of his attention to the status of games with regard to the discourse of high art (2008, p. 22), and the notion of games cultures as subcultures, where players are compared to different religious or ethnic groups found in a contemporary Western metropolis (p. 25). As a result, further subdivisions are discussed here primarily in terms of hardcore and casual gamers (pp. 26–28). Clearly, video games do have a potential to generate cultures based on shared identity, artefacts, practices, etc. However, highlighting this aspect without simultaneously acknowledging various cultures that are brought into games

---

[6]While game rules, or gameplay, may seem autonomous, Mäyrä himself notes that gameplay is regulated by internal as much as external, socio-cultural rules (p. 19), while Salen and Zimmerman emphasize that "the internal structures of a game—rules, forms of interaction, material forms—mirror external ideological contexts" (p. 516).

[7]On the "tiered" approach to video game components, see Bogost (2009).

by players, or incorporated by designers, may leave us with a view of culture as still a rather homogenous, unifying system.[8]

To be sure, Mäyrä's model makes room for an inquiry into the question of video game multiculturalism. However, the perspective adopted requires such an inquiry to be located under a broader heading of anthropological or cultural studies, where it remains only implied (Mäyrä, 2008, pp. 23–24). Thus, despite the stress put on the cultural embedment of games, what is brought into games from the outside remains vague, and the ways in which games reproduce their cultural background may escape attention. Such an approach may be compared, for example, with that on game design adopted by Salen and Zimmerman (2004), who emphasize the view that culture is "a system of shared ideas, values, and behaviors" (p. 509), which automatically enter games. Consequently, understanding cultural rhetorics of gender, race, ethnicity, colonialism or imperialism is immediately seen as pertinent to learning meaningful game design (Salen and Zimmerman, 2004, p. 523). Or, it could be compared to that of David Myers, adopted in his 2014 review of video game research. The spatial limits of the account necessitate a general approach: issues related to multiculturalism are not mentioned, even though the game/player/context model of game studies is adopted. However, Myers represents games research as "a currently eclectic field" (p. 333) in which influences from cultural studies and relativist approaches are strong (p. 332), without simultaneously delimiting the way in which culture and video games are to be understood (or specifying core and secondary elements). As a result, it appears that research into multiculturalism could be accommodated within the outline he thus provides more easily and without certain tensions.

It appears, then, that what is necessary to illuminate the intersection between games and multiculturalism most fully is a model of game studies that does justice to the specificity of video games as a medium, but at the same time views them holistically, without introducing a hierarchy of components. One such possible model is advocated by, again, Bogost (2009), who distinguishes between five "focuses" of video game studies: (1) reception and operation, concentrating on user experience; (2) interface; (3) form and function, including rules, gameplay, and the representative/semiotic layer; (4) code; and (5) platform. Within this model, investigation takes place on multiple levels, including physical qualities of the game carrier, ideologies represented throughout the story, the question of intellectual property, the historical context the game embodies and the meaning that is ascribed

---

[8]Mäyrä speaks of diversity at a point, stressing that games are nowadays played by people of different social background, gender and age. However, he performs a strange move describing this diversity in terms of "more diffuse gaming behaviors" (p. 26), often associated with casual gamers, that are different from "clearly identifiable gaming subcultures" (p. 26) apparently represented by hardcore gamers. Such a conceptualization of diversity as "casual" is suspicious, considering, e.g., the fact that both categories are gendered and associated with a superior/inferior dichotomy (Newman and Vanderhoef, 2014, pp. 383, 384–5). On the other hand, Mäyrä's call for the study of casual gamers as "the 'invisible majority'" (p. 26) of gamers, which significantly contributes to games cultures, is certainly valuable.

to it within a given culture. It is not difficult to point to various areas within this framework where we could study multiculturalism; also, it assumes the irreducibility of various aspects of games and their functioning. As a result, it allows for noticing an array of relationships or correlations between various levels of games' existence, delving into which opens a path to a more complete understanding of the phenomenon at hand.

It is often stressed that games partake in identity formation (see e.g. Everett, 2014, p. 398; Hammar 2015). Perhaps one benefit of studying video games from such a perspective as multiculturalism (see also Warnes, 2005, p. 3) is that it makes clear what we overlook if our understanding of this multifaceted medium is a limited one. There is much at stake while speaking of cultural diversity in video games, and not acknowledging the centrality of multiculturalism to the medium may result in passing over several topical issues at the heart of video games, player cultures and the industry, and culture in general. As Salen and Zimmerman (2004) note regarding design, relying on cultural conventions without interrogating them may impede innovation as much as lead to reproducing "destructive ideologies tied to racism, sexism, and xenophobia" (p. 512). The same refers to research, both into games and into multiculturalism.

3   Areas of Study

There are many directions that we may take while studying video games from the perspective of multiculturalism. We may take some clues from design. Salen and Zimmerman (2004) note: "[g]ames are designed objects that engage culture on several levels. As systems of representation they *reflect* culture, depicting images of gender ..., as well as portrayals of race and class" (p. 507). As already mentioned, representation, or *reflection*, is an obvious level to investigate. At the same time, the authors mention that cultural contexts affect both representation and gameplay, and also point to the fact that games can, in turn, affect cultural contexts (2004, p. 507). This partly stems from the fact that "*games are social contexts for cultural learning*" (Salen & Zimmerman, 2004, p. 516) and thus they reflect and reproduce ideological values, and partly refers to games' potential to *transform* their contexts through conscious and innovative design (pp. 507–508). Thus, further levels of investigation—designers as a professional group, the design process, the experience and the effects of games—become apparent.

These levels not only require a multidisciplinary approach, but also can be further broken down in a net of correlated areas which extend well beyond the borders of the magic circle. For example, as Salen and Zimmerman (2004) investigate games as "open culture," they stress that design/rules can never determine the entire cultural effect of gameplay, which is also dependent on the player (p. 538). This immediately draws our attention to players and their contribution to the game, also in the sense of changing the game's structure to extend its meaning (see e.g. Salen and Zimmerman's discussion of Will Wright's *The Sims*, 2004, pp. 539–544).

Another direction to pursue could be then linked with such questions as whether a game permits players to become producers in a way that allows them for enhancing cultural diversity or allowing for better identification. Investigating such a question, could, in turn, entail tackling legal matters like property rights, companies support of extra-game communities (see e.g. Kocurek, 2014, pp. 368–369), open source software (see Salen & Zimmerman, 2004, pp. 544–546.), "metagaming" activities (see Salen & Zimmerman, 2004, p. 540) as well as the impact on player interaction, for example in an online environment. From another perspective, we may examine ways in which rules of a game limit diversity, and ways in which players engage in resistance tactics, for example through modding (see Salen & Zimmerman, 2004, pp. 559–564). Biases brought inside the game environment by players themselves is yet another possible area.

An example of a systematic theoretical approach to the study of cultural diversity in relation to video games, one that runs through many planes of games' functioning, may be found in the work of a sociologist and digital games researcher, Aphra Kerr. In her 2010 "Beyond billiard balls: Transnational flows, cultural diversity and digital games," Kerr addresses both academics and regulators, and, reviewing the existing games research to date, focuses on the possible areas within the digital games industry where cultural diversity might be promoted and enhanced. As she observes, "there is some resistance to applying this concept [i.e. of cultural diversity] and associated policies to transnational media ... especially in relation to new forms of content like digital games" (p. 19), which remain, in most cases, a self-regulated industry (p. 2). She also notes that, in 2010, the study of cultural diversity in the context of video games still remains underdeveloped[9]—in spite of investigation into gender diversity and issues, specific national game development industries, or cultural hybridity of video games' content[10] (pp. 4–6).

Significantly, Kerr is concerned with a functional re-deployment of the concept of cultural diversity, as defined by the academic and policy-making discourses, in the context of specifically digital games. Paying attention to the global dimension of the industry, she frames cultural diversity as "less about protecting national cultures and more about promoting a diversity of opinions, languages, ethnicities and races" (2010, p. 2). In her opinion, what needs to be recognized is the fact that particular kinds of cultures are promoted by specific policies; that cultures are not stable but tend to mix and interact, and hence preservation in not necessarily to be seen as an ultimate goal; and that international distribution and power relations in the industry need to be treated on equal terms with the production of content (p. 4). Consequently, Kerr proposes a three-fold model of research into cultural diversity in relation to digital games, based on Denis McQuail's three categories of

---

[9]In fact, she speaks of "the lack of existing work on cultural diversity in games" (p. 6).
[10]Kerr refers here to the work by Mia Consalvo (2006) on the Japanese *Final Fantasy* series, which Consalvo sees as representative regarding how the video game industry proves culturally hybrid in providing a mix of American and Japanese culture.

diversity.[11] This model advocates the study of: (1) diversity of production; (2) diversity of content and representation; (3) diversity of game players (p. 6). With respect to all three categories, Kerr suggests crucial areas of interest, or "gaps" (p. 2), as she terms them, in need of further exploration.

When it comes to production, Kerr points to the interests of the publishers, market demand, economic issues and marketing matters as vital areas for consideration. As she observes, to study cultural diversity in the context of digital games production "one needs to attempt to differentiate between where the production is geographically located and where the ownership and control of production and publishing is located. One needs also to separate hardware and software" (p. 8). She also draws our attention to the division of the industry into four basic segments: that of the console market, PC market, MMOGs, and casual/mini games (p. 7). It is significant, for instance, that the console segment, being the biggest, is dominated by a handful of American and Japanese companies, which control the game selection process. Thus, greater diversity might be expected to reside in the other segments (p. 7). When it comes to console software publishers, Kerr enumerates the US, Japan and France as the countries where the top companies are located, each representing a "supra-region," "demarcated by technological, economic, social and cultural barriers" (p. 8). The crucial role that the publishers play in the game production cycle is granted to them through funding schemes (p. 9). Other questions that emerge in the area of production are the diversity of the workforce in development companies, or national/government support schemes and their criteria (pp. 10–11).

With regard to the diversity of content/representation, Kerr points to a number of further issues in need of study. She emphasizes the diversity of game genres, looking particularly at the question of genre preferences depending on gender, age, market, or platform, as well as the role of localization in the flow of genres between different markets. Another question is that of cultural influences, be they national (e.g. British humor in UK games), fictional (e.g. in *GTA*, set in a city modelled on US metropolises, but developed in Scotland) or hybrid (e.g. mixing American and Japanese cultures in *Final Fantasy* series). And yet another is that of the representation of linguistic diversity in video games, a matter worthy of investigation taking into consideration, for example, the rise of Asian game development. The issue of representation emerges further in relation to the practice of modding, especially in the context of copyrights, as well as regarding game characters, stories or gameplay themselves (pp. 12–16).

Finally, as far as players are concerned, what calls for attention is a whole array of questions such as culturally (and market-) conditioned reasons for playing and effects of play, demographics of the players and players' preferences (as much as the agendas behind player surveys), habits of players, contexts and constraints of gaming, game culture and its gendering, player communities (including manifestations of

---

[11]McQuail's categories of diversity in the media comprise diversity of provision, diversity of content/representation and diversity of audiences (2005, p. 197, cited in Kerr, 2010, pp. 2–3).

sexism and racism), identity formation, promotion and the access to video games (Kerr, 2010, pp. 16–18).

The study of production, representation/content and players may be seen as roughly corresponding to both Mäyrä's and Bogost's models for studying games. Different areas of study indicated by Kerr converge with particular areas they discuss, simultaneously broadening our perspective to a considerable extent; consequently, studying the intersections emerges as a way to significantly deepen our overall understanding of the phenomenon of games.

4   A Brief Insight into the Current Research

In what follows, we shall focus on two outlets of critical research into video games: a number of chosen texts available at DiGRA's digital library and several chapters from *The Routledge Companion to Video Game Studies*. Both of them are valuable resources which provide an interesting insight into the existing games research dedicated to multiculturalism. DiGRA's library, extensive as it is, testifies to the fact that diversity as regards video games has diverse meanings, but its multicultural aspect is also pointed to as topical. The same refers to the companion, though its status as a comprehensive and educational text simultaneously draws our attention to certain issues and tensions that may emerge in the process of delimiting a field of knowledge.

Edited by prominent researchers, Wolf and Perron, and published in 2014, the companion frames itself as a comprehensive resource, one of only few in the field. Its goal is defined as "to address the on-going theoretical and methodological development of game studies, providing students, scholars, and game designers with a definitive look at contemporary video game studies" (2014, p. i), which marks it as a significant text in the process of knowledge-making. The companion includes chapters which cover cultural diversity, especially those on femininity, masculinity and race, gathered with a few other chapters in Part VI of the companion, under the common heading of "Sociological Aspects," which is a somewhat limiting move, as might be claimed.[12] These chapters do analyse their topics from the points of view enumerated by Kerr; it is not, however, difficult to notice that certain other chapters in the same section, as well in other sections, make—or, by contrast, seem to require references to cultural diversity.

Carry Heeter's "Femininity" and Michael Z. Newman and John Vanderhoef's "Maculinity" both provide an overview of research into gender issues. Heeter (2014) considers games themes, playable characters, and the visual representation of women, noting the continuing dominance of the masculine perspective, but also points to differences in representation depending on game genres, especially with

[12]Interestingly, Lukacs (2014) in "Sociology" stresses that sociological methodologies, while they have much to offer, have been so far applied only partially in game studies, and their potential is still greatly underestimated (p. 407).

regard to casual games (pp. 373–375); varying preferences and motivations as regards boys and girls, and sexual harassment of female players in online environments, grounded in culturally codified gender roles that map on game spaces (pp. 375–377); and finally the overwhelming dominance of men in the workforce (pp. 377–378). Newman and Vanderhoef (2014) consider, among others: the early association of games' contents with boys' culture, the links between masculinized technology and the construal of gamer identity as predominantly male, the impact of marketing and media on upholding the masculine ideal, the gendering of hardcore gamer culture and casual games, and the impact of "crunch" time on companies' workforce makeup (pp. 380–385).

The possible areas for research, however, may be found also in several other chapters. For example, the chapter on "Community" by Carly A. Kocurek, also found in Part VI of the companion, both covers the diversity of communities formed in and around games and draws our attention to areas where this diversity intersects with multiculturalism. Among those areas, Kocurek points to internet forums as spaces of exchange between companies and players that provide valuable insight into companies' policies concerning diversity, or mentions the correlation between different types of gamer communities and their attitudes towards discriminatory behaviours (2014, pp. 370–371). As she stresses, investigating this correlation may help to better understand "the differing gaming interests of [community] members, but also varying standards for community engagement and participation and individual behavior" (2014, p. 371).

On the other hand, we could also easily imagine how the theme of cultural diversity might be usefully introduced into such chapters as those devoted to characters or performance (also Part VI), or players/gamers (Part III: "Playfulness Aspects"). For example, Frédéric Clément's chapter on players generally presents the classification of players as based on the way they interact with games. The chapter does not provide information on how categories of players/gamers/gameplayers (introduced by Perron) (Clément, 2014, pp. 199–200), or socializers, killers, achievers and explorers (introduced by Richard Bartle) (pp. 200–201), or the differences between hardcore gamers and casual gamers (interrogated e.g. by Juul) (pp. 201–202) might correspond to cultural, national or social background of people whom they describe. The lack of such a contextualization is somewhat striking. The notions of hardcore and causal gamers are heavily gendered ones, as mentioned above, as much as they are evaluative. The very definitions of players, as concerned less with game objectives than with exploration and free movement, and gamers, as taking up the challenges and determined to win, might be referred to specifically gendered contexts which automatically link with culturally predefined behaviours. Similarly, it might be interesting to see what categories manage to escape implicit biases—or try to overtly address gender, national or economic backgrounds.[13]

---

[13]An attempt at linking aptitude, styles of play, motivation and game preferences to gender differences was made for example by Noble, Ruitz, Destefano, and Mintz (2014). They note that hardcore gamers constitute approx. 10% of gamers, dominate the designer sector (para. 1), and may be seen in terms of "early adopters" of technology (para. 2). As such, they have different

Our aim is not to claim that each and every chapter, where possible, should refer to the multicultural aspect of the question discussed. It seems, however, that some might particularly benefit from providing a reference, thus significantly broadening the readers' perspective and illuminating certain implicit tendencies and influences at work. We could concede that such influences are, in fact, illuminated elsewhere, in the chapters corresponding to the topic, and the whole matter is one of organization. The companion is certainly multidimensional and diverse in the offered perspectives—and thus indisputably useful. Nonetheless, is appears that omitting to highlight certain links in certain places may invite a hasty assumption that certain phenomena may be safely considered without a reference to sometimes crucial broader contexts. This, in turn, may lead to formulating totalizing (or partial) conclusions and further assumptions. On the other hand, the fact that diversity could beneficially illuminate certain topic, but is not referred to, may point to the continuing need for further research, and an intensification thereof.

The remaining part of the section looks at a few more strands of possible inquiry in the question of multiculturalism in video games context, based mostly on a brief review of several conference proceedings texts found in DiGRA's library. Among these, race and ethnicity are certainly worth considering—here, we shall take Anna Everett's chapter from the Routledge companion as a starting point.

While Kerr views preserving national cultures as not necessarily a major effort while catering for cultural diversity in video games, the way video games represent cultural heritage appears nonetheless a worthy object of study. To give one brief example, Balela and Mundy (2011) consider two case studies, Ubisoft's *Assassin's Creed 1* (2007) and *Unearthed: Trail of Ibn Battuta* (2013), produced in Saudi Arabia by Semaphore, and focus specifically on the representation of Arabic culture. The games are analysed from the perspectives of narrative, architecture, character design and clothing and intangible artefacts, and then interrogated with regard to the questions of cultural appropriation, Hollywoodization, beautification, game dynamics and rules constraints, and finally ideological constraints.[14]

Salen and Zimmerman (2004) mention imperialism and colonialism as cultural rhetorics that deserve attention. Lammes (2003) provides an interesting account of *Civilization III* from this perspective. Analysing game leaders, Lammes unveils the conception of civilization that the game relies on: upward progress from nature to culture, taking us on a journey from the Roman Empire to the contemporary Western metropolis (2003, pp. 122–123). The history of civilization in the game, as it turns out, is represented as "linear and uniform [...] white and male" (Lammes, 2003, p. 123). Moving on to the game's rules, Lammes points to the fact that the emphasis

---

(Footnote 13 continued)

preferences than casual players, but what needs to be considered are also such categories as age, ethnicity, gender (para. 17) and country (para. 18).

[14]Such research appears particularly pressing noting the ubiquitous biased representation of Muslims. This, in turn, points to a broader issue worthy of investigating: the impact of political ideologies and rhetoric on representation. See also e.g. Billingslea (2014) on the political aspect of enemies in games (pp. 92–93).

on expanding borders, the way in which the game allows for exploiting foreign villages, the general manner of mapping known and unknown spaces, etc., all "[bear] on several white western histories of exploration and expansion" (2003, pp. 126–127), which makes the game a particularly postcolonial one.

What is also a promising path of inquiry is the interrogation of attempts at introducing multiculturalism in video games. Curlew (2005) provides such an interrogation of *The Sims*, a ground-breaking game known for introducing equality of sexes, availability of different races, and the possibility of same-sex relationships, as well as for providing extensive opportunities for the player to create their own content for the game (p. 1). Yet as Curlew observes, egalitarianism of *The Sims* seems to result not so much from socio-cultural and political changes, as from "the commercial appropriation of difference": "*The Sims* amounts to an exploitation of diversity initiated by targeting untraditional markets to better tap into the consuming potential of millions of non-white, non-male, non-heterosexual people" (2005, p. 1).

Moving on to race and ethnicity, writing in 2014, Everett discusses a number of useful perspectives of study. Situating her considerations in the context of Obama's era, she notices that, [h]aving emerged now as a media industry giant and a potent cultural force, the video/computer games industry and the narrative texts it creates, promote, sell, and profit from both racist and antiracist cultural values" (2014, p. 398). Thus she draws our attention to an inherent duality reflected in video game contents, production and players' attitudes.

To begin, Everett briefly surveys contemporary games that introduce MPCs (main playable characters) and OPCs (optional playable characters) representing people of colour, noting these have become widely available.[15] Simultaneously, she also points to business models of expanding target audiences as a reason. Focusing on Latino Americans, she emphasizes they constitute a high percentage of player community and are represented in a number of acceptable, though often stereotypical roles across various games; still, their representation, as in the case of other traditionally under-represented demographics, remains "woefully incommensurate with their demographic percentages in society, and with the industry's own market shares" (p. 339). Furthermore, Everett comments on the emergence of non-white male MPCs that manage to transgress "gaming's privileged masculine archetypes of heroic whiteness" (p. 339), and discusses black female playable characters, who still tend to reproduce stereotypes, but nevertheless manage to depart from the typical representation of black women as "non-playable victims of violence" (pp. 400, 402–404).

Focusing on players, Everett mentions the study of Kishonna Grey into oppositional play strategies applied by groups of black and Puerto Rican female players in response to racism and sexual harassment in Xbox Life's player communities

---

[15]See also e.g. Hitchens's (2011) more detailed survey into First-Person Shooter (FPS) avatars and their characteristics concerning race, gender and background. For an earlier survey into the representation of gender and race/ethnicity in video games, see e.g. Jansz and Martis (2003). It should be noticed that while the possibility for the representation of the player's actual identity is a crucial thing, the diverse ways in which players approach, play and experiment with identities in video games and online environments is equally worthy of attention.

(pp. 400–401). She also devotes considerable attention to player participatory cultures, which engage in forms of cultural activism through social media, as well as through modding and otherwise enhancing pre-programmed games environments (pp. 402–404). Another matter is the market's growing awareness of the Arab, Muslim, and Middle East markets, and the ubiquitous representation of Muslims as extremists and terrorists. Here, Everett draws our attention to the attempts to counter anti-Arab games undertaken by Syrian and Lebanese studios, and the resulting emergence of games for the Middle East Market, aimed as self-representation, such as *Special Force* (2003), *Under Ash* (2002), or *Under Siege* (2005) (p. 405).[16]

The range of perspectives of study into race and ethnicity listed above may be easily extended once we reach for more narrowly focused texts on the topic. For example, DiSalvo et al. (2009) provide a valuable insight into the cultural play practices of African American young males (p. 2). At the same time, their study draws our attention to the fact that the degree to which particular racial/ethnic groups engage with computer sciences has its impact on the percentage they make in the video game industry.

When it comes to content and representation, there seems to broad range of possible inquiries. Dymek and Lennerfors (2005), in their interrogation of *GTA* series, propose to analyse racial stereotypes represented by the games from the perspective of the theory of humour. In turn, Kafai, Cook and Fields's (2007) study into the community of *Whyville.net*, a multi-user virtual environment, provides an interesting multifaceted analysis of the representation issues faced by the game's adolescent population, players' interaction with the game's creators, and the measures taken to introduce variety.

Finally, we must acknowledge that a continuing analysis of research matters as much as the study of content, production and players. This is made clear for example by Hammar in his study of 2015. Hammar stresses the lack of systematic research on the actual racial makeup of players, simultaneously pointing to occasional studies that confirm Hispanics and African Americans to constitute a substantial percentage of gamers, which is reflected neither in the workforce nor games contents (pp. 4–5). Similarly, he stresses the need for both surveying the representation of sexuality, and researching the representation of gender in correlation with other categories (pp. 5–6). In the first place, however, he focuses on the ways in which different groups are marginalized in both internal and external spaces generated by video games (see pp. 7–9), and calls on moral agents—publishers and developers, but also the press, players and researchers—to work against the *status quo* (p. 1, 10–12).

---

[16]A more detailed account of *Under Ash*, a Syrian game featuring a young Palestinian hero who partakes in the struggle against Israeli soldiers and settlers, may be found in Gee (2004, pp. 148–152).

5   Conclusion

From the perspective of multiculturalism, video games constitute a promising field of inquiry. Simultaneously, they appear to be still much in need of a continuing research. Compelling and complex phenomena as they are, games and their spaces invite multiculturalism as much as they raise issues connected with representation, learning, cultural resistance, the experience and bounds of play and players' agency, the limits imposed on the industry by current politics or economy, as much as by itself, and many others, not excluding those related to academic research. Examining them equals better understanding the culture(s) we live in and by as much as the medium itself. As such, it certainly benefits both multiculturalism, and game studies.

References

Aarseth, E. (2001). Computer game studies, year one. *Game Studies, 1*(1). http://www. gamestudies.org/0101/editorial.html

Aarseth, E. (2015). Meta-game studies. *Game Studies, 15*(1). http://gamestudies.org/1501/articles/ editorial

Aarseth, E. (2014). Ludology. In M. J. P. Wolf, & B. Perron (Eds.), *The Routledge companion to video game studies* (pp. 185–189). New York, NY, Abington, England: Routledge.

always_black. (2006). Bow, nigger. In K. Salen & E. Zimmerman (Eds.), *The game design reader: A rules of play anthology* (pp. 602–608). Cambridge, Mass., London, England: The MIT Press.

Balela, S. M. & Mundy, D. (2011). Analysing cultural heritage and its representation in video games. In *Proceedings of DiGRA 2011 conference: Think design play* (pp. 1–16). http://www. digra.org/wp-content/uploads/digital-library/92_BalelaMundy_Analysing-Cultural-Heritage-and-its-Representation-in-Video-Games.pdf

Billingslea, S., II. (2014). It's just a game, or is it?: A study of racism in game and character design. In D. Stobbard & M. Evans (Eds.), *Engaging with videogames: Play, theory and practice* (pp. 91–100). Oxford, England: Inter-Disciplinary Press.

Bleja, D. (2015, June 5). The melting pot and the salad bowl: Why the Witcher 3 is a step forward for ethnic diversity in games [blog post]. Retrieved from http://www.gamasutra.com/blogs/ DaveBleja/20150605/245285/The_Melting_Pot_and_the_Salad_Bowl_Why_the_Witcher_3_ is_a_step_forward_for_ethnic_diversity_in_games.php

Bogost, I. (2006). *Unit operations: An approach to videogame criticism.* Cambridge, Mass., London, England: The MIT Press.

Bogost, I. (2007). *Persuasive games: The expressive power of videogames.* Cambridge, Mass., London, England: The MIT Press.

Bogost, I. (2009, September). Videogames are a mess. In *Plenary lecture given at DiGRA 2009 conference*, West London, UK. Retrieved from http://bogost.com/writing/videogames_are_a_ mess/

Clément, F. (2014). Players/gamers. In M. J. P. Wolf, & B. Perron (Eds.), *The Routledge companion to video game studies* (pp. 197–203). New York, NY, Abington, England: Routledge.

Consalvo, M. (2006). Console video games and global corporations. *New Media & Society 8*(1), 117–137.

Curlew, A. B. (2005). Liberal sims?: Simulated difference and the commodity of social diversity. In *Proceedings of DiGRA 2005 conference: Changing views—worlds in play* (pp. 1–7). http:// www.digra.org/wp-content/uploads/digital-library/06276.47199.pdf

DiSalvo, B. J., Guzdail, M., Mcklin, T., Meadows, C., Perry, K., Steward, C., et al. (2009). Glitch game testers: African American men breaking open the console. Breaking new ground: Innovation in games, play, practice and theory. In *Proceedings of DiGRA 2009* (pp. 1–7). http://www.digra.org/wp-content/uploads/digital-library/09287.35217.pdf

Dymek, M. & Lennenfors, T. (2005). Among pasta-loving mafiosos, drug-selling Columbians and noodle-eating triads—Race, humour and interactive ethics in Grand Theft Auto III. In *Proceedings of DiGRA 2005 conference: Changing views—worlds in play* (pp. 1–12). http://www.digra.org/wp-content/uploads/digital-library/06276.49210.pdf

Everett, A. (2014). Race. In M. J. P. Wolf, & B. Perron (Eds.), *The Routledge companion to video game studies* (pp. 396–406). New York, NY, Abington, England: Routledge.

Frasca, G. (1999). Ludology meets narratology: Similitude and differences between (video)games and narrative. *Parnasso, 3*, 365–371. Retrieved from http://www.ludology.org/articles/ludology.htm

Frasca, G. (2003a). Simulation versus narrative: Introduction to ludology. In M. J. P. Wolf & B. Perron (Eds.), *The video game theory reader* (pp. 221–235). London, England, New York, NY: Routledge.

Frasca, G. (2003b). Ludologists love stories, too: Notes from a debate that never took place. In M. Copier & J. Raessens (Eds.), *Level up: Digital games research conference proceedings* (pp. 92–99). Utrecht: DiGRA, University of Utrecht.

Gee, J. P. (2004). *What video games have to teach us about learning and literacy.* New York, NY, Basingstoke, England: Plagrave Macmillan.

Hammar, E. L. (2015). Ethical recognition of marginalized Groups in digital games culture. In *Proceedings of DiGRA 2015: Diversity of play: Games—cultures—identities* (pp. 1–17). http://www.digra.org/wp-content/uploads/digital-library/215_Hammar_Ethical-Recognition-of-Marginalized-Groups-in-Digital-Games-Culture.pdf

Heeter, C. (2014). Femininity. In M. J. P. Wolf, & B. Perron (Eds.), *The Routledge companion to video game studies* (pp. 373–379). New York, NY, Abington, England: Routledge.

Hitchens, M. (2011). A survey of first-person shooters and their avatars. *Game Studies, 11*(3). http://gamestudies.org/1103/articles/michael_hitchens

Huizinga, J. (2006). Nature and significance of play as a cultural phenomenon. In K. Salen & E. Zimmerman (Eds.), *The game design reader: A rules of play anthology* (pp. 96–120). Cambridge, Mass., London, England: The MIT Press.

Jansz, J., & Martis, R. G. (2003). The representation of gender and ethnicity in digital interactive games. In M. Copier & J. Raessens (Eds.), *Level up: Digital games research conference proceedings* (pp. 260–269). Utrecht: DiGRA, University of Utrecht.

Jenkins, H. (2006). Game design as narrative architecture. In K. Salen & E. Zimmerman (Eds.), *The game design reader: A rules of play anthology* (pp. 602–608). Cambridge, Mass., London, England: The MIT Press.

Juul, J. (2003). The game, the player, the world: Looking for a heart of gameness. In M. Copier & J. Raessens (Eds.), *Level up: Digital games research conference proceedings* (pp. 30–45). Utrecht: DiGRA, University of Utrecht.

Kafai, B. J., Cook M. S. & Fields, D.A. (2007). "Blacks deserve bodies too!" design and discussion about diversity and race in a tween online world. In *Situated play, Proceedings of DiGRA 2007 Conference* (pp. 269–277). http://www.digra.org/wp-content/uploads/digital-library/07312.14099.pdf

Kerr, A. (2010). Beyond billiard balls: Transnational flows, cultural diversity and digital games. In E. Elgar (Ed.), *Governance of digital game environments and cultural diversity: Transdisciplinary enquiries*, Cheltenham, England (pp. 47–73). Retrieved from http://eprints.maynoothuniversity.ie/2902/1/AK__cult_div_09.pdf (paginated 1–21).

Kocurek, A. C. (2014). Community. In M. J. P. Wolf, & B. Perron (Eds.), *The Routledge companion to video game studies* (pp. 364–372). New York, NY, Abington, England: Routledge.

Lammes, S. (2003). On the border: Pleasure of exploration and colonial mastery in Civilization III Play The World. In M. Copier & J. Raessens (Eds.), *Level up: Digital games research conference proceedings* (pp. 120–129). Utrecht: DiGRA, University of Utrecht.

Lukacs, A. (2014). Sociology. In M. J. P. Wolf, & B. Perron (Eds.), *The Routledge companion to video game studies* (pp. 407–414). New York, NY, Abington, England: Routledge.

Mäyrä, F. (2008). *An Introduction to game studies: Games in culture*. Los Angeles, London, New Delhi, Singapore, Washington DC: Sage.

Mäyrä, F., Van Looy, J. & Quandt, T. (2013). Disciplinary identity of game scholars: An outline. In *Proceedings of DiGRA 2013: DeFragging game studies* (pp. 1–16). http://www.digra.org/wp-content/uploads/digital-library/paper_146.pdf

Moosa, T. (2015, June 3). Colorblind: On the Witcher 3, Rust, and gaming's race problem. *Polygon*. Retrieved from http://www.polygon.com

Myers, D. (2014). Research. In M. J. P. Wolf & B. Perron (Eds.), *The Routledge companion to video game studies* (pp. 331–338). New York, NY, Abington, England: Routledge.

Newman, M. Z., & Vanderhoef, J. (2014). Masculinity. In M. J. P. Wolf & B. Perron (Eds.), *The Routledge companion to video game studies* (pp. 380–189). New York, NY, Abington, England: Routledge.

Noble, R., Ruitz, K., Destefano, M. & Mintz, J. (2003). Conditions of engagement in game simulation: Contexts of gender, culture and age.In *Proceedings of the 2003 DiGRA international conference: Level up*. http://www.digra.org/wp-content/uploads/digital-library/05150.05387.pdf

Pearce, C. (2005). Theory wars: An argument against arguments in the so-called ludology/narratology debate. In *Proceedings of DiGRA 2005 conference: Changing views—worlds in play* (pp. 1–6). http://www.digra.org/wp-content/uploads/digital-library/06278.03452.pdf

Romero, B. (2009). *Train* [game description]. Retrieved from http://www.blromero.com/train/

Romero, B. (2011). *Gaming for understanding*. TED talk. https://www.ted.com/talks/brenda_brathwaite_gaming_for_understanding?language=en

Ryan, M.-L. (2001). Beyond myth and metaphor—The case of narrative in digital media. *Game Studies*, *1*(1). http://www.gamestudies.org/0101/ryan/

Salen, K. & Zimmerman, E. (2004). *Rules of play: Game design fundamentals*. Cambridge, Mass., London, England: The MIT Press.

Taylor, T. L. (2006). *Play between worlds: Exploring online game culture*. Cambridge, Mass., London, England: The MIT Press.

Ubisoft Montreal. (2007). *Assassin's creed* [Video game]. Retrieved from http://store.ubi.com

Ubisoft Quebec. (2015). *Assassin's creed: Syndicate* [Video game]. Retrieved from http://store.ubi.com

Warnes, C. (2005). Baldur's gate and history: Race and alignment in digital role playing games. In *Proceedings of DiGRA 2005 conference: Changing views—worlds in* play (pp. 1–6). http://www.digra.org/wp-content/uploads/digital-library/06276.04067.pdf

Watson, C. W. (2000). *Multiculturalism*. Buckingham, Philadelphia: Open University Press.

Author Biography

Agnieszka Kliś-Brodowska, PhD, is an assistant professor at the Department of Rhetoric in Culture and the Media, Institute of English Cultures and Literatures, University of Silesia in Katowice, Poland. Her research interests include Gothic fiction, especially with regard to critical discourse on the Gothic in the 20th and 21st century and the question of (constructing) genre definition, literary criticism, poststructuralism (of Michel Foucault), and recently video game studies as a research field.

An Haughty Sniff Versus a Spoonful of Sugar, or Who Is Mary Poppins?

Dorota Malina

Abstract "Who is Mary Poppins? In our mind's eye we see Julie Andrews in a pastel Edwardian dress, […], as saccharine as the spoonful of sugar that helped the medicine go down. […]. The original Mary Poppins was not cheery at all. She was tart and sharp, plain and vain. That was her charm; that—and her mystery"—writes Valerie Lawson (Mary Poppins, she wrote: The life of PL Travers. Simon and Schuster, p. 143, 2013). Mary Poppins, an iconic nanny created by Travers, is the main protagonist of a seven volume series. The books quickly became children's classics and the source of various translations and adaptations. In my article I intend to explore the notion of the literary character's identity across some of them. I want to focus specifically on comparing the picture of Mary Poppins that emerges from the original text with that in the Polish translation by Irena Tuwim and the famous 1964 Disney musical. By analyzing the changes between the versions I propose to demonstrate that each translation constitutes an act of rereading the original for the purposes of a new audience. Looking at the changes that have been made, one can learn a lot not only about the new identity of the literary protagonist but also about the identity of the target culture which emerges in confrontation with "the other."

Keywords Adaptation · Children's literature · Identity · Intersemiotic translation

1 Introduction

The Mary Poppins saga written by Travers has been translated into seventeen languages, adapted to screen and appropriated by pop culture. The goals of my article are to establish the picture of Mary Poppins that emerges from two literary texts (the original books and their Polish translations) and one cultural product (the 1964 Disney musical) with the view of determining how the heroine's identity

D. Malina (✉)
Chair of Translation and Intercultural Communication, Philological Department,
Jagiellonian University, Al. Mickiewicza 9a, 31-120 Kraków, Poland
e-mail: framboise.kr@gmail.com

© Springer International Publishing AG 2017   157
J. Mydla et al. (eds.), *Multiculturalism, Multilingualism and the Self: Literature and Culture Studies*, Issues in Literature and Culture,
DOI 10.1007/978-3-319-61049-8_12

changes in what are supposedly "equivalent texts." Rather than bemoaning the lack of fidelity in subsequent representations, I argue, following Hermans (2007), that "a translation, for as long as it remains a translation, cannot be equivalent to its source" (p. 25) and the changes can be treated as a proof of the original text's viability.

First, on the basis of the first three volumes of Travers's books (*Mary Poppins, Mary Poppins Comes Back, Mary Poppins Opens the Door*)[1] I sketch the portrait of the famous nanny, focusing both on *what* she is like and *how* she is presented. Then, I analyse Irena Tuwim's Polish translations (*Mary Poppins, Mary Poppins wraca, Mary Poppins otwiera drzwi*) in order to establish how the change of means of presentation (notably the language but also the cultural background) affects the portrait. In the following Sect. 1 look at Stevenson's (1964) musical, which I treat as a case of intersemiotic translation. In concluding remarks, drawing insights form Theo Hermans's theory of translation I propose that both translations, necessarily non-equivalent, do "flesh out the interpretative potential" (Hermans, 2007, p. 30) of the text by constructing new incarnations of the mysterious nanny.

2 Travers's Mary Poppins

According to Neil Gaiman, "Mary Poppins defies explanation" (Grilli, 2007, p. xiii). Victoria Neumark concurs, pointing out the heroine's mysterious origins and deliberate gaps in Travers's story: "There is a hint of awe around Mary Poppins, an aura of pagan divinity. Who is she, really? Where does she come from, so suddenly, and why?" (Eccleshare and i Blake, 2009, p. 475). Given that she features in six books, one cookbook and twenty-six vignettes (*Mary Poppins from A to Z*), she remains bafflingly mysterious and, as such, continuously fascinates readers and scholars alike.

Volume one (*Mary Poppins*) establishes the pattern that recurs throughout the series: the middle-class Banks family is in crisis: the house is in chaos, the children are unruly, the servants incompetent and the parents on the verge of a nervous breakdown. Suddenly, the East Wind blows in a mysterious visitor who refuses to give references (deeming them old-fashioned), ignores all their questions and immediately brings order to the messy nursery. Then she efficiently combines the mundane with the magical, introducing her charges into the universe of fantastical creatures and quirky relatives whilst all the time teaching them manners and leading by example (which is easily done, since she is a paragon of all virtues). When the time comes, she leaves, without giving notice or saying goodbye. In the words of Neil Gaiman: "The patterns of the first three Mary Poppins books are as inflexible as those of a Noh play" (Grilli, 2007, p. xiv).

---

[1]The first three volumes are crucial since, as the author explains, the nanny paid only three visits to the Banks Family. Subsequent adventures "should be understood to have happened during any of the tree visits" (Travers, 2008, p. 503).

Chapter "Fear of Multilingualism and the Uses of Nostalgia in Ivan Vladislavić's *The Restless Supermarket*" of the first volume, which usually contains the exposition of "the play," demonstrates both the character's inscrutability and the way it is constructed. Mary Poppins first enters the scene at 17, Cherry Tree Lane on a windy afternoon. The children, Jane and Michael, are looking through the window:

"There he is!" said Michael, pointing suddenly to a shape that banged heavily against the gate.

Jane peered through the gathering darkness.

"That's not Daddy," she said. "It's somebody else."

Then the shape, tossed and bent under the wind, lifted the latch of the gate, and they could see that it belonged to a woman, who was holding her hat on with one hand and carrying a bag in the other. As they watched, Jane and Michael saw a curious thing happen. As soon as the shape was inside the gate the wind seemed to catch her up into the air and fling her at the house. It was as though it had flung her first at the gate, waited for her to open it, and then lifted and thrown her, bag and all, at the front door (Travers, 2013, p. 15.)

The nanny, arriving amidst a gale, remains unidentified for a relatively long time— first mistaken for the father, then a few times referred to as "shape." Her arrival is immediately characterized as "curious," an adjective that frequently recurs throughout the series. What also reappears are markers of epistemic modality (Palmer, 1986, p. 54)—all the "seems" and "as ifs"—indicating that most of what is known about the heroine belongs to the domain of conjecture.

The same is true when later the children are peeping through the banisters at the newcomer—they see certain characteristics (her shiny black hair, which makes her resemble a Dutch Doll and her extraordinary trick of sliding up the banisters), hear various noises (notably her dismissive sniff and her stern voice) but ultimately the nanny remains unknowable: they keep gazing "at the strange new visitor" (Travers, 2013, p.17), who has "something strange and extraordinary about her—something that was frightening and at the same time most exciting" (Travers, 2013, p. 19).

Indeed, the stories about Mary Poppins deploy what Fowler (1977) calls external perspective, where "words of estrangement" such as modals, references to appearance, surface, looking and observing "convey an air of mystery" about a character (p. 93). According to Fowler "this externality leads to alienation, the creating of an inhuman gap between the observer and the character: the character is unknowable, unreachable, scarcely a member of the human race" (p. 94).

There is undoubtedly something otherworldly about Mary Poppins. In her book *Myth, Symbol and Meaning in Mary Poppins*, a poppinsologist Grilli (2007) analyses her in terms of various liminal figures she embodies—she is notably a shaman (partly human and partly belonging to a world beyond, providing children access to the other side), trickster or mother earth. The analysis of the archetypes comprised in the figure of Mary Poppins is beyond the scope of this paper. For its purposes it is sufficient to state that the heroine serves as a link between the middle-class nursery and the universe beyond, including the magical one. The way she is presented makes her intriguing and inscrutable and "No one ever knew what Mary Poppins felt about it for Mary Poppins never told anything..." (Travers, 2013, p. 21).

There is another reason why a discussion of archetypes is not essential in a paper on translation between two languages from relatively close cultures—if an archetype is "a symbol, theme, setting or character type that recurs in different times and places in myth, literature or folklore" (Baldick, 2001, p. 19), it is quite likely that archetypical facets of Mary Poppins will be interpreted in a similar fashion in both contexts (since the patterns are deemed "universal"). Her narcissistic nature, for example, and constant self-admiration in mirrors refers to the archetype common to both cultures.

What is more relevant here are cultural stereotypes and references to typically British concepts also present in the stories. Grilli (2007) evokes the sociocultural figure of a dandy and that of a governess, which, being rooted in a particular context, are potentially challenging for translators (pp. 54–6, 119–133).

Dandyism, a sociocultural and artistic movement popular in the 19th century chiefly in France and England, was characterized by artificiality and refinement. Dandies, mostly though not exclusively men, were engaged in what Baudelaire (1945) termed *cult de soi-même* or cultivation of one's own manners and appearance (p. 88). Interestingly, far from being just an expression of vanity, dandyism often constituted an act of rebellion, subversive criticism of societal norms conducted from within the society. A dandy was seeking to subvert social norms, "behaving not in a way that was opposite to the bourgeoisie, but following the manners they considered proper to the extreme, thus making them appear absurd" (Grilli, 2007, p. 55). Dandies were thus extremely well-mannered and always immaculately dressed. Their preoccupation with external appearance was such that, as Baudelaire said, they wanted "to live and die before a mirror" (1887, para. 5).

Many of these characteristics apply to Mary Poppins, who considers herself absolutely perfect. The nanny is constantly looking at herself in mirrors and shop-windows, usually assessing and admiring a new piece of clothing:

> Mary Poppins put her hat straight at the Tobacconists Shop at the corner. It had one of those curious windows where there seem to be three of you instead of one, so that if you look long enough at them you begin to feel you are not yourself but a whole crowd of somebody else. Mary Poppins sighed with pleasure, however, when she saw three of herself, each wearing a blue coat with silver buttons and a blue hat to match. She thought it was such a lovely sight that she wished there had been a dozen of her or even thirty. The more Mary Poppinses the better (Travers, 2013, pp. 30–31.)

Self-admiration and a strong narcissistic note that come across in this (and many similar) passages, so far from the typical British self-deprecation, make Mary Poppins a somewhat rebellious figure: she is not a modest frumpy spinster or austere governess, but a woman happy with the way she looks.

Mary Poppins is, of course, also a nanny (this is what Mrs. Banks advertises for) or a governess (according to Grilli). Although, in fact, she does not quite fit into either category. She does replace Katie Nanna and fulfills nanny duties such as tidying up the nursery or feeding the toddlers but, contrary to the stereotype, she is not warm or maternal. In fact, she is rather cold and often cross:

"Mary Poppins, are we *never* going home?" [Michael] said crossly.

Mary Poppins turned and regarded him with something like disgust.

(Travers, 2013, p. 82)

"That's Mary Poppins' favourite seat. She will be cross!"—exclaimed Michael.

"Indeed? And when was I ever cross?" her voice inquired behind him.

The remark quite shocked him. "Why, you are often cross, Mary Poppins!" he said. "At least fifty times a day!"

"Never!" she said with an angry snap. "I have the patience of a Boa Constrictor! I merely Speak My Mind!" (Travers, 2013, p. 401.)

Interestingly, although the custom was to address nannies by their first name (hence Katie), Mary Poppins is never just "Mary." According to Grilli (2007), this shows that "no other character is permitted to enter into an overly intimate relationship with the governess, nor will she answer to any title suggestive of her social position or marital status" (p. 5).

The scholar sees Mary Poppins as the embodiment of the sociocultural figure of the governess, which, unlike a nanny, focuses mostly on educating children. In Grilli's view Travers chose this profession deliberately as this made the heroine inherently strange—an outsider inside a family, unmarried and yet financially independent. She claims that "Travers pushes the strangeness of the governess to the extreme and exaggerates her paradoxical sense of familiarity by enriching it with the disturbing echoes of myth and antiquity" (2007, p. 20).

Mary Poppins doubtlessly has many features of a governess but she lacks the essential one: she has no desire to teach the children anything. She kindles their curiosity by uncovering the world of magic to them but she refuses to explain what they have seen. Almost every adventure ends with Mary Poppins's flat denial that anything has happened:

"But you came down on—I don't know—what! Where did you come from?'Ow did you get'ere? That's what I want to know!"

"Curiosity killed the cat!" said Mary Poppins primly (Travers, 2013, p. 165.)

"How often does your Uncle get like that?"

"Like what?" said Mary Poppins sharply, as though Michael had deliberately said something to offend her.

"Well—all bouncy and boundy and laughing and going up in the air."

"Up in the air?" Mary Poppins' voice was high and angry. "What do you mean, pray, up in the air?"

Jane tried to explain.

"Michael means—is your Uncle often full of Laughing Gas, and does he often go rolling and bobbing about on the ceiling when—"

"Rolling and bobbing! What an idea! Rolling and bobbing on the ceiling! You'll be telling me next he's a balloon!" Mary Poppins gave an offended sniff.

But the look that passed between them said: "Is it true or isn't it? About Mr. Wigg. Is Mary Poppins right or are we?"

But there was nobody to give them the right answer (Travers, 2013, p. 40.)

Summing up, Mary Poppins is a mysterious, in-between figure: an outsider inside a family, stern and practical but also magical, a spinster and a dandy, a governess that refuses to provide explanations. To depict her, Pamela Travers very skillfully uses various alienating techniques that make the heroine unknowable and perennially fascinating.

3   Tuwim's Agnieszka

Irena Tuwim translated the Mary Poppins books (four out of six volumes) between the 1930s and the 1960s, in the cultural context that differed considerably both from the one depicted in the novels and the one they were written in. People during the interwar and then communist Poland had very different "private encyclopedias" (Tabakowska, 1995, p. 77), i.e., background knowledge which they used to "supply the missing ground" (ibid.) necessary for interpretation. It is widely recognized that texts are underdetermined, that they contain blank spaces which need to be filled with the reader's knowledge and imagination (Jahn, 2007, p. 94). A translator is, of course, the first reader who needs to imagine the textual world in order to convey it in the target language. According to Katan (2014), translators are not only "human dictionaries" performing purely linguistic operations but "cultural interpreters and mediators" who create understanding between people (p. 3). They themselves, therefore, need to have not only high linguistic competence but also great inter-cultural awareness. Incidentally, Katan, unlike many scholars, does provide a useful definition of culture. In his model, culture is:

> a system for making sense of experience ... A basic presupposition is that the organization of experience is not "reality" but is a simplification and distortion which changes from culture to culture. Each culture acts as a frame within which external "signs" of reality are interpreted (Katan, 2014, p. 3.)

Consequently, calling on the traditional distinction between foreignization and domestication (Munday, 2013, p. 144), translating is seen as "shifting frames"— either making them explicit to show how the foreign culture frames reality (in foreignization) or removing them and trying to frame "the same" reality with the target culture's frames (in domestication).

Irena Tuwim was a self-confessed domesticator. She argued that "in order to give children linguistically accomplished works, translators must be given considerable leeway and in many cases they need to adapt rather than translate" (Balcerzan and Bokiewicz 1977, p. 129, transl. DM). A lot has been written (cf. Adamczyk-Garbowska, 1988; Borodo, 2006; Woźniak, 2012) on the sometimes extreme way she domesticated her translations, bringing London to Warsaw, replacing Guy Fawkes with the Polish król Ćwieczek and naming Donald Duck

Kiwajko. Particular attention has been devoted to *Winnie the Pooh*, who, according to Kozak (2009) has been polished and neutralized so as to retain only a tentative link with Milne's original. The purpose of this section is to analyse whether in Tuwim's translation, Mary Poppins essentially remains herself or whether in the process of adaptation she loses her identity.

If identity be understood literally, according to the first dictionary meaning —"who someone is: the name of a person" (MWD) then the latter is true. In the first edition of Tuwim's translation Mary Poppins was called Agnieszka, which she remained until the 1960s when, because of the release of the movie and at the author's request, the original name was restored. According to Monika Biały (2014), Tuwim's motivation for renaming the heroine was two-fold. On the one hand it was a part of her domestication strategy, on the other—an act of self-censorship on the part of the translator who had to work under the communist regime:

> Agnieszka is a typical Polish name, this is why it can be suggested that the translator purposely wanted to make the whole story more familiar to the target audience. What is more, in socialist Poland all the signs of the Western? world were unwelcome and translators had to submit to the current authority in order to have their books published (p. 177.)

When asked about her decision Tuwim herself stated that she "wanted to bring the heroine closer to the readers" and Agnieszka seemed to be "the most appropriate and suitable name" (Tuwim, 1985, p. 5, transl. DM). Tuwim was consistent in her strategy of bringing characters closer to the reader and reframing English reality with Polish frames—most other protagonists of *Mary Poppins* have names changed into forms of address that would be more conventional in Poland (hence the cook Mrs. Brill becomes Jakubowa[2] and a poodle Andrew—Duduś).

It is a relatively common practice to change proper names in translations for children as names are often punny and meaningful. Translators, willing to preserve this playfulness, invent new names, therefore Horrid Henry becomes Koszmarny Karolek and Thackeray's Spinachi—Szparagino. The surname Poppins is also meaningful—according to Grilli (2007) it is suggestive not only of the fact that "the governess ... will literally *pop in*to the lives of the Banks children (she will suddenly become part of them, but only for a short time), but also points to the little explosions and subsequent shocks heralded by the verb *to pop*" (p. 5).

Irena Tuwim does not attempt to preserve this, admittedly subtle, onomastic hint. Moreover, she does not give the nanny a surname either although, as has been indicated before, the fact that the nanny is always addressed by her full name and surname in the original text marks her unusual social status. However, following in Shakespeare's footsteps ("name, which is no part of thee") and given that the name did ultimately revert back to the original one, it is perhaps worth looking at other dimensions of the heroine's identity.

As has been stated before, the main feature of Mary Poppins is that she is neither one thing nor the other. She is both a slightly unusual, yet in many ways

---

[2]Marking her, incorrectly, as the wife of Mr. Jacob.

conservative English nanny and a magical, otherworldly figure. Arguably, in order to preserve Mary Poppins's uniqueness this duality has to stay intact. Given that the world of fantasy and fairies belongs to the "universal republic of childhood" (Hazard, 1944, p. 146), what seems considerably harder to convey is the Englishness of Mary Poppins.

The heroine, though magical and elusive, is also quite clearly situated within the British class system—she is a nanny and/or a governess to a middle-class family and she must abide by a set of well-established conventions: e.g., she eats and sleeps with the children, has one afternoon off every week. Travers constructs her identity also through her possessions, to which she is very attached[3] and which become characteristic of her as they recur in the series. Hence Mary Poppins always has her (extremely roomy) carpet bag, she brings her own Sunlight soap (traditional British laundry soap) and is partial to Yorkshire pudding, most of which were neutralized in Tuwim's translation. Agnieszka simply brings a cake of soap (kawał mydła) and eats ham and cheese gratin (zapiekanka z szynką i serem).

Such neutralization of culture-specific elements is consistent with Tuwim's general translational strategy. Does she, however, preserve the unknowability of the nanny, her otherworldliness created by means of alienation techniques? Or maybe, like many translators, she subtly changes the point of view into that of an omniscient translator (Tabakowska, 2003, p. 325).

The "entrance scene" seems to faithfully render the children's fascination:

– O, idzie—zawołał nagle Michaś, wskazując na jakąś postać [pointing to a figure], która oparła się ciężko o furtkę. Janeczka wpatrywała się przez chwilę w zapadające ciemności.

To nie Tatuś!—powiedziała—to ktoś inny [it is somebody else].

Gdy postać [the figure] miotana wiatrem nacisnęła klamkę furtki, dzieci zobaczyły, że jest to kobieta [a woman], która jedną ręką przytrzymywała kapelusz a w drugiej dźwigała dużą torbę.

Wówczas też Janeczka i Michaś ujrzeli, że dzieje się rzecz dziwna. Gdy tylko postać [the figure] znalazła się za furtką, w ogrodzie, wiatr jakby uniósł ją w powietrzu i przywiał aż do samego domu.

Wyglądało to trochę tak, jakby wiatr przywiał tę postać najpierw do furtki, poczekał, aż ją otworzy, a następnie uniósł postać [the figure] w powietrzu i rzucił razem z torbą do drzwi frontowych (Travers, 2014, p. 10.)

In this excerpt Irena Tuwim reconstructs the alienation effect—since Polish lacks articles, she uses indefinite pronouns (jakaś, ktoś) to introduce a mysterious guest. Like Travers, she consistently refers to the guest as "postać" [a figure], emphasizing that at this stage of the story she remains unidentifiable. The only reservation one might have is that Travers's "shape" is more elusive than Tuwim's "figure," as the latter already identifies the referent as human. Tuwim also uses

---

[3]Like another embodiment of middle-class values in children's literature i.e., Mary Norton's *The Borrowers* (Travis, 2007, p. 188).

verbs of estrangement, filtering the observation through the consciousness of the children: "wyglądało to troche tak jak" [It was as though].

Like her English prototype, Polish Mary Poppins is rather cold and unaffectionate, loath to compromise or give any explanations. Inevitably, there are slight shifts—for example in the original she looks at Michael "with disgust." In the Polish translation it becomes a "look of contempt" (spojrzała na niego z pogardą). Also, Tuwim's penchant for diminutives sometimes slightly dilutes the nanny's edginess. Nevertheless, overall Tuwim brilliantly reconstructs Mary Poppins's mannerisms and brusqueness both in relation to the children and adults:

> - Jak często przytrafia się to twojemu wujowi?
> - A co takiego?—zapytała szorstko, jakby Michaś umyślnie próbował jej dotknąć. […] Mój wujek tarzał się i turlał? Także pomysł! Jak wy śmiecie (Travers, 2014, p. 34.)
> - Mary!—zawołała pani Banks.—Oddałaś swoje najlepsze rękawiczki na futrze? Oddałaś je?
>
> Mary Poppins pociągnęła nosem.
>
> - Moje rękawiczki to moja rzecz i robię z nimi, co mi się podoba!—odpowiedziała wyniośle Travers, 2014, p. 123.)

4 Robert Stevenson's Musical

Disney's 1964 musical adaptation has been widely commented on (cf. Cuomo, 1995), not least because, according to Travers herself, it contained little of the essence of her books—in a letter to her publisher she wrote that "Disney through and through, spectacular, colorful, gorgeous but all wrapped around mediocrity of thought, poor glimmerings of understanding and over-simplification" (Lawson, 2013, p. 96). In Ariel Dorfman's opinion, the films of Walt Disney, including Mary Poppins, are dominated by the "infantilization of the adult" (ibid., p. 55). Talking about the motivation behind writing her book Grilli (2007) states that she wanted "to try and right the wrongs of the Disney film, which, while making this governess very popular, reduced her intriguing nature to a spoonful of sugar and much frivolity" (p. 25). It is frequently the case that film adaptations of books, especially popular ones, are criticized for not doing justice to the original, typically for making it more shallow and one-dimensional.

However, as scholars point out, what has to be taken into account in any assessment is the different specificity of the medium. Cinematic adaptation of a novel can be seen as a case of intersemiotic translation or transmutation that is "an interpretation of verbal signs

by means of signs of nonverbal sign systems" (Jakobson, 1992, p. 139). Shifting the verbal into the visual brings gains and losses. On the one hand, "a picture is worth a thousand words"; it can give what language cannot, namely a full visualization with Ingarden's empty spaces filled out (Tabakowska, 2015, p. 137). On the other, language provides what images cannot—deliberate ambiguity, lack of specificity, room for imagination, it can express nuanced feelings so that textual clues cannot always be "translated into pictures" (Tabakowska, 2015, p. 137). According to Król (2006), most fantasy adaptations become "too literal" since the mystery has to be shown and the distance between what is known and what is revealed diminishes (2006, p. 79).[4]

Like any translation, Disney's *Mary Poppins* constitutes a reading of the original. As has been stated above, according to some the reading is so fanciful and far from the original that it preserves only tangential links with Travers's books. Others claim that it is a legitimate interpretation, which, like any translation, tries to make the work relevant to a new audience. What O'Sullivan (2005) wrote about the adaptation of *Pinocchio* applies to the Mary Poppins movie as well: "Disney's version can still be understood in relation to the norms and projections of American society at the time when the film was made (p. 121).

What heroine emerges from this Americanized transmutation of Mary Poppins?

Critics are unanimous in stating that as interpreted by Julie Andrews, Mary Poppins is definitely sweeter and more cheerful. Gone is the cold and rather brusque nanny, who never explains anything and always sniffs disapprovingly, enter a sunny, smiley beauty who every now and again breaks into song (one of which, rather tellingly is about a spoonful of sugar).

Due to the limitations of this paper no detailed analysis of the movie will be offered here. There are, however, two elements that are worth commenting on since they play a significant role in building Mary Poppins' American identity.

Firstly, the language—as has been said before, in the book Mary Poppins is rather reluctant to explain anything. In fact, she speaks relatively little, usually limiting herself to giving commands and scolding. In the movie, she is somewhat more talkative (although most dialogues are taken from the book) and has a playful attitude to words. In the famous episode of the picnic inside the painting, she says that a word which best expresses her joy is "Supercalifragilisticexpialidocious"—a sonorous neologism (absent in the book—Travers's Poppins never expressed any feelings, let alone joy), which subsequently becomes a refrain of a song.

Secondly, the departure scene—every book in the *Mary Poppins* series ends with the heroine's taking French leave. She never gives notice to the parents or says goodbye to the children. Jane and Michael usually sense the wind changing and are anxious that their favorite nanny will disappear, which she inevitably does, leaving the parents furious and the children inconsolable ("'Mary Poppins is the only person I want in the world!' Michael wailed, and flung himself on to the floor"—Travers, 2013, p. 135).

In the movie it is the nanny who is looking teary-eyed at the children before flying away propelled by her umbrella. And although she says (to herself or to the parrot-head that is the handle of her umbrella): "Practically perfect people never permit sentiment to muddle their thinking," we can clearly see (what the parrot comments on) "how she feels about these children."

---

[4]Król analyses C.S. Lewis' *The Lion, the Witch and the Wardrobe* and its movie adaptation.

Beautiful, more talkative and sentimental—is Disney's Mary Poppins still substantially the same as Travers's creation? The relationship is complex, as evidenced by Neil Gaiman's reminiscences:

> I encountered Mary Poppins, as so many of my generation and those who followed it did, through the film. ... Thus I was delighted to find, as a five- or six-year-old, a Puffin paperback edition of *Mary Poppins* by Travers with a picture of pretty Julie Andrews flying her umbrella on the cover. The book I read was utterly wrong—this was not the Mary Poppins I remembered—and utterly, entirely right (Grilli, 2007, p. 13.)

Similar sentiments are expressed by Kathryn Hughes:

> Walt Disney took a small, difficult book—not yet a classic in the way that *Winnie-the-Pooh* or *Peter Pan* were when he got his hands on them—and he stripped it down to its component parts and reimagined. The film became the yang to the book's yin.

5   Conclusion

This controversial yet admittedly rather marginal debate on the legitimacy of different Mary Poppinses is bound with many issues central to Translation Studies. In the words of Cronin (2006), nowadays "translation must be at the centre of any attempt to think about questions of identity" (p. 4).

The question about a literary figure's identity in translation can thus be seen as yet another way of asking about translational equivalence. In older accounts "equivalence was the result of sameness or similarity of meaning, however defined. It sought to infer equivalence from semantic relations between texts" (Hermans, 2007, p. 23). Later pragmatic, goal-oriented approaches were adopted, which "posited equivalence in pragmatic terms as sameness or similarity of use value" (ibid.). However, now many scholars point to the institutional dimension of equivalence—it is not established on the basis of inherent features of two texts but proclaimed by an appropriate authority. In the words of Theo Hermans: "Equivalence between a translation and its original is established through an external, institutional perlocutionary speech act. Rather than being an inherent feature of relations between texts, equivalence is declared" (2007, p. 24). Ultimately, therefore, whether Polish and American Mary Poppinses are equivalent to their English ur-heroine is a moot point. As Neil Gaiman stated: she is right and wrong at the same time, different like Kathryn Hughes' yin and yan, and yet somehow belonging together. To a large extent it is a matter of belief—do we accept a Mary Poppins who knows Król Ćwieczek or ads a smile and a spoonful of sugar to everything? Ultimately the question of identity remain as mysterious as the nanny herself.

References

Adamczyk-Garbowska, M. (1988). *Polskie tłumaczenia angielskiej literatury dziecięcej: problemy krytyki przekładu.* Wrocław: Ossolineum.
Balcerzan, E., & Bokiewicz, J. (1977). *Pisarze polscy o sztuce przekładu 1440–1974.* Wydawnictwo Poznańskie: Antologia. Poznań.
Baldick, C. (2001). *Concise dictionary of literary terms.* Oxford: Oxford University Press.
Baudelaire, C. (1887). Mon cœur mis à nu. Retrieved from http://www.bmlisieux.com/archives/coeuranu.htm
Biały, P. (2014). Snow White gets black hair and brown eyes. *STUDIA NEOFILOLOGICZNE X* (p. 173–186). Częstochowa.
Borodo, M. (2006). Children's literature translation studies?-zarys badań nad literaturą dziecięcą w przekładzie. *Przekładaniec, 16,* 12–23.
Cuomo, C. (1995). Spinsters in sensible shoes. In E. Bell & L. Haas (Eds.), *From mouse to mermaid: The politics of film, gender, and culture* (pp. 212–223). Bloomington: Indiana University Press.
Cronin, M. (2006). *Translation and identity.* Oxon: Routledge.
Eccleshare, J., & i Blake, Q. (2009). *1001 children's books you must read before you grow up.* Londyn: Quintessence.
Grilli, G. (2007). *Myth, symbol, and meaning in Mary Poppins.* The governess as provocateur. Transl. J. Varney. New York and London: Routledge.
Hazard, P. (1944). Books, children and men, trans. *Marguerite Mitchell (Boston: Horn Book, 1944), 40.*
Hermans, T. (2007). *The conference of the tongues.* Manchester: Jerome Publishing.
Jahn, M. (2007). Focalization. In The Hermans (Ed.), *Cambridge companion to narrative* (pp. 94–108). Cambridge: Cambridge University Press.
Jakobson, R., Schulte, R., & Biguenet, J. (1992). Theories of translation: An anthology of essays from Dryden to Derrida.
Katan, D. (2014). *Translating cultures: An introduction for translators, interpreters and mediators.* London: Routledge.
Kozak, J. (2009). *Przekład literacki jako metafora: między logos a lexis.* Warszawa: PWN.
Król, Z. (2006). Suszone śliwki. *Res Publica, 3,* 79–81.
Lawson, V. (2013). *Mary Poppins, she wrote: The life of PL Travers.* Simon and Schuster.
Munday, J. (2013). *Introducing translation studies: Theories and applications.* London: Routledge.
O'Sullivan, E. (2005). *Comparative children's literature.* London: Routledge.
Palmer, F. (1986). *Mood and modality.* Cambridge: Cambridge University Press.
Stevenson, R., (Director). (1964). *Mary Poppins [Motion Picture on DVD].* United States: Walt Disney Studio.
Tabakowska, E. (1995). *Gramatyka i obrazowanie. Wprowadzenie do językoznawstwa kognitywnego.* Kraków: Polska Akademia Nauk.
Tabakowska, E. (2003). Trzech Gabrieli: słowo i obraz jako przekład (o dwóch przekładach *Zmarłych* Jamesa Joyce'a). In I. Bobrowski (Ed.), *Anabasis: prace ofiarowane profesor Krystynie Pisarkowej* (pp. 317–328). Wydawn: Lexis.
Tabakowska, E. (2015). *Myśl językoznawcza z myślą o przekładzie. Wybór prac.* Kraków: WUJ.
Travers, P. L. (2013). *Mary Poppins-the complete collection.* London: HarperCollins.
Travers, P. L. (2014). *Mary Poppins-kolekcja* (I. Tuwim, Trans.). Warszawa: Jaguar.
Travis, M. (2007). Mixed messages: The problem of class in Mary Norton's Borrowers Series. *Children's Literature in Education, 38*(3), 187–194.
Tuwim, J. Listy do Toli Korian. *Dialog: miesięcznik Związku Literatów Polskich* 30.5(1).
Woźniak, M. (2012). Puchata przepustka do sławy. Pochwała Ireny Tuwim. *Przekładaniec,* 115–134.

Author Biography

Dorota Malina is a PhD student in linguistics at the Jagiellonian University in Kraków. She does research in children's literature translation. She is especially interested in the notion of the point of view in writing and translating for children. Her broader interests include Cognitive Linguistics as well as cultural and ethical aspects of translation.

Reading Ethnic American Children's Literature and the Questions of Cultural Authenticity

Ewa Klęczaj-Siara

Abstract Children's literature featuring non-white characters has always been essential to multicultural education provided in American schools. It has been celebrated for offering multiple perspectives and fostering intercultural under-standing. However, definitions of multiculturalism are oftentimes far from straightforward. The presence of non-white characters does not always give much authenticity to the represented culture. The author's perspective, the intended audience as well as the contextual and literary traditions from which the books arise are the actual measures of their legitimacy. Drawing on Rudine Sims's division of ethnic children's literature into "socially conscious" books, "melting pot" books and "culturally conscious" books, the paper explores the issue of authenticity by looking at a number of ethnic American children's picture books. It focuses specifically on African American children's literature, which has always been in the center of scholarly debates concerning the concept of cultural authenticity.

Keywords Multicultural literature · Ethnic literature · African American children's literature · Cultural authenticity

1 Introduction

The meaning of the term "multicultural literature" has generated numerous controversies within the last few years. One view on this issue suggests that multicultural literature "should include as many cultures as possible with no distinction between the dominant and the dominated" (Gilton, 2007, p. 2). Another approach stresses the importance of racial and ethnic issues in multicultural literature (Gilton, 2007, p. 2). The latter view is what most readers associate with multicultural children's books, in America frequently referred to as ethnic children's literature.

E. Klęczaj-Siara (✉)
Casimir Pulaski University of Technology and Humanities in Radom, Radom, Poland
e-mail: ekleczaj@tlen.pl

© Springer International Publishing AG 2017
J. Mydla et al. (eds.), *Multiculturalism, Multilingualism and the Self: Literature and Culture Studies*, Issues in Literature and Culture,
DOI 10.1007/978-3-319-61049-8_13

Given the popularity of current debates on cultural diversity in the United States, American multicultural children's literature is still relatively rare. The results of the study conducted by the Cooperative Children's Book Center reveal that about ten percent of the approximately 5000 children's books published in the U.S. annually are about people of color, and only five percent are written by people of color. There is a large proportion of ethnic children's books written by authors from different cultures. For example, in 2015, 261 books were written about African Americans, and only 86 of them by African American authors or illustrators. Out of the 41 books published about Native Americans, only 17 were written by people from the relevant cultures. Out of 81 books with Latino content, 42 were created by Latino authors or illustrators. Of the 111 books published about Asian/Pacific Americans, 86 were written by people from those cultures.

With such a large number of books written by authors from outside the culture portrayed, cultural authenticity emerges as a vital as well as complicated issue. There is no single definition of the concept. Violet Harada provides a list of criteria defining books as authentic. These are: the absence of stereotypes, derogatory language, and parodied speech; the presence of accurate illustrations and historical or cultural information (Harada, 1995). Weimin Mo and Wenju Shen question these criteria arguing instead that cultural authenticity pertains to cultural values and norms held by a social group. They contrast cultural authenticity with cultural facts arguing that not all cultural practices that exist in a culture are part of the central code of the culture (Mo & Shen, 1997, p. 87). Kathy G. Fox and Dana L. Short decide that "cultural authenticity cannot be defined, although 'you know it when you see it' as an insider reading a book about your own culture" (Fox & Short, 2003, p. 4).

Many children's literature scholars have been involved in the so called "insider/outsider" debate over cultural authenticity, which is simultaneously a debate over the quality of ethnic children's literature. Dona Gilton outlines three schools of thought on the concept of ethnic children's literature. The first one implies that "Multicultural literature should be written by all," and the author's cultural background should make no difference (Gilton, 2007, p. 81). According to the second one, "Only members of a culture should write their own story," and their background determines how well they describe the culture under consideration (Gilton, 2007, p. 82). However, members of one group vary greatly in their opinions of the culture. Not all of them know or identify with all aspects of their own culture, and some may produce stereotypes of their own. As Henry Louis Gates rightly observes, authenticity can be "faked" well enough to fool some cultural insiders (as cited in Gilton, 2007, p. 83). Gilton explains the third approach in the following way: "Background makes a definite difference as people write about a culture new or unknown to them.... However, people not indigenous to a group can learn enough about a culture new to them to do a good job.... Also, some cultural group members may not know their own culture that well and may make errors writing about or illustrating a story about their own culture or a related one" (Gilton, 2007, p. 82).

Idealizing one's own culture by ethnic authors is also an enemy to cultural authenticity. Members of ethnic minorities will rarely portray their own groups in a negative way, especially when most information on them published by mainstream authors has been based on stereotypes. However, if ethnic authors concentrate only on positive aspects of their cultures, their books become distorted and lead to historic inaccuracy.

Thus cultural authenticity is not as straightforward as it appears. There are many questions related to the issue of cultural authenticity, including what experiences authors need to have to write authentic books, how a book's purpose and use may relate to this question, the intended audience of the books, and the issue of social responsibility versus writers' freedom of expression.

Kathryn Lasky sees the question of authenticity as a form of censorship and a kind of restriction upon the author's freedom to write (Lasky, 1996). In this respect cultural authenticity might be perceived as a personal attack on the author's creativity and writing skills. Dana L. Fox and Kathy G. Short argue that "the question reflects larger issues of power structures and a history of negative misrepresentations of people of color in children's literature" (Fox & Short, 2004, p. 375). In their view the authors of "authentic" children's books should take into consideration the historical context of racist stereotypes as well as the false images of African American characters in children's books by white authors. Besides, African Americans' expectations to see positive portraits of themselves in children's literature are equally important.

2   Cultural Authenticity in African American Children's Literature

Conveying accurate and authentic portrayals of one's culture has always been important to the creators of African American children's literature. For almost a century they have been trying to replace the stereotyped portrayals of blacks with new inoffensive images. Although the first texts with positive black child characters were published in mid-1800s, the most important moment in the development of African American children's literature was the emergence of the first periodical for black children, "The Brownies' Book," published in 1920 and 1921 by well-known African American scholar William E.B. Du Bois. The magazine was produced in response to the lack of authentic information about African American people in mainstream materials. Dianne Johnson describes the context in which Du Bois and other scholars decided to create "The Brownies' Book":

> They wanted African American children and young adults to know about the history and achievements of Negro people. They wanted Negro children to know that even though black people in America had endured many struggles, they also had achieved many goals. For them it was important to have a magazine that taught black children about the lives of other black people, because most of the other children's magazines, movies, schoolbooks,

and picture books in 1920 portrayed black people as being ugly and rarely, if ever, doing anything important. (Johnson 1996, p. 13)

In order to change such negative perceptions of blacks in America and create a more authentic picture of their lives and culture, the founders of "The Brownies' Book" outlined seven objectives for their project:

(a) To make colored children realize that being <<colored>> is a normal, beautiful thing.
(b) To make them familiar with the history and achievements of the Negro race.
(c) To make them know that other colored children have grown into beautiful, useful and famous persons.
(d) To teach them a delicate code of honor and action in their relations with white children.
(e) To turn their little hurts and resentments into emulation, ambition and love of their homes and companions.
(f) To point out the best amusements and joys and worthwhile things of life.
(g) To inspire them to prepare for definite occupations and duties with a broad spirit of sacrifice (Du Bois, 1919, p. 286.)

According to many scholars of African American children's literature, these objectives can still be used as measures of cultural authenticity as well as guidelines for contemporary authors, both white and colored, writing books for and about black children. Rudine Sims, a leading scholar of African American children's literature, combined her own experience of children's literature with Du Bois's concept to create a framework dividing ethnic children's literature into three categories: melting pot, socially conscious, and culturally conscious literature (Sims, 1982).

3 Socially Conscious Books

Socially conscious books, most of which were published before 1970s, are primarily addressed to non-black readers. The presence of the white character, who gets into positive relationships with black people, is an essential element of the story. Generally the books portray people of color from the white perspective. As Gilton observes, "The main point of these books is the reaction of white people to people of color, who are seen as problems or challenges to be solved. These books mean well, but include subtle stereotypes of their own" (Gilton, 2007, p. 86). Sims labels the books "social conscience books" because they are supposed to create a social conscience and develop empathy for people from outside their own culture. Then she refers to some of the books as "backlash books" because they are also intended to develop African American tolerance towards other minority groups (Sims, 1982, p. 17). There are several types of stories offered in the socially conscious books. The stories of school desegregation and the accompanying changes in children's lives are the most popular ones (e.g. N. Carlson, *The Empty Schoolhouse*, 1965). Many of the books focus on the attempts of individual black and white children to make friends with each other in the new circumstances (e.g.

F. Randall, *The Almost Year*, 1971; F. Heide, *Sound of Sunshine, Sound of Rain*, 1970). In some of the stories both blacks and whites are working together to effect political changes (e.g. N. Carlson, *Marchers for the Dream*, 1969).

Socially conscious books convey a number of attitudes and assumptions about being black in America. Although they generally help to increase the visibility of African American characters in the world of children's books, many of them fail to effect any social change. The authors' perspective frequently leaves the reader with the belief that the existing social order is acceptable. For instance, evoking the motifs of the defeated black woman or the absent black father supports the existing stereotypes of African Americans. According to Gilton, such an approach does not challenge the racial views of the readers (Gilton, 2007, p. 29).

4   Melting Pot Books

Melting pot literature is not culturally specific although it concerns the lives of children of color. However, the books do not concentrate on the differences between characters of different races. Because most of them are picture books, and illustrations are frequently the only means of indicating the race of the characters, melting pot books do not focus on such issues as racial prejudice, discrimination or conflict. Instead they emphasize the concept of integration. Most of the books have both black and white characters living in the racially integrated settings. They face different kinds of problems that are usually beyond the racial conflict. Sims divides melting pot books into three categories: books with non-Afro-Americans as main characters, books about whites, with African Americans playing some important role, and stories about the relationship between a white child and a black one, usually presented as seen through the eyes of the white child (Sims, 1982, p. 34).

Unlike socially conscious books, melting pot books ignore subcultural differences, which, among others, is implicit in the language the characters use. All the African Americans are speakers of standard English. Sims concludes that the absence of Black English can be interpreted as an indicator of the assumption of homogeneity that marks melting pot books (Sims, 1982, p. 43). However, in some of the texts one can find other details indicating the black characters' racial identity, for instance, the racially marked setting of the book, standardized roles of the characters, or references to African American cultural traditions. In most cases, even if the authors try to keep a color-blind perspective, subconsciously they internalize the negative past images of African Americans.

The Snowy Day (1962), written and illustrated by Ezra Jack Keats, is a typical example of a melting pot book. It is generally known as the first full-color American picture book to feature a black child by a non-black author. The main character is an inner-city African American boy, Peter, who is playing in the snow. One may wonder why a white author decided to write about a black child at the peak of the civil rights movement in America. Keats had personal reasons for that. During the Depression of the 1930s he grew up in Brooklyn, where he had a chance to interact daily with children of different ethnicities, all living in poor tenement houses. Later on in his life, as an author and illustrator, Keats became particularly alarmed by the fact that very few children's books featured black characters. He decided to change that with *The Snowy Day*. Michelle Martin refers to the words of the author, which she treats as a turning point in the development of African American children's literature:

> My hero would be a Black child. I made many sketches and studies of Black children. . . .
> I wanted him to be in the book on his own, not through the benevolence of white children
> or anything else. The important thing is that the kids in a book have to be real — regardless
> of color. I don't like to emphasize the race thing, because what's really important is the
> honesty. (Martin, 2004, p. 51)

Many literary critics acclaiming Keats's picture book refer to Peter as "the American Everychild in a brown face and a red snowsuit" (Bishop, 2007, p. 116). Keats's book says nothing about ethnicity of its characters. However, visual details of the book raise questions about presenting racial stereotypes. For instance, the boy's mother, who is overweight and always wears a bright house dress, is reminiscent of the stereotyped "mammy" figure.

Melting pot books are the most universal in their approach to racial issues. Nonetheless, as Sims observes, "This universality seems to be achieved in a rather facile manner, by viewing Afro-Americans with a tunnel vision that permits only one part of the duality of growing up Afro-American to be seen at a time" (Sims, 1982, p. 41). The authors of melting pot books create kids who are Afro-Americans in appearance only, who reflect only the non-Afro side of the African American duality. Ignoring the sociocultural differences between white Americans and African Americans may also signify something undesirable. It may be a means of conferring a kind of invisibility on black characters.

5   Culturally Conscious Books

Unlike socially conscious or melting pot books, culturally conscious books on African Americans are usually written by people belonging to the described ethnic group. Gilton characterizes the books in the following way:

> These books are written from the points of view of ethnic children, include more specific
> cultural details than do the melting-pot books, and include fewer stereotypes than the
> socially conscious books. Many reflect the perspectives of ethnic writers writing for their
> own children, as well as for those from other groups. (Gilton, 2007, p. 86)

For these reasons culturally conscious books come closest to what we can call "authentic" African American children's literature today. They celebrate the distinctiveness of African American life and culture. They primarily speak to African American children about themselves though they are not closed to non-black readers. Sims explains the meaning of the label "culturally conscious" in the following way:

elements in the text, not just the pictures, make it clear that the book consciously seeks to depict a fictional Afro-American life experience. At minimum this means that the major characters are Afro-Americans, the story is told from their perspective, the setting is an Afro-American community or home, and the text includes some means of identifying the characters as black — physical descriptions, language, cultural traditions, and so forth. (Sims, 1982, p. 49)

Culturally conscious books also reflect other cultural behaviors, institutions, and traditions that are part of Afro-American life experiences, such as Black church services, extended families or respect for elders.

The setting of the books, which corresponds to the general geographic distribution of the Black population, is another important element of culturally conscious literature. There is a considerable number of urban books presenting low income families, as well as books focusing on the southern rural communities. The picture of the city is usually depressing. While in most cases the protagonists emerge hopeful, their experiences are rather grim. In spite of the conditions depicted, the books emphasize the strengths and resources available within the individual and the support from family and friends that enable people to cope.

Tar Beach written and illustrated by Faith Ringgold is one of the most successful picture books focusing on black experience in America's most "black" setting. Published in 1990 by Crown Books, it was an immediate success as *Tar Beach* was a Caldescott honor Book and winner of the Coretta Scott King Award for illustration, among numerous other honors. *Tar Beach* is based on Ringgold's experiences of growing up in Harlem, a place which had a great impact on the author's sense of reality. It tells the story of an African American family whose father lost his job since he was black and was excluded from the trade unions. However, it was him who built the Union Building, which now he has no right to enter. The mother of the family struggles with the family's lack of financial resources by leading a modest lifestyle. Their daughter, Cassie, is not resigned though. One starry night, as her parents are having dinner with their neighbors on the roof of their apartment block, which they call "tar beach," the girl imagines that she can improve the situation of her family by flying in the stars above the roof of the building. Cassie in *Tar Beach* seems to be able to change the social order of the 1930s. She is depicted flying above the buildings and the bridge as if she was ruling the Harlem community. It is a highly symbolic scene in which she says: "Now I have claimed it [the bridge]. All I had to do was fly over it for it to be mine forever. ... I can fly. That means I am free to go wherever I want for the rest of my life" (Ringgold, 1991, unpaged). By the act of flying she wants to find a job for her father, and thus improve the economic situation of the whole family.

Although Ringgold aims this message at all her readers, the book has roots in African American history and culture. The flying motif is a direct reference to the folk belief that slaves had the ability to fly out of the fields, and back to Africa. The family's dining with their neighbors is connected with the African American community spirit, and the food (the southern staples) they are eating—peanuts, fried chicken, watermelon—reminds the readers of their African roots.

Culturally conscious literature frequently depicts the southern rural experience, which is another thing that gives credibility to the stories of black characters. The books illustrating black lives in the American South are usually affirmations of unity and black family love, which is a counter narrative to the existing stereotypes of black communities. Moreover, the illustrations capture the beauty of the land as well as the rituals of black life in the rural South. Nikki Giovanni demonstrates the point in her picture book *Knoxville, Tennessee*, illustrated by white artist Larry Johnson. The book includes a number of authenticating details: an extended black family, close relationships between people of different generations, references to religion, and beautiful illustrations showing landscapes of the American South. Both the narrative text and the illustrations represent the setting. While the verbal representation of the setting is reduced to a few nouns—the garden, the mountains, and the church—the range of pictorial solutions used in the accompanying illustrations provides additional information to the story. The panoramic views of the rural South, with white buildings, church towers, and the profusion of natural surroundings, reflect the author's romantic view of her birthplace, and can be apprehended as a symbol representing her nostalgia for the past.

Implicit in the scenery is also the author's resistance to the existing social and political constraints imposed on black communities, which are debunked with such a dreamlike vision of black life in America. With *Knoxville, Tennessee*, Giovanni initiates a discussion of the role of the African American church. The illustrated version particularly emphasizes this point. The pictures present black people enjoying themselves on a church picnic, sitting outside the church and listening to a church choir, or socializing at the church homecoming. While for many sociologists examining the influence of the church on black communities the black church represents both the concept of separation and the concept of integration, Giovanni's story exemplifies only the unifying force of the institution that gives its members a sense of belonging and a feeling of racial pride. Given the fact that the book was based on the author's personal experience of growing up in the South, the image of the church congregation should be regarded as the central code of the black culture. Another authenticating detail is the motif of the quilt, which appears as an important component of the illustrations in *Knoxville, Tennessee*. The quilt on which the girl character is sitting alone or with her grandmother creates a sense of security and links her with the past. In many African American picture books, the quilt is interconnected with the figure of the grandmother, and like her, it is used as a metaphor of keeping family history, with the scraps of cloth that make the quilt functioning as reminders of important people and events in the family.

Except for the stories of everyday life of African Americans, many culturally conscious children's books focus on the issues of black looks and identity. Being despised by others due to one's skin color or hair texture is common experience to many Afro-Americans. In order to resist such behaviors, many contemporary black authors, drawing on their personal experience, are producing children's books aimed at countering negative attitudes toward skin color or Afro hair.

One of the earliest children's books written on the significance of hair textures among African Americans is Carolivia Herron's autobiographical *Nappy Hair* (1997). Judging by the illustrations it is probably set in the rural South. Although the book gave rise to a national conversation on Afro hair, it should be credited for a number of details speaking for the unique presentation of black experience. The story is based on the African American call-and-response pattern. Uncle Mordeca, a senior of the family, declares that Brenda'a hair is the nappiest hair in the world, and throughout the book the family members, like one chorus, respond to Uncle's statements. The whole family, like a church congregation, becomes integral to the performance of the tale. Introducing the call–and–response pattern gives a lot of credibility to the book. It is evidence of the author's familiarity with black folk rituals of talking. Interestingly, the language of the characters is marked with distinctive grammar, lexicon and style reflecting the features of Black English, which somehow defines African American identity (Lester, 2007, p. 105). Moreover, in the book there are examples of exaggerated language, proverbial statements, plays on words, image making and metaphor, such as "Combing your hair is like scrunching through the New Mexico desert in brogans in the heat of summer," the use of rhyme, rhythm, and repetitive sounds: "Why you gotta be so mean, why you gotta be so willful, why you gotta be so ornery, thinking about giving that nappy, nappy hair to that innocent little child?" (Herron, 1997, unpaged). Another detail that indicates the author's awareness of Afro-American traditions is naming. In the culturally conscious books, many characters' names reflect some understanding of Afro-American naming traditions (e.g. Mordecai, Cassie), as well as some terms of address that are popular in some Afro-American communities. Children are often referred to as "Baby," mothers are called "Mama," siblings are often called "Sister" or "Brother" within the family.

Culturally conscious books differ significantly from socially conscious books as well as melting pot books in terms of the imagery they use to describe a variety of skin colors of Afro-Americans. Whereas most white authors make a general distinction between black and white characters, gradations in skin color are almost always an obligatory part of an Afro-American's description of another Afro-American. Sims observes two interesting tendencies in culturbooks:

> One is to describe shading — light brown, reddish brown, dark brown, copper colored, olive, sandy brown, oak brown, light skinned. The other is to use positive imagery (and often food-related) to paint the person accurately... Such descriptions of skin color are indicative of an awareness of the naturalness of such descriptions among Afro-Americans and perhaps indicative of an effort to create and promote positive associations with the darkness that carries so many negative connotations in the English language. (Sims, 1982, pp. 70–71)

Although the main theme of Herron's book is the beauty of the child's hair as well as the trouble connected with handling this type of hair, there is a considerable amount of Afro-American history which is skillfully woven into the texture of the story. The black readers are reminded that their ancestors were brought to America as slaves, and their hairstyle is a form of legacy of this forced relocation. Interestingly, the child character challenges any efforts to straighten her hair, described in the book as "the kinkiest, the nappiest, the fuzziest, the most screwed up, squeezed up, knotted up, tangled up, twisted up, nappiest … hair you've ever seen in your life" (Herron, 1997, unpaged). Brenda's hair thus becomes a metaphor of resistance—"an act of God that came straight through Africa" that cannot "be hot-pressed into surrender" (Herron, *Nappy Hair*, unpaged). The accompanying illustrations of Brenda and her family play an important role here. As Lester observes, they "exude confidence, self-knowledge, and historical awareness" (p. 104). Cepeda pays attention to various black skin tones and hairstyles: Brenda's family members are different shades of brown and have braids, dreadlocks, and Afros.

With its visual appeal, its cultural celebration of black hair, its revisionist history, and its emphasis on black community, *Nappy Hair* authenticates important details of black life in America. Nonetheless, several scholars question the credibility of some of the book's illustrations. For instance, the picture featuring a group of family members trying to straighten the girl's hair with different kinds of cosmetics seems to stand in opposition to the book's general concept of celebrating black hair. This situation, however, is authentic in many black families who absorb white people's attitudes to black hair.

Carolivia Herron, Faith Ringgold, Nikki Giovanni and many other contemporary African American authors expanded the canon of American children's literature with stories that authenticate the real cultural context in which black children live their lives. Bishop concludes that "This authentication is realized through weaving into the texts and illustrations Black rhetorical styles, realistic details of everyday living, a focus on family and family relationships, and cultural traditions" (2007, p. 123). The primary audience of those books are black children. However, the stories are also a great source of information for readers of other races and ethnicities.

Recent studies in African American children's literature indicated great improvements of picture books. Most of the recent publications can be defined as culturally conscious literature. The book characters are presented in positive, nonstereotypical ways. They usually assume a pro-active role in resolving their own problems. Derogatory language is absent from those works. Historical information is accurately presented in all the titles. Moreover, there is a myriad of cultural details that are authentically described. Finally, African American characters and places are realistically depicted through illustrations.

6   Conclusion

Not all of the successful African American picture books have been created by writers or illustrators of the same culture. In fact, there is a growing number of publications whose authors come from different cultural backgrounds than those depicted in the books. These writers have successfully crossed cultural gaps to write outside their own experience. It must be stated, though, that the authors writing outside their own culture may do so for different reasons than the "insiders." The authors of color usually write within their own culture with the intention of enhancing the self-esteem of children of color and in order to challenge existing stereotypes and dominant assumptions about their culture, as well as to pass on the central values and stories of that culture to children. Authors writing outside their own cultures often focus on building awareness of cultural differences and improving intercultural relationships. These differing intentions result in different stories for different audiences and different evaluations of authenticity.

In her later study on children's literature, Bishop notes that multicultural children's books can be described as "specific" or "universal" depending on the extent to which they illustrate a culturally-specific or universal theme (Bishop, 2003). Some authors intentionally create "generic books" which are based only on universal experiences, and unlike the authors of culturally-specific books, they do not mark the ethnicities of their characters by means of actions, attitudes, appearances or dialogue. Hence Bishop argues that generic books can be evaluated entirely on literary criteria rather than authenticity since they do not portray any specific cultural experience. Yet, there are scholars who believe that every single book should be assessed for both literary criteria and cultural authenticity. For instance, Yenika-Agbaw (1998) strongly criticizes the "generic books" arguing that they are based on the assumption that there is a homogenous human experience. Marginalizing specific cultural details, in her view, leads to further marginalization and exclusion of the minority cultures while maintaining the superiority of the dominant culture. Such an approach does not authenticate the presented stories and facts.

Although cultural authenticity may not matter to scholars of literature, it does matter to educators, specifically in the multicultural environments. As Kathy Short and Dana Fox observe in their critical review on multicultural children's literature, "all children have the right to see themselves within a book, to find within a book the truth of their own experiences instead of stereotypes and misrepresentations" (Short & Fox, 2004, p. 381). Since literature serves as an important tool to learn about oneself and other cultures, it should not provide distorted images of selected ethnic and racial minorities. Thus the concept of cultural authenticity is essential to build intercultural understandings as well as to challenge monocultural perspectives that characterize many school settings.

References

Bishop, R. S. (2003). Reframing the debate about cultural authenticity. In D. L. Fox, & K. G. Short, (Eds.), *Stories matter: The complexity of cultural authenticity in children's literature*. Urbana. IL: National Council of Teachers of English.

Bishop, R. S. (2007). *Free within ourselves: The development of African American children's literature*. Portsmouth, NH: Heinemann.

Du Bois, W. E. B. (1919). *The True Brownies. The Crisis* (No. 18, pp. 285–286).

Fox, D. L., & Short, K. G. (Eds.). (2003). *Stories matter: The complexity of cultural authenticity in children's literature*. Urbana, IL: National Council of Teachers of English.

Fox, D. L., & Short, K. G. (2004). The complexity of cultural authenticity in children's literature: A critical review. In J. Worthy (Ed.), *53rd Yearbook of the National Reading Conference*. Oak Creek, Wisconsin: National Reading Conference, Inc.

Gilton, D. L. (2007). *Multicultural and ethnic children's literature in the United States*. Langham, MD: The Scarecrow Press.

Harada, V. H. (1995). Issues of ethnicity, and quality in Asian-American picture books, 1983–93. *Journal of Youth Services in Libraries, 2*, 135–149.

Herron, C. (1997). Nappy Hair. Illustrator J. Cepeda. New York: Dragonfly Books.

Lasky, K. (1996). To Stingo with love: An author's perspective on writing outside one's culture. *The New Advocate, 9*(1), 1–7.

Lester, N. A. (2007). *Once upon a time in a different world: Issues and ideas in African American children's literature*. New York: Routledge.

Martin, M. H. (2004). *Brown gold: Milestones of African American children's picture books, 1845-2002*. New York and London: Routledge.

Mo, W., & Shen, W. (1997). Reexamining the issue of authenticity in picture books. *Children's Literature in Education, 28*(2), 85–93.

Ringgold, F. (1991). *Tar beach*. New York: Scholastic.

Sims, R. (1982). *Shadow and substance: Afro-American experience in contemporary children's fiction*. Urbana IL: National Council of Teachers of English.

Yenika-Agbaw, V. (1998). Images of West Africa in children's books: Replacing old stereotypes with new ones? *The New Advocate, 11*, 203–218.

Author Biography

Ewa Klęczaj-Siara received her PhD in American Literature at the University of Lublin in 2014. Her dissertation was published as a monograph *Pokochać czerń. Dziedzictwo myśli W.E.B. Du Boisa w książkach dla dzieci Nikki Giovanni, Faith Ringgold i bell hooks* in 2015. Her academic interests encompass ethnic American children's literature. More currently, her research focuses on the intersection of race and gender in contemporary African-American children's picture books. She has presented papers on children's literature at major conferences, including the International Research Society for Children's Literature (IRSCL). She teaches American Studies at the University of Technology and Humanities in Radom.

Native American Lives in Between Cultures in Selected Contemporary Self-narratives

Edyta Wood

Abstract This paper explores Native American perspectives emerging from a selection of contemporary American Indian self-narratives. The discussion is based on *The Lone Ranger and Tonto Fistfight in Heaven* and *The Absolutely True Diary of a Part-Time Indian* by Sherman Alexie (Spokane/Coeur D'Alene) and *Crazy Brave* by Joy Harjo (Mvskoke/Creek). These autobiographical stories offer insights into the questions of identity surrounding the dilemmas of Native Americans themselves vis à vis their own tribal community and vis à vis white culture in the United States. The self-narratives explore American Indians' responses to traditional ways and dealing with the contemporary context of American culture and confronting the white world. The authors of these autobiographical stories share the experience of the struggles negotiating these issues within themselves as Native Americans and the outside world revealing the conflicted selves and the reality of American Indian lives in between worlds.

Keywords Sherman Alexie · Joy Harjo · Native American · American Indian · Self-narrative

1 Introduction

> We Indians have LOST EVERYTHING. We lost our native land, we lost our languages, we lost our songs and dances. We lost each other. We only know how to lose and be lost (Alexie, 2007, p. 173.)

With very little presence of Native American authentic representations in popular culture, American literature, or American consciousness in general, it seems to be quite appropriate and justified that contemporary indigenous writers would choose the form of self-narrative to write about their experience. Through writing

E. Wood (✉)
Institute of Modern Languages and Applied Linguistics, Kazimierz Wielki University in Bydgoszcz, ul. Grabowa 2, 85-601 Bydgoszcz, Poland
e-mail: edytawood@ukw.edu.pl

© Springer International Publishing AG 2017
J. Mydla et al. (eds.), *Multiculturalism, Multilingualism and the Self: Literature and Culture Studies*, Issues in Literature and Culture,
DOI 10.1007/978-3-319-61049-8_14

such autobiographical books about the reality and perspectives of modern-day Indians, they are determined to make sure that the voices of Native Americans are represented in a way that is true to life.

Autobiography occupies a special place in Native literature. David Brumble in his *American Indian Autobiography* emphasizes the importance of what he calls preliterate autobiographical narratives and points out the need to "understand the early, oral autobiographical narratives in order to fully appreciate the autobiographies of the later, literate Indians" (as cited in Tatonetti, 2009, p. 280). These stories were told in particular tribes in their tribal languages as part of storytelling within the oral tradition. They evolved as a result of colonization when some were written down by white ethnographers. These white co-authors not only translated them (or had someone else as an interpreter), but also adapted them in the process to better suit the white audience. These autobiographies often took the form of "as told to" narratives. Unavoidably, the process of mediation and interpretation must have led to some distortions, and it was difficult to distinguish the original intent of the Native author and the intervention of the white editor. These autobiographies, then, were written through the lens of the white person who took the agency of authorship instead of the original Native author. Perhaps the best-known case is that of John Neihardt, the editor of what was supposed to be the autobiography of Black Elk (*Black Elk Speaks*, 1932), who admitted that he influenced Black Elk's original words so that they could be understood by the white audience. He openly stated that "the beginning and ending are mine" (cited in DeMallie, 2014, p. 250).

Another type of Native autobiographical narrative is self-written by indigenous authors. An important figure who produced autobiographical stories was Zitkala-Ša (1876–1938, otherwise known as Gertrude Simmons Bonnin), who learned English at a boarding school to which, like many other Native children, she had been forcefully taken. She mastered the English language to the point that she became an accomplished author and used it also for political causes in the fight for Native people's rights. Through her writing and actions, she paved the way for modern Native writers who can be in control of the message conveyed, having a sense of agency and thus turning Native Americans as people and characters in their stories into full subjects in their own right. Carpenter (2004) argues that Zitkala-Ša's writing "produces a bicultural context in order to reconfigure the representation of Native Americans and their cultural status" (p. 1). This enabled Native authors to transform what Powell calls "their object-status within colonial discourse into a subject-status, a presence instead of an absence" (as cited in Carpenter, 2004, p. 2).

This self-representation, however, does not come without complications for Native authors. The limited presence of Native American perspectives caused by the dominating role of Euro-American culture, let alone the sheer number of indigenous people in the United States, require a greater sense of responsibility as to what precisely to represent and how exactly it should be achieved.

Contemporary Native American writers are often acutely aware of their role since their tribal communities and some fellow indigenous authors hold them responsible for their actions and views expressed. They are expected to position themselves clearly vis à vis their own culture and white culture as well as to show their response to colonialism and stereotypes of American Indians. There is a noticeable tribalist or nationalist approach in Native American communities and in some circles of Native literary critics in which the roles of indigenous writers are strictly prescribed. Martínez (2014) explains that the Native intellectual needs to be politically involved, maintaining links with his or her tribe without "giving into the dominant society's preconceptions of Indians" (p. 30). Figures such as Clyde Warrior or Vine Deloria Jr. emphasized the role of indigenous authors in "affirming the language of sovereignty and determination" (p. 39).

Both authors whose works have been selected here, Sherman Alexie, a Spokane/Coeur D'Alene Indian author, and Joy Harjo, a Mvskoke Indian writer, realize the immense social, political, and ethical responsibility that they bear as indigenous authors writing about their own communities. Sherman Alexie feels that "[t]he responsibilities of being an Indian writer are enormous. Even more so than any other group of people because we have so much to protect" (Purdy & Alexie, 1997, p. 16). In a conversation with Caldwell (2009), Alexie offers a perspective which sounds like a manifesto for Native writers:

> We do have a cultural responsibility above and beyond what other people do, more than other ethnic groups, simply because we are so misrepresented and misunderstood and appropriated. We have a serious responsibility to tell the truth. And to act as (and I hate to use the word because people put it on me, and I don't like the responsibility) role models. We are more than just writers. We are storytellers. We are spokespeople. We are cultural ambassadors. We are politicians. We are activists (p. 58.)

Joy Harjo echoes this imperative as a Native author when she writes that she feels that she "was entrusted with carrying voices, songs and stories to grow and release into the world, to be of assistance and inspiration. These were my responsibility ... We enter into a family story and then other stories based on tribal clans, on tribal towns and nations, lands, countries, planetary systems and universes. Yet we each have our own individual soul story to tend" (Harjo 2012, p. 20).

The very form of autobiography further complicates the act of writing for Native writers since it touches upon core questions of identity. Erdinast-Vulcan (2008) asserts that "what is at stake here is not just the spectrum of literary representations of subjectivity" and quotes Eakin who claims that it "is not merely something we read in a book," but as "a discourse of identity, delivered bit by bit in the stories we tell about ourselves day in and day out, autobiography structures living" (p. 5). Sherman Alexie points out what this may involve for indigenous authors: "As an Indian, you don't have the luxury of being called an autobiographical writer often. You end up writing for the whole race" (Nygren, 2005, p. 152).

The autobiographical books written by Sherman Alexie, *The Lone Ranger and Tonto Fistfight in Heaven* and *The Absolutely True Diary of a Part-Time Indian*, as well as *Crazy Brave* written by Joy Harjo are forms of self-narratives, personal stories that are embedded in the larger story of their tribes and Indian cultures. They also address how indigenous people fit or do not fit in the mainstream white-dominated society. The personal experiences of growing up Indian are interwoven with experiences central to Native Americans, like removal, displacement, dispossession, broken treaties, near annihilation of their cultures and people. These two authors struggle with questions of identity trying to find their role in their own community and their place in white people's culture in America. They give a complex picture of dilemmas facing modern-day Indians living their lives in between cultures being strangers not quite in a strange land, but in their own land.

2 Sherman Alexie

Sherman Alexie, born in 1966, grew up on the Spokane reservation in Wellpinit, Washington. This experience made a powerful imprint on his life, his self-perception and understanding of the situation of Indians in the United States. *The Lone Ranger and Tonto Fistfight in Heaven* is a collection of short stories first published in 1993, which Alexie calls autobiographical. In an interview with *The New Yorker* (Alexie & Walter, 2013) he admits that it is not "an autobiography of details but an autobiography of the soul." *The Absolutely True Diary of a Part-Time Indian*, published in 2007, tells the story of growing up on the Spokane Indian reservation from the point of view of a fourteen-year-old Spokane Indian boy named Arnold Spirit born in the early nineties. This is, in fact, the story of Sherman Alexie, with the difference that it was moved to more contemporary times. In his characters, Alexie reflects many of his own issues surrounding the question of being Indian. The figures in these books show an array of different attitudes toward tradition and dealing with everyday life as an Indian in modern-day America. Alexie paints a painful picture of poverty, hunger, unemployment, and a sense of hopelessness afflicting the community on the reservation. Sometimes he shows the anger, rage, tensions and frustration of his characters, who have to deal with the past, but also with the harsh reality of modern tribal life, the effects of, as he writes, the situation that "[f]or hundreds of years, Indians were witnesses to crimes of an epic scale" (Alexie, 1994, p. 3).

In this context of futility and hopelessness, drinking is a self-destructive response to the reality of Indian life, which plagues its communities. Alexie describes the reaction of Victor, a character in *The Lone Ranger*, observing his father drinking: "Victor watched his father take a drink of vodka on a completely empty stomach. Victor could hear that near-poison fall, then hit, flesh and blood, nerve and vein. Maybe it was like lightning tearing an old tree into halves. Maybe it was like a wall of water, a reservation tsunami" (Alexie, 1994, p. 6). Alcohol is like a painkiller and poison at the same time: "he wanted to drink so much his blood could make the entire tribe numb" (1994, p. 90).

Many tragedies and deaths are caused by drinking in the Indian communities that Alexie portrays. In both books he describes tragic situations from his own life like his alcoholic father, who would disappear for days causing him sorrow and distress, his older sister, who died in a house fire when she fell asleep drunk after a party, his grandmother, who ironically had never drunk herself but died in a car accident caused by a drunk Indian driver, and Alexie's own problems with drinking. He seems to be deeply troubled by this issue. In *The Absolutely True Diary*, he clearly shows his frustration and sadness to the point of lamentation through his teenage protagonist who "cried because so many of my fellow tribal members were slowly killing themselves and I wanted them to live. I wanted them to get sober" (2007, p. 216). Arnold Spirit, in the face of a series of alcohol-related deaths in his immediate circle, was adamant about never drinking himself: "I wept and wept and wept because I knew I was never going to drink and because I was never going to kill myself" (2007, p. 217).

Some Native American critics fault Alexie for his portrayal of indigenous people in relation to the problem of alcoholism. Evans (2001) discusses the criticism of a group of Native critics such as Louis Owens, Gloria Bird and Elizabeth Cook-Lynn who raise the problem of Alexie "perpetuating damaging stereotypes, including that of the drunken Indian" (p. 4). Evans, however, counters that Alexie's "fictional realism in his portrayal of alcohol on reservation life meets head-on the facts of real Indian existence and experience" (2001, p. 4). Also Hafen (1997), a Native American woman herself, confirms Alexie's portrayal of reality when she writes about her own community where "like Victor, many drifted in and out of alcoholic rehabilitation" (p. 4). She admits that "my own sister lost her life in that struggle ... I identify with Alexie's personal revelations as they point to statistical trends in Native populations" (p. 76). Alexie himself in interviews responds to the criticism of his presentation of the role of alcohol in tribal community explaining his perspective that alcoholism is simply a fact, a reality in reservation life (Moyers & Ablow, 2013). He expresses his exasperation saying "people thought I was writing about stereotypes, but more than anything I was writing about my own life" (Nygren, 2005, p. 152). Probably the key aspect here to consider would be Alexie's intent. Given his own struggle, and his family's ongoing struggle on both sides of the problem (his mother having been a counselor on the Spokane reservation for decades), it may be assumed that his own pain testifies to his compassion rather than contempt for his fellow tribal members.

Alexie articulates his own conflicted feelings of being Indian, which show a larger picture of Native Americans and their self-perception. He explores challenging questions of identity, writing "I had to figure out what it meant to be a boy, a man, too. Most of all, I had to find out what it meant to be Indian, and there ain't no self-help manuals for that last one" (1994, p. 211). He shows the ambivalent and painful elements of a love-hate relationship, describing poignantly the internal struggle which then finds an external expression in the interactions between Indians. These bonds can be strong and close, but they can also cause pain and confinement. When commenting on one of the many fights on the reservation, Alexie points out that "strangers would never want to hurt each other so badly" (1994, p. 2). In one of the short stories in *The Lone Ranger and Tonto* entitled "Crazy Horse" he describes an encounter at a powwow between a young Indian man and a young Indian woman which turns into a date where both of them judge each other's degree of being a real Indian. They watch for each other's Indian ways, or the lack of them, reflected in each other's physical appearance, their way of dressing with regard to what is authentic or not, and most importantly, being a warrior or not. What is reflected here is a kind of loathing and self-loathing in confronting each other's Indianness. The young man, Victor, fearing that probably he does not measure up as a "warrior," sabotages the relationship by showing contempt to the woman by saying "You're nothing important (...) You're just another goddamned Indian like me" (1994, p. 41). The characters' internal dialogues, however, show that even though at first they saw each other as falling short of the ideal, later they decide that the other one is, in fact, perfect. What went on in the young woman's mind was that "[s]he thought he was Crazy Horse" (1994, p. 41). Victor leaves, but then lingers watching the Winnebago for hours and wishing "he was Crazy Horse" (1994, p. 42).

Even if the characters in Alexie's books may show an ambivalent attitude to being Indian, they still grapple with the questions of tradition and tribal legacy in general, showing a host of responses. Alexie shows his appreciation for traditional singing and dancing, which he refers to as "great, beautiful, in fact" (2007, p. 17). He writes about modern-day powwows, which are a combination of tradition with tribal singing, dancing, storytelling and frybread, and contemporary American culture with hot-dogs, hamburgers, and a variety of cars. Alexie describes the scenery of "the parked cars, vans, SUVs, RVs, plastic tents, and deer-hide tepees" (2007, p. 20). This image may be symbolic of the lives of many Native Americans which are often a mix of both worlds.

One of the most traditional characters in *The Lone Ranger and Tonto* is Thomas-Builds-the-Fire, who is perceived by the older generation as "magic" and the younger generation as simply disturbed. The narrator sees him as both "magic and crazy" (1994, p. 20). Thomas's stories involve some of the tribal myths and legends, and also address the contemporary situation. The narrator shows some distance and humor in Thomas's stories, for example, describing his drug-induced vision when Thomas says, "Victor—I can see you. You're beautiful. You've got braids and you're stealing a horse. Wait no. It's not a horse. It's a cow" (1994, p. 14). There are times, however, when his stories take a more serious tone when he, for instance, tells a story of how he will toss Victor's father's ashes into the water: "And your father will rise like a salmon, leap over the bridge, over me, and find his way home. It will be beautiful" (1994, p. 74). This story integrates a very symbolic element for Spokane Indians who were fishermen, the salmon, and the central figure for Alexie, his father, who he has been trying to come to terms with, also through his stories.

Sometimes these visions and myths encapsulate the Native American experience in general and a personal or family experience in particular, recounting the nightmares that Native Americans are haunted by. Alexie mentions the painful past of encounters with white people, recalling how: "[t]hose blankets they gave us, infected with smallpox, have killed us" (1994, p. 17), or the dramatic experience of boarding schools: "I remember the nightmare about the thin man in a big hat who took the Indian children away from their parents. He came with scissors and a locked box to hide all the amputated braids. But we danced, under wigs and between unfinished walls, through broken promises and around empty cupboards" (1994, pp. 194–195).

Alexie, however, shows some characters that seem to be perfect examples of how to be Indian in the contemporary world. Norma-Many-Horses in *The Lone Ranger and Tonto* combines the traditional Indian ways with the ability to integrate elements of white people's culture. The narrator recollects how Norma "could dance Indian and white. And that's a mean feat, since the two methods of dancing are mutually exclusive" (1994, p. 200). Perhaps what Alexie writes about her ability to reconcile these two seemingly irreconcilable dancing styles is what he would envision as an approach to life worthy of imitating for his fellow tribal members. He writes that Norma was "a cultural lifeguard, watching for those of us that were so close to drowning" (1994, p. 199). Despite her young age, she was called "grandmother" in the community out of respect. Alexie's own grandmother, who appears in *The Absolutely True Diary*, is another person he deeply admires. She is presented as the embodiment of what the writer believes is best in a human being generally and also specifically as a role model of being Indian. What he shows as best in her was her tolerance, which Alexie points out was a virtue of Native people in the past: "in the old days, Indians used to be forgiving of any eccentricity ... Of course, ever since white people showed up ..., Indians have gradually lost all of their tolerance ... But not my grandmother" (2007, p. 155). She also ended her life with the message of forgiveness, forgiving the driver who had fatally injured her.

Tolerance, however, was painfully missing in Alexie's experience of growing up on a reservation. In *The Absolutely True Diary of a Part-Time Indian* he writes about the dramatic circumstances of his childhood and adolescence. The protagonist, Arnold Spirit, like Alexie, was born with hydrocephalus ("too much cerebral fluid" or in more simple terms "water on the brain" (2007, p. 1) and as a baby underwent successful surgery, but still suffered from other related health problems. Because of his disproportionately large head, stutter, lisping and epileptic seizures, he stood out as different and became a target of bullying on the reservation. He writes "I was a human punching bag" (2007, p. 62) and "I'm a zero on the rez" (2007, p. 16). Being different, suffering from health-related problems, and being bullied turned him into a bit of a recluse. He spent a lot of time at home reading books.

The rest of his reality, however, was the same as his fellow tribal members in terms of poverty, sometimes even hunger, and a general lack of prospects. The way he writes about hunger from the point of view of Arnold Spirit, it does not seem like it was the worst problem. As Arnold reflects, "[a]nd sure, sometimes, my family misses a meal, and sleep is the only thing we have for dinner," but "being hungry makes food taste better. There is nothing better than a chicken leg when you haven't eaten for (approximately) eighteen-and-a-half hours. And believe me, a good piece of chicken can make anybody believe in the existence of God" (2007, p. 8). Later, however, Arnold describes an incident that was more painful for him than occasional hunger. This was when he could not help his dog that he was very attached to, as he puts it, "the only living thing that I could depend on" (2007, p. 9). His family could not afford to take his dog to the vet, so to ease the pet's agony,

Arnold's parents decided that he needed to be shot. "So I heard the boom of my father's rifle when he shot my best friend. A bullet only costs two cents, and anybody can afford that" (2007, p. 14).

This poverty, lack of opportunities, and a sense of hopelessness that Arnold observes on the reservation lead him to believe that "you're poor because you're stupid and ugly. And then you start believing that you're stupid and ugly because you're Indian. And because you're Indian you start believing you're destined to be poor" (2007, p. 13). Alexie, in his own life, could observe how his parents, who were smart and gifted people, did not have any opportunities to develop their talents and this was a fairly accurate picture of the community on the Spokane reservation.

The relationships within the tribal community that Alexie portrays are quite complex and certainly not one-dimensional and, similarly, the interactions with the outside world of white Americans are not simply clear-cut and black-and-white, either. Usually, however, those encounters are defined in opposition to the tribal community, as hostile to it, and approached as the world of enemies. This attitude of Alexie's Indian characters to white people is often justified by the past encounters that are still alive in their memory, as well as first-hand experiences of facing humiliation, dehumanization, prejudice and ridicule. In *The Lone Ranger and Tonto*, in the short story of the same name, Alexie describes an encounter with the police. The Indian character, who was simply driving around town, is stopped by a police officer who reprimands him with the words: "You're making people nervous. You don't fit the profile of the neighborhood" (1994, p. 183). In his mind, the Indian character responds: "I wanted to tell him that I didn't really fit the profile of the country but I knew it would just get me into trouble" (1994, p. 183). Such trouble is a recurring theme, as the author shows how frequently Indians thought of encounters with whites as simply life-threatening. In another passage where two Native characters are dealing with a fellow tribal member, Dirty Joe, who passed out drunk in the middle of a white carnival, Alexie shows how frightened they are facing the white world. The author voices this fear writing that "we wear fear now like a turquoise choker, like a familiar shawl … We sat there beside Dirty Joe and watched all the white tourists watch us, laugh and point a finger, their faces twisted with hate and disgust. I was afraid of all of them, wanted to hide between my Indian teeth, the quick joke" (1994, p. 55).

Nonetheless, there are also white people who play an important and positive role in Alexie's journey of finding his place in the world. Paradoxically, it is the pathetic figure of a white reservation school teacher in *The Absolutely True Diary*, Mr. P, who encourages a fourteen-year-old boy, Arnold Spirit, to leave the reservation and continue his education elsewhere. He advises the boy to "go somewhere where people have hope" (2007, p. 43). The teacher, who himself confesses that he hurt many Native students psychologically and physically, probably driven by a sense of guilt and wanting to compensate for the wrongs he had committed, pleads with the young reservation student to transfer schools. Mr. P shows appreciation for his young student's intelligence and gifts and this is what pushes Arnold Spirit to face the challenge, finding the determination to pursue a better life.

Transferring to a white school in Reardan, a nearby town, the boy puts himself in the risky situation of facing hostility from two sides—his own tribe treating him like a traitor and enemy, and white people approaching him like an alien. Because of his choice, Arnold faces even more loneliness and isolation. On the one hand, he faces contempt and hatred from his community, including his best friend turning into his worst enemy, and on the other hand, he faces insults and sneers from white students and teachers. In response to the latter, he is determined to defend Indians, identifying himself with them. In response to a racist joke Arnold Spirit declares: "I wasn't just defending myself. I was defending Indians, black people and buffalo" (2007, p. 65).

In his protagonist, Alexie shows the duality and the ambivalence that became part of his life. Arnold's fellow tribal members accused him of being "an apple," that is "red on the outside and white on the inside" (2007, p. 132). Arnold saw himself divided, as it were, between these two worlds: "Traveling between Reardan and Wellpinit, between the little white town and the reservation, I always felt like a stranger. I was half Indian in one place and half white in the other. It was like being Indian was my job, but it was only a part-time job ... I felt like two different people inside one body" (2007, p. 61).

Dealing with the dilemma of being an outcast in his own community tormented Arnold, but it also strengthened his belief that he could not be confined by the reservation. Despite all the scorn, Arnold Spirit managed to function in the white school and generally earn respect in that environment. It was playing basketball and overcoming his fears that gave him a sense that this was, in fact, what it meant to be brave. The basketball games in which he played with the white team from Reardan against the reservation school in Wellpinit, when he confronted fellow tribal members, were symbolic of the battles Arnold needed to fight in himself and the duality he had to face. He felt the imperative to test himself in the painful confrontation, facing hatred and contempt from his former friends. After defeating them he felt proud, but was also tortured by guilt and shame as if he was to blame for the tragedies afflicting his fellow tribal members.

Arnold Spirit entered the white world with feelings of inadequacy, inferiority, apprehension, or even utter terror. Even though his father was supportive and encouraging, saying "[t]hose white people aren't better than you" (2007, p. 55), Arnold initially was afraid that this was not true and felt that his father was "the loser Indian father of a loser Indian son living in a world built for winners" (2007, p. 55). But his parents, who themselves had been deprived of realizing their dreams, wanted their son to have a better life than they had. They were proud of him. The most important words that Arnold heard from his father were "You're so brave. You're a warrior" (2007, p. 55). Despite the precariousness of his choice to enter the white world, Arnold mostly saw it was the right decision.

To be a warrior in the modern world, Alexie seems to say, is to face challenges, overcome fears and transcend boundaries between the two worlds—the world of the reservation and tribal community on the one hand, and that of white people on the other. In *The Absolutely True Diary of a Part-Time Indian* Alexie points out that "Indians have forgotten that reservations were meant to be death camps ... I was the only one who was brave and crazy enough to leave the rez … I realized that, sure, I was a Spokane Indian. I belonged to that tribe. But I also belonged to the tribe of American immigrants. And to the tribe of basketball players" (2007, p. 217). Even though the protagonist believed that he needed to leave the reservation, he still longed for being forgiven, expressing his deep yearning in the words: "I hoped and prayed that they would someday forgive me for leaving them. I hoped and prayed that I would someday forgive myself for leaving them" (2007, p. 229). His best friend, Rowdy, a fellow tribal boy, gave him a sort of absolution saying that Arnold was like an old-time nomad like Indians used to be.

3   Joy Harjo

Joy Harjo, born in 1951 in Tulsa, Oklahoma, is a member of the Mvskoke nation (Creek). She published her memoir *Crazy Brave* in 2012 after working and reworking it for fourteen years. When interviewed by Indian Media Today Network (Lemay, 2012, p. 38), she shared her feelings of being "horrified by it, actually, at the thought of revealing anything … That's why it took 14 years." Harjo felt the responsibility toward her family and her ancestors to pass down the story, to remember: "I am one of the oldest living relatives of our family line. My generation is now the door to memory. This is why I am remembering" (Harjo, 2012, pp. 20–21). She felt obligated to be the one to remember and honor her ancestors. Being strongly rooted in her own family story, Harjo shows a powerful connection to tribal history, and so the words of her dedication of her book seem simply natural: "To the warriors of the heart/To my teachers in the East, North, West, and South, Above and Below" (2012). It seems she was determined to use all of her creative energy to meticulously craft her own personal story immersed in the larger story of her tribe, of Native people, and of women (Lemay, 2012). In her personal narrative, the author of *Crazy Brave* integrates poetry for which she has the most profound appreciation and incorporates traditional and tribal elements thus showing her deep respect toward her Native heritage.

Harjo is proud of her ancestors, writing "I am born of brave people" (2012, p. 28). These brave people include on her father's side tribal leaders in the Mvskoke (Creek) nation who are still appreciated in their community. One of them was among the leaders of "the Red Stick War (…) the largest Indian uprising in the country" (2012, p. 21). Another relative, a Seminole warrior, "refused to sign a treaty with the United States government" (2012, p. 21). On her mother's side there were poor Cherokee and Irish ancestors. Her mother came from a family of sharecroppers, which made her unwelcome by her father's more prominent family. What those two sides of the family did have in common, however, was the experience of removal and displacement, the Trail of Tears, which was still alive in the memory of the tribes that had experienced it. Harjo was born and grew up in Tulsa, Oklahoma, where the displaced tribes ended their tragic journey.

Harjo attributes a great role to her ancestors who provide her with links to the past serving her as her guides and guardians in life. She feels particularly close to those with whom she shares some characteristics and talents. She believes that each of these ancestors is her guardian, who, as she writes, "reminds me of those older generations of Creek people who stayed close to the teachings... They teach by story, images, and songs" (2012, p. 31). This connection with her ancestors, present in her life and writing, is a reflection of a broader trend in Native literature. Nixon (2006) points out "the fluidity of Native storytelling through migrations and generations, as the past through memory becomes an intricate part of the present" (p. 7).

In *Crazy Brave*, Harjo recounts the story of her life, including its turbulent parts, with compassion and honesty. The author shows herself as a conflicted combination of her elusive and mysterious father whose character she compares to "water" and her magnetic, creative, clear-headed mother described as "fire." She admires both of them. She writes about her mother's beauty, "that mix of Cherokee and European that dazzles" (2012, p. 23) and her talent for singing. At the same time, she was quite attached to her father, whom she describes as "a handsome god (...) whose slick black hair was always impeccably groomed" (2012, p. 17), a man who had charisma and sensitivity. This period of a fairly happy childhood, however, did not last long. Her father's drinking, his occasionally violent temper directed at her mother, and his being a womanizer, led to her parents' divorce when Harjo was eight years old. It was painful for her to witness her father's aggressive behavior toward her mother, but it was also hurtful for her not to have him around. She found some excuses for his actions, writing that "[h]e was angry because his mother died of tuberculosis when he was a baby, because his father beat him, because he was treated like an Indian man in lands that were stolen away along with everything else" (2012, p. 53).

Harjo's life took a more dramatic turn when her mother remarried, and her stepfather, who at the stage of courting her mother seemed to be a charming man, turned out to be abusive toward his wife and children. He did not to seem to have any redeeming quality and was described as simply evil. Her home seemed like a place where she was trapped along with her mother and siblings. Since her stepfather was a white employed man, Harjo's mother felt completely powerless. Describing the situation, Harjo writes how, "[m]y mother confided that there was no way we could leave. He said he would kill her and her children if she divorced him, he'd leave our bodies in a burning house. He said it would look like an accident" (2012, p. 59). In her memoir, she expresses how she lived in utter terror, especially when she was alone with her stepfather because she "felt like prey" (2012, p. 69) fearing sexual abuse. In the relationship with her stepfather Harjo experienced oppression, which could also be seen as symbolic of the Indian oppression from white people. In her own home, which she characterized as "the domestic prison" (2012, p. 70) created by her stepfather wielding his unlimited power over the family, she was deprived of the possibility to express herself emotionally and simply feel free.

As a result of being confined at home, she tried to find some freedom elsewhere. Harjo writes about the liberating experience of growing up in an urban environment in Oklahoma alongside Native and white people. She refers to school as "a refuge from home" (2012, p. 69). At school, she was able to mingle with students from different backgrounds. "I made friends across the various islands of school cultures (...) My friends were other Indian students as well as non-Indian students. I defied categories. I was considered 'the brain' and 'the artist' all at once" (2012, p. 69). Despite this ability to be part of different circles of people, though, she still "had always felt different than others" (2012, p. 80).

She appreciated knowledge, learning and books, and she excelled academically feeling that the exploration of knowledge was like a liberating experience opening doors to more freedom. She also tried to replace the bleakness of her home and the emotional void after losing her father with passionate reading. Books offered imaginary journeys to different worlds, Harjo found, in which "[e]ach book was its own matrix and it contained a world you could carry in your hands" (2012, p. 50). She also took delight in art and creativity, showing a passion for drawing, photography, theater, and, like her mother, singing and music in general. However, all her artistic leanings were thwarted by her stepfather, who expected her to focus entirely on household chores.

As part of her seeking, Harjo also tried to find her religious home. In her heart and soul she saw parallels between the Christian faith and the Native spiritual world. She describes her experience of Christianity as such, as well as the church congregation of which she was a member. Commenting on the Bible, Harjo relates how she sees the Old Testament as analogous to indigenous tribal laws for the peoples in the Middle East. Her view of the New Testament, which she found inspiring, shows further parallels. She perceived Jesus as comparable to "old-time medicine people who spoke in metaphor, in poetry" (2012, p. 78). Yet despite finding her own way to reconcile Native and Christian traditions, in the congregation, however, she often felt awkward and alienated. Many children avoided her, would not sit next to her, because she was Indian and because her parents were divorced. She also felt that the Bible was misinterpreted to demonstrate "the superiority of white people, to enforce the domination of women by men" (2012, p. 78). What she found particularly hurtful was her church congregation's "prohibition on dancing and the warnings against prophecy and visions" (2012, p. 78). She did not feel welcome and included by the congregation, which seemed to her very unfair, especially that she took pride in her ancestors among whom there were also Christian clergymen.

Alienated at home, at school and in her church, Harjo reveals how much she needed to find "a place where I would belong, where I would be normal" (2012, p. 82). She was determined to attend a school with other Native students like her. She found such an environment in Santa Fe, New Mexico, at the Institute of American Indian Arts, a high school for talented Native students from all across the United States. There, she could thrive, feeling that her life "was no longer a solitary journey" (2012, p. 86). She could relate to the experience of fellow students. "We were all 'skins' traveling together in an age of metamorphosis, facing the same traumas from decolonization. We were direct evidence of the struggle of our ancestors" (2012, p. 86). This environment was a place where she could release her creative energy through music, painting, sculpture, traditional pottery and dramatic arts, which she found invigorating and which helped build her self-confidence. Even there, however, the struggles and divisions among Native people were apparent, and some traumas surfaced, revealing the emotional and domestic problems that many of them shared. However, despite these elements of dysfunction, Harjo emphasized the constructive role of art that they created together or alongside each other.

In her memoir, however, the author does not avoid addressing the problem of alcohol in her own life and in the lives of other Native people in her immediate environment. She shares her own episodes of being drunk. Haunted by feelings of despair, she would occasionally reach for alcohol: "The more I drank, the more I didn't care that I couldn't sing in the house anymore or try out for the play. I drank more to fly above the rude story. I drank to obliterate my life" (2012, p. 76). Her stance on alcohol, however, is very clear: she sees drinking as destructive and something one should be wary of. She comments on alcohol that like other substances derived from plants, it can be a powerful medicine, and that "[a]ll these plant medicines... are potent healers. There's a reason they're called spirits... If you abuse them, they can tear holes in your protective, spiritual covering" (2012, p. 77). She could see the damage caused by alcohol in the men she loved. Her first husband, who was a Cherokee Indian, turned out to be immature and unable to keep a job owing to his drinking. With a small child that they had, she was forced to humiliate herself going through the garbage in more affluent neighborhoods to find something for survival. Harjo also writes about struggling in another relationship with a Pueblo Indian poet, who seemed charming and talented, but who once they were married would have abusive outbursts when drunk. Both of these marriages failed and the difficulties she experienced in these relationships caused her serious emotional problems.

Beyond her own individual experience, Harjo could see how Native people were scarred by the experience in their lives as American Indians, feeling lost, confused, and traumatized. She writes about the distressing state of Native people:

> These fathers, boyfriends, and husbands were all men we loved, and were worthy of love. As peoples we had been broken. We were still in the bloody aftermath of a violent takeover of our lands. Within a few generations we had gone from being nearly one hundred percent of the population of this continent to less than one-half of one percent. We were all haunted (2012, p. 158.)

Harjo shows her position regarding the political situation of Native people, writing about her own political involvement in the American Indian Movement, which was inspired by the Civil Rights Movement of African Americans, but still maintained its distinctiveness. She explains her attitude within the broader context of the Native political stances commenting how "[t]hough black America inspired us, Indian peoples were different. Most of us did not want to become full-fledged Americans. We wished to maintain the integrity of our tribal cultures and assert our individual tribal nations. We aspired to be traditional-contemporary twentieth-century warriors, artists, and dreamers" (2012, p. 139).

Along with Native rights, Harjo also supported the women's rights movement, although her situation as a Native woman was more complicated. She could see that her role in her own community was marginalized, pointing out how in Native communities women were more subjugated and sidelined than white women in their environments. Harjo describes her reduced position: "I was a woman, and my tribe wasn't even from here. I was not a real person" (2012, p. 156). Despite the challenges, she believed in the feminist struggle and thought that Native women were good examples of contemporary warriors. She points out, however, the lack of recognition for the role of indigenous women voicing the question: "[a]nd what of the wives, mothers, and daughters whose small daily acts of sacrifice and bravery were usually unrecognized and unrewarded? These acts were just as crucial to the safety and well-being of the people" (2012, p. 150). This complicated position as a Native woman lends Harjo's writing part of its richness. As Andrews (2000) points out, Harjo "depicts her own complex status… who is a part of different communities and is continually crossing various kinds of borders and boundaries—both literal and figurative—in her writing" (p. 201).

Harjo, who struggled with emotional problems and traumas in her own life, being haunted by her personal problems and the awareness of the broader context of Native people's pain, managed to find fulfillment in creative work, especially poetry, music, and painting. Most importantly, she freed herself from fear by writing poetry in which she let go of pain, anxieties, and suffering. Poetry provided her with a doorway to her ancestors, writing that "the spirit of poetry" is "a kind of resurrection light, it is the tall ancestor spirit" and that "in spirit nothing is ever far away" (2012, p. 164).

She concludes her book with a discovery that her life brought her to focus on compassion and forgiveness for herself and others. Her message is to "Ask for forgiveness. Let all the hurts and failures go. Let them go" (2012, p. 171).

4   Conclusion

Joy Harjo and Sherman Alexie voiced important messages about themselves and Native people in their autobiographical writing. They chose different paths as Native writers, and their backgrounds were different. Harjo chose to embrace her tribal heritage and to seek the environments in which she could live, study, and be creative alongside other Native people. Even though she grew up in an urban environment among indigenous as well as white people, she gravitated to what provided her with the connection with her ancestors. For her, being a woman added another layer to the host of challenges Native people often have to deal with. For Alexie, on the other hand, ridding himself of the limitations of the reservation was liberating. Both needed to negotiate the world of Native people and the white world, turning to creativity to find ways to express themselves and reach a sense of fulfillment. What seems to be most meaningful to both is sharing their stories and their journeys through life.

Harjo's and Alexie's autobiographical stories are rooted within the larger stories of their tribes. Bearing in mind the responsibility that is involved in reflecting the experience of often underrepresented or stereotypically represented Native Americans, they bring them to the foreground through their stories as people of flesh and blood, as subjects, not objects. These self-narratives, with the authors sharing their struggles and facing hard truths, humanize indigenous people, giving them real faces that the readers may be able to see for the first time. For many non-Natives, these autobiographical stories may provide rare opportunities to become familiar with contemporary reservation life, in the case of Alexie's books, or with urban Native lives in Harjo's memoir. For American Indians, these may be opportunities to relate to these stories that are written down, but that are first and foremost lived. Because these stories are written, published, and read by many, they can also show that the people they portray, in fact, matter. They are empowering both for the authors and for Native Americans as a whole in their lives in-between worlds. They validate the experience of American Indians whose voices have often been muted.

References

Alexie, S. (1994). *The lone ranger and tonto fistfight in heaven.* New York, NY: Harper Perennial (originally published 1993 by Atlantic Monthly).

Alexie, S. (2007). *The absolutely true diary of a part-time Indian.* New York, NY: Little, Brown.

Alexie, S., & Walter, J. (2013). *The lone ranger and Tonto fistfight in heaven turns twenty.* The New Yorker. Retrieved from http://www.newyorker.com/books/page-turner/the-lone-ranger-and-tonto-fistfight-in-heaven-turns-twenty

Andrews, J. (2000). In the belly of a laughing god: Reading humor and irony in the poetry of Joy Harjo. *American Indian Quarterly, 24*(2), 200–218. Retrieved from http://www.jstor.org/stable/1185871

Caldwell, E. K. (2009). *Dreaming the dawn. Conversations with native artists and activists.* Lincoln, NE: University of Nebraska Press.

Carpenter, R. (2004). Zitkala-Sa and bicultural subjectivity. *Studies in American Indian Literatures, 16*(3), 1–28. doi:10.1353/ail.2004.0032

DeMallie, R. J. (2014). John G. Neihardt and Nicholas Black Elk. In J. G. Neihardt (Ed.), *Black Elk speaks. The complete edition* (pp. 242–266). Lincoln, NE: University of Nebraska Press.

Erdinast-Vulcan, D. (2008). The I that tells itself: A Bakhtinian perspective on narrative identity. *Narrative, 16*(1), 1–15. doi:10.1353/nar.2008.0005

Evans, S. (2001). "Open containers": Sherman Alexie's drunken Indians. *American Indian Quarterly, 25*(1), 46–72. doi:10.1353/aiq.2001.0004

Hafen, P. J. (1997). Rock and roll, redskins, and blues in Sherman Alexie's work. *Studies in American Indian Literatures, 9*(4), 71–78. Retrieved from http://www.jstor.org/stable/20739426

Harjo, J. (2012). *Crazy brave.* New York, NY: W. W. Norton

Harjo, J. (2014). *A life in poetry. Talk given at the chicago humanities festival.* Retrieved from http://joyharjo.com/a-life-in-poetry/

Lemay, K. (2012). Brave truths. *Indian country today media network*. Retrieved from http://joyharjo.com/wp-content/uploads/2014/01/38BookshelfOPT.jpg

Martínez, D. (2014). Neither chief nor medicine man: The historical role of the "intellectual" in the American Indian community. *Studies in American Indian Literatures, 26*(1), 29–53. doi:10.1353/ail.2014.0011

Moyers, B., & Ablow, G. (2013). Sherman Alexie on living outside cultural borders. *Moyers and Company*. Retrieved from http://billmoyers.com/segment/sherman-alexie-on-living-outside-borders/

Nixon, A. V. (2006). Poem and tale as double helix in Joy Harjo's A map to the next world. *Studies in American Indian Literatures, 18*(1), 1–21. doi:10.1353/ail.2006.0014

Nygren, Å. (2005). A world of story-smoke: A conversation with Sherman Alexie. *MELUS, 30*(4), 149–169. Retrieved from http://www.jstor.org/stable/30029639

Purdy, J., & Alexie, S. (1997). Crossroads: A conversation with Sherman Alexie. *Studies in American Indian literatures, 9*(4), 1–18. Retrieved from http://www.jstor.org/stable/20739421

Tatonetti, L. (2009). The both/and of American Indian literary studies. *Western American literature, 44*(3), 276–288.

Author Biography

Edyta Wood is a senior lecturer in the Institute of Modern Languages and Applied Linguistics of Kazimierz Wielki University in Bydgoszcz, Poland. Her academic interests include teaching American culture, with a focus on the perspectives of Native Americans and African Americans.

Printed by Printforce, the Netherlands